A Checklist of

American Newspaper Carriers' Addresses, 1720–1820

Compiled by
Gerald D. McDonald,
Stuart C. Sherman,
and Mary T. Russo

Worcester, Massachusetts
American Antiquarian Society
2000

LIBRARY OF CONGRESS CATALOGING-IN-PUBLICATION DATA

McDonald, Gerald D. (Gerald Doan), 1905–
    A checklist of American newspaper carriers' addresses, 1720–1820 / by Gerald D. McDonald, Stuart C. Sherman, and Mary T. Russo.
        p. cm.
    Includes bibliographical references and index.
    ISBN 0-944026-16-8 (alk. paper)
    1. Newspaper carriers' writings, American—Bibliography. 2. American poetry—Colonial period, ca. 1600–1775—Bibliography. 3. Newspaper carriers' writings, Canadian—Bibliography. 4. New Year—North America—Poetry—Bibliography. 5. American poetry—1783–1850—Bibliography. 6. Broadsides—North America—Bibliography. I. Sherman, Stuart C. II. Russo, Mary T. III. Title.

Z1229.N44 M37 1999
[PS153.N57]
016.811'080892097—dc21   99-049392

Table of Contents

Foreword
iv

Introduction
vii

List of Illustrations
xiii

Arrangement and Acknowledgment
xiv

Symbols and Sources
xv

Carriers' Addresses
1

Canadian Carriers' Addresses
133

Bibliography
143

Indices

Location Index
146

Newspaper Name Index
153

First Line Index
159

Name Index
170

Foreword

READER, the contents of this volume represent the work of nearly two centuries by collectors and bibliographers. Like the gathering up of an institutional collection or the compilation of any bibliography, it is an amalgam of the efforts of many individuals. In particular, this volume is the fruit of a long-standing collaboration between staff members of the libraries of the American Antiquarian Society and Brown University. The poetical effusions recorded here were addressed by news carriers to their customers at the turn of each year in expectation of a reward for services performed during the previous and forthcoming years. They are the ephemeral remnants of an ancient custom followed not only by news carriers, but by the lamplighters and other tradesmen in Europe and America, from the seventeenth into the early years of this century. In our own day, the custom of tradesmen giving annual calendars to their customers may well be a vestige of that tradition. The American Antiquarian Society received its first examples of these broadside verses in 1812 when Isaiah Thomas gave his collections of American books and newspapers to found the Society. Addresses were bound up in the volumes of the Boston, New York, and Philadelphia newspapers that he had begun to collect during the last decades of the eighteenth century. Succeeding generations of Society librarians have continued their eager pursuit of individual examples of news carriers' addresses, as well as the files of newspapers that generations of men and boys delivered to their subscribers. Doubtless, Brown University's collection of carriers' addresses began in a similar way—scattered examples bound up in runs of newspapers. However, in the later nineteenth century, when C. Fiske Harris, a businessman of Providence, began his collection of American poetry, carriers' addresses were systematically included in the great collection that in 1884 found its way to the university library. Over the next few decades it was greatly expanded. In 1929 S. Foster Damon was appointed the curator of the Harris Collection of American Poetry and Plays, and from that time forward the Harris Collection increased remarkably in intellectual vigor and in magnitude. Carriers' addresses were not ignored by Damon, by his successor Roger E. Stoddard, or by Stoddard's successors in the position. Other significant collections exist beyond the major ones at the American Antiquarian Society and Brown: the New York Public Library, The New-York Historical Society, and the Huntington Library among them.

This checklist of carriers' addresses had its genesis in the mid-1930s, when Gerald D. McDonald wrote to R.W.G. Vail, then AAS librarian, to ask advice on a policy of inclusion for such a compilation. McDonald, who spent his entire professional career at the New

York Public Library, was then an assistant in its rare book division, later rising to be chief of that division, then chief of the division of American history and genealogy, and finally, chief of special collections. Some three years before he died, McDonald informed us that, although the checklist, then thirty years in the making, was not quite finished, he thought that the end was in sight. Unfortunately, he had not yet completed the work at his untimely death in 1970 in Paris during a book acquisition trip for the New York Public Library. Following Gerald McDonald's death, his sister, Margery McDonald Henderson, sent his manuscript to the Society. With it came her generous gift of $4,000 to help defray the cost of publishing the checklist over which McDonald had labored so long. However, it was not yet ready for publication and it lay fallow for several years before another member of the Society, Stuart C. Sherman, volunteered to take up the work once more. Sherman was then the librarian of the John Hay Library at Brown where he presided over the Harris Collection. AAS agreed to his proposal and McDonald's manuscript was sent to Providence in order that Sherman could complete it. Although Sherman made considerable progress on the project, intending to cover the years 1721–1957, his obligations toward his bibliography of whaling logbooks and ill health prevented him from completing this work before his death in 1983.

In 1982 Sherman delivered his revision and expansion of McDonald's manuscript to his colleague Mary T. Russo, curator of broadsides at the John Hay Library. At that time, the Society and Brown agreed to get on with the work in an energetic manner and to bring the first segment covering the years 1720–1820 to completion. Roger E. Stoddard of the Houghton Library and curator of rare books at Harvard, Samuel Allen Streit, assistant university librarian for special collections at Brown University, and John B. Hench, the American Antiquarian Society's director of research and publication, were appointed as an advisory committee. Brown University contributed part of Ms. Russo's time over a period of six years to the task of completing the work. She organized, revised, and expanded its size and scope, particularly in the field of physical description. She was assisted from time to time by Ajay Nagpal and Rita H. Warnock. Jennifer Lee and John Mignault of the John Hay Library at Brown subsequently provided much helpful assistance in computer matters relating to this checklist. M. Sheila McAvey, then the Society's assistant editor, shepherded the book through various editorial metamorphoses. Ronald Labuz, professor of advertising design at Mohawk Valley Community College and scholar of nineteenth-century American graphic design, along with colleagues and students at the college, volunteered to design and typeset the book from disks keyboarded at Brown. Preparation for the press was completed at The Stinehour Press, Lunenburg, Vermont. Thus, the volume you have before you is the collaborative work of many persons accomplished during a period of nearly seventy years.

The materials recorded herein have been collected by many other persons over a period of two hundred years. It has been said that good scholarship requires a long period of time to ripen adequately. This *Checklist of American Newspaper Carriers' Addresses* surely proves the truth of that maxim! Those of us who remain to witness its publication record here our gratitude to the late Gerald Doan McDonald, its progenitor; to the late Stuart Capen Sherman, its contributor; to Mary T. Russo, its completor; and to the late Margery McDonald Henderson, its benefactor.

MARCUS A. McCORISON
President emeritus
American Antiquarian Society
March 15, 1999

Introduction

WHAT we now call carriers' addresses were printed pieces, usually broadsides, that carriers of newspapers distributed on New Year's Day to extend greetings, usually in the form of verse, to their customers and to solicit a gift in reward for the dependable delivery of newspapers during the previous year. The carriers were frequently the printer's apprentices, or printer's devils as they were known in the eighteenth century, who generally served only for room and board. Later, carriers were paid, but only meager salaries at best. Carriers therefore eagerly awaited this annual tip, and customers obliged. Newspaper carriers were not the only tradesmen to attempt to convert verse into a cash gift at year's end. In the later decades of the eighteenth century, American watchmen, carters, street sweepers, bootblacks, lamplighters, and baker's apprentices started to follow the lead of newspaper carriers in producing annual messages. Never as numerous as carriers' addresses, these verses appeared sporadically in urban areas through the nineteenth century. A number of carriers left testimony to the significance of their New Year's windfall. The noted editor Joseph T. Buckingham recalled distributing to thirty or thirty-five subscribers to the *Greenfield* (Mass.) *Gazette* an address written by Samuel Elliot in 1797, when Buckingham was seventeen. Buckingham remembers his youthful elation with the results of his New Year's appeal: 'O Croesus! how mean and insignificant was thy grandeur. . . . I counted my wealth,—six dollars and seventy-five cents,—all in quarters and eighths of a dollar,—and locked it in my chest! Never before had I been the owner of so much money,—never before so rich.' Likewise, Samuel Woodworth, the author of the 'Old Oaken Bucket,' served an apprenticeship at the *Columbian Centinel* in Boston. In a letter written to his family when he was seventeen, he listed items purchased with the ten dollars he received in tips on New Year's Day in 1802: a pair of candlesticks and an almanac for his parents and clothing for himself. The lines devoted to graphic depictions of the carrier as the poor but honest youngster who endured many a hardship as he delivered the news in all sorts of weather are not only touching but informative about the lives of these apprentices.

Who could deny a generous tip to the youngster whose New Year's verse greeting recounted the hardships undergone by the faithful carrier in winter weather:

> Bedouins of the street are they, tenting anywhere
> Pitching camp upon the cobblestones
> Braving rain and snow and sleet and winter's chilly wind;
> Lighting fires to warm their frozen bones.

Moreover, the customary plea at the end of one address revealed that the delivery of newspapers was not exclusively a male preserve. The greeting in the *American Telegraphic* of Newfield, Connecticut, in 1799 was written by Polly:

> To you, generous patrons, see Polly appear,
> To congratulate you on the birth of a year.
> A song—a mixture of humor and folly,
> At a season like this, is expected from Polly.
> For carriers must sing, whether female or male,
> On New Year's Day, or their purses will fail.

This pleasant custom of carriers' New Year's broadside greetings persisted in America for roughly two hundred years, from 1720 to its decline after 1900. Still, as late as the 1930s, carriers from the *Providence* (R.I.) *Journal* were extending the traditional New Year's verse to their customers. Other examples can be found even later, such as the 1942 *Grand Rapids* (Mich.) *Herald* newspaper greeting in the form of a pamphlet, and calendars presented by Chicago papers in 1957 and 1959. Gerald D. McDonald was the first and foremost investigator of these ephemera. In his 'New Year's Addresses of American Newsboys,' in *Bookman's Holiday* (New York: New York Public Library, 1943) McDonald traces the origin of the custom to England. On Boxing Day, December 26, apprentices in the various trades carried boxes from house to house to collect donations from the master's customers. McDonald declares that as early as 1666, a London bellman (i.e., a watchman) presented a printed broadside of verses to the people of his district. Both Clarence S. Brigham, in his *Journals and Journeymen: A Contribution to the History of Early American Newspapers* (Philadelphia: University of Pennsylvania Press, 1950), and McDonald concur that English newsboys' verses appeared later. Brigham states that none can be found before 1720. McDonald also pointed out that, in America, Aquila Rose, a Philadelphia compositor and poet, first penned verses for an appeal distributed by the printer's apprentices. Although no copy of what may well be the first carrier's address (1720) is extant, the verse is included in Rose's collected works, as are his poems for New Year's Day in 1721 and 1722. The American Antiquarian Society holds the earliest surviving example of a carrier's address issued as a broadside, that of the *American Weekly Mercury*, a Philadelphia newspaper, for 1735. From the opening lines asserting the indispensability of the news to the closing hint for a gratuity, this early appeal set the tone for the addresses to come:

> There's not an ear that is not deaf
> But listens to the news;—
> But, if you think my time misspent,
> Then give me ne'er a penny.

Generally printed on single sheets of paper, carriers' addresses were vulnerable to damage and loss. A few were printed on white or colored satin, perhaps to be given to the wealthiest customers. The *Salem* (Mass.) *Gazette* in the early 1800s often printed the same address on both paper and silk. And the *Quebec Gazette*, which contained by English- and French-language verse, seems to have produced two printings on occasion, with a copy of the French verses printed separately on satin. But whether on paper or silk, on single sheets or in pamphlet form, it is amazing how many of these ephemera have survived. Many were slipped or tipped into bound volumes of the newspapers, others were framed, therefore surviving the ravages of time. As the verses grew in popularity and as subscribers to newspapers lived farther from the city of publication, newspaper publishers began to print the carriers' greetings not only as broadsides but in the pages of their regular issues immediately following New Year's Day. The *Boston Gazette* of January 5, 1809, explains: 'The following address was on Monday last, presented by our faithful carriers, to the patrons of the *Gazette*, in town. That their merits both as poets as well as post-boys, may be known to our distant as well our neighboring friends, we have been induced to place their well-written address in the columns of this paper.' Frequently carriers' addresses were picked up by other papers in the same or distant cities and reprinted, sometimes with textual changes. For example, the *Massachusetts Centinel* in Boston printed a carrier's address on January 7, 1789, but credited it to the *American Mercury* of Hartford of that year.

One reason for creating an elaborate finding aid for carriers' addresses is to provide a scholarly access to a substantial body of local American poetry. Although most of these verses were published anonymously, they are important as cultural artifacts and deserving of study. Unfortunately, most addresses provide no clues to authorship. The style of some indicate that they were written by educated individuals—a local poet perhaps or the newspaper editor. Those that are shorter and simpler may have been written by the carrier. Some authors enjoyed expounding on varied topics, others composed the verse in slapdash fashion. We find carrier Lawrence Swinney's name printed as the author of the 1767 address of the *New-York Gazette*, while Daniel Jones appears to be the writer, as well as the carrier, of the {Boston} *Disciple and Theological Review* address of 1816. Some well-known authors wrote addresses on behalf of the carrier and apprentices. Brigham, in *Journals and Journeymen*, declared it reasonable to assume that Benjamin Franklin wrote many of the pre-Revolutionary War verses for the *Pennsylvania Gazette*. Philip Freneau contributed addresses to twelve papers in Philadelphia, New York, New Haven, and Charleston between 1783 and 1798. Theodore Dwight, Richard Alsop, Lemuel Hopkins, and Joel Barlow, members of the group known as the 'Hartford' or 'Connecticut Wits,' turned out many political satires that were popular as carriers' addresses. William Cobbett wrote addresses for his paper, *Porcupine's Gazette* in Philadelphia. William Biglow contributed verse for Boston and Salem papers, and Samuel Woodworth was a frequent contributor of addresses for various New York papers. McDonald reveals that Daniel Webster wrote the New Year's address for the *Dartmouth Gazette* (Hanover, N.H.) in 1803, signing the piece 'Icarus.' Most often, the subject matter of the verses provides a survey of the social and cultural events of the previous year. Moreover, the verses express the candid opinions of their authors, frequently from the perspective of the common man. Verse content ran the gamut from odes to the old and new year, to commendations of civic virtue, or the recitation of some local scandal. The verses often included praises for the newspaper, reports of political campaigns, pleas for temperance, complaints about taxes, invocations of heroes, commemorations of battles, and discussions of fashions or new inventions. Thus any conceivable topic was fair game for the New Year's rhymer, but somewhere in the verse there was usually the request for a gratuity for the faithful carrier. The following selections exhibit some of the variety of the carriers' addresses. The (Philadelphia) *Pennsylvania Gazette* in 1771 extended this praise for Britain's stance for liberty in a conflict with Spain over the Falkland Islands:

> But gracious George, to whose blest Scepter's giv'n
> Bright Mercy's Ray, prime Attribute of Heav'n
> With Ear paternal hears their mournful Cries,
> Up to his Throne in piteous Accents rise.

In contrast, four years later, in 1775, the author of the carrier's greeting of the *Pennsylvania Journal* of Philadelphia pictures Britain as the oppressor of its children's rightful legacy of liberty:

> When Britain first at Heaven's Command,
> Arose from out the azure Main,
> This was the Charter of the Land,
> And guardian Angels sung the Strain
> 'Rule Britania, Britania rule the Waves,
> Britons never will be Slaves.'
> But now what guardian Angel will,
> Sing this once favor'd Strain to thee,
> Whose greatest Pleasure is to Kill,
> Thy children's hopes of Liberty:
> Vain is their Empire o'er the Waves,
> Who'd sink their Subjects into Slaves.

Though a serious tone usually prevailed, the greeting could be satiric, humorous, patriotic, or sentimental. For example, the deep sense of loss and anguish upon the death of George Washington finds expression in these elegiac lines from Hartford's *Connecticut Courant* in 1800:

> O widow'd country! what protecting form,
> Shall ope thy pathways thro' the gathering store!
> What mighty hand thy trembling barque shall guide
> Thro' faction's rough, and overwhelming tide!
> The hour is past—thy Washington, no more.

Authors frequently criticized city fathers, as in the address of the *Mercantile Advertiser* of New York in 1819.

> In pairs, in herds, the swine we meet
> Dispersed o'er alley, land and street
> Rolling in filth of ev'ry name
> And flushing every cheek with shame! . . .
> To witness a disgusting sight. . . .

Indeed, the New Year's broadside addressed any and all topics of the day, from pestilence to slavery or war. When a fever raged in Philadelphia in 1807, *Poulson's American Daily Advertiser* articulated the fears engendered by the disease in a graphic personification:

> Dread Pestilence with lurid eye
> And heart consuming breath
> Deep horror lurking in his sigh
> His touch the stroke of Death.

As early as 1820, slavery aroused foreboding in the newsboys' greetings. Verses in *Poulson's American Daily Advertiser* expressed passionate feelings:

> Slavery, the bane and curse of every land,
> The foulest stain upon the Christian hand,
> Freeman and Christians, check the monstrous claim,
> Fraught with your ruin, infamy and shame.

The format of the address was generally straightforward, although variations did occur. The address of the *Massachusetts Gazette and Boston News-Letter* for 1769 was in the form of a dialogue between two newsboys. Occasionally, the address appeared in prose. The author of the address in the (New Haven) *Connecticut Journal* of 1795 admitted that 'the muses have absolutely refused me their aid, and I am doomed to silence, or to address you in prose.' Not all of the addresses were presented in English. The earliest French-Canadian address recorded here is that of the *Quebec Gazette* of 1767. German-language broadsides had a long tradition, particularly in the Pennsylvania counties of Lebanon and Lancaster. The earliest German address listed in this bibliography appeared in the 1765 *Wochentlichte Philadelphische Staatsbote.* As printing techniques improved, the single sheets of the addresses became increasingly elaborate. Decorative borders of type furnished the earliest ornamentation, followed by simple woodcuts, then initial block letters and tailpieces; typographic elements sometimes ran riot over the page. The attractiveness and exuberance may have ensured the survival of some of these ephemera. Some clearly reflect current taste in the graphic arts. In their day, the addresses served a purpose, bringing, on a very personal level, warm greetings at the beginning of the New Year from the newspaper carriers to their customers. To treat the carrier's address as a curiosity or merely as a desirable collector's item is to miss the true significance of what the contents tell us about the times. The widespread appeal of the verses and their popularity over a long period provide a spontaneous and contemporary perspective on historical, political, and social events in the various regions of the country. Since the greeting included a review of local and national events, it served to broaden the horizons of its readers, while appealing at the same time to feelings of civic pride and patriotism. Because they provide a view of the preceding year from the vantage point of a particular locality, these addresses can serve the social historian. In addition, the style and themes of the verse furnish material for the literary scholar. For the printing historian, they are a source revealing changes in American journalistic styles, tastes in design, and technological advances, such as in the methods and techniques of printing, illustrations, typography, and the use of color. The poetic remnants of these ephemeral New Year's greetings thus present a fascinating record of the country and its people in the eighteenth and nineteenth centuries. Perhaps suspect as exact history, the carrier's address nevertheless invites us to share the fears, hopes, and dreams of past eras. As Gerald McDonald so aptly wrote, 'Collectively, these addresses are a march of time with the history of one hundred years done in meter.'

Mary T. Russo
North Smithfield, R.I.
August 9, 1991

List of Illustrations

1. McDonald 4. *American Weekly Mercury*, Philadelphia, Pa., 1735. 2

2. McDonald 104. *South Carolina and American General Gazette*, Charleston, S.C., January 1, 1768. 15

3. McDonald 127. *Massachusetts Spy*, Boston, Mass., January 1, 1771. 19

4. McDonald 291. *American Apollo*, Boston, Mass., January 1, 1794. 40

5. McDonald 312. *New York Weekly Museum*, New York, January 1, 1795. 44

6. McDonald 363. *Porcupine's Gazette*, Philadelphia, Pa., 1798. 52

7. McDonald 383. *Connecticut Courant*, Hartford, Conn., January 1, 1800. 56

8. McDonald 440. *Newport Mercury*, Newport, R.I., January 1, 1803. 64

9. McDonald 475. *Salem Register*, Salem, Mass., January 1, 1805. 69

10. McDonald 523. *Readinger Adler*, Reading, Pa., January 1, 1807. 76

11. McDonald 605. *Tickler*, Philadelphia, Pa., January 1, 1810. 88

12. McDonald 894. *Idiot*, Boston, Mass., January 1, 1819. 126

Arrangement and Acknowledgment

THIS bibliography contains a listing of carriers' addresses from the years 1720 through 1820 printed in what is now the continental United States. While some Canadian addresses are included, this list should not be considered all-inclusive of Canadian material.

The arrangement is chronological; the date the address was presented determining its place in the list. All supplied information is enclosed in square brackets. Numbers in the indices refer to entry numbers.

A typical entry includes:

> date
>
> place of publication
>
> name of newspaper (as in Brigham; variant names found in titles have 'see reference' to name used in index)
>
> title of address
>
> first line
>
> size of sheet in centimeters, height preceding width; size of printed area, in parentheses; brief physical description
>
> location of no more than four copies; notes on copies examined; reprint notes
>
> author attribution; miscellaneous notes
>
> * signifies copies examined
>
> ◊ signifies supplied date
>
> [n.p.n.] no paper name

Acknowledgment

THE kind assistance of the staffs of numerous libraries and historical societies across the country has made the compilation of this bibliography possible. Over a long period, they permitted us to examine material, supplied details, provided photocopies, and gave generously of their time. Their help has been greatly appreciated.

I would also like to express my gratitude to my associate Rita Warnock for her support and assistance. Thanks also is extended to Andrew Kidd, Ajay Nagpal, and Denis Nepveu, Brown University students, who patiently provided careful data entry.

MARY T. RUSSO

xiv

Symbols and Sources

CSmH	Henry E. Huntington Library and Art Gallery, San Marino, California.
CaNSHa	Public Archives of Nova Scotia, Halifax, Nova Scotia.
CaOA	Bibliothèque des Archives publiques au Canada, Ottawa.
CaOOP	Library of Parliament, Ottawa.
CaQMBN	Bibliothèque nationale du Quebec, Montreal, Quebec.
CaQMM	McGill University, Montreal, Quebec.
CaQQL	Bibliothèque de la Legislature de la Province de Québec, Quebec, Quebec.
CaQQS	Seminaire de Québec, Quebec, Quebec.
CtHi	Connecticut Historical Society, Hartford, Connecticut.
CtSoP	The Pequot Library, Southport, Connecticut.
CtY	Yale University, New Haven, Connecticut.
DLC	Library of Congress, Washington, D.C.
DeHi	Historical Society of Delaware, Wilmington, Delaware.
ICHi	Chicago Historical Society, Chicago, Illinois.
ICU	University of Chicago, Chicago, Illinois.
In	Indiana State Library, Indianapolis, Indiana.
InU	Indiana University–The Lilly Library, Bloomington, Indiana.
MB	Boston Public Library, Boston, Massachusetts.
MBA	Boston Athenaeum, Boston, Massachusetts.
MH	Harvard University, Cambridge, Massachusetts.
MHi	Massachusetts Historical Society, Boston, Massachusetts.
MSaE	Essex Institute, Salem, Massachusetts.
MWA	American Antiquarian Society, Worcester, Massachusetts.
MdBE	Enoch Pratt Free Library, Baltimore, Maryland.
MdHi	Maryland Historical Society, Baltimore, Maryland.
MeHa	Hubbard Free Library, Hallowell, Maine.
MeHi	Maine Historical Society, Portland, Maine.
MiD-B	Detroit Public Library–Burton Collection, Detroit, Michigan.
MiU-C	University of Michigan–William L. Clements Library, Ann Arbor, Michigan.
MoHi	Missouri State Historical Society, Columbia, Missouri.
N	New York State Library, Albany, New York.
NAlI	Albany Institute of History and Art, Albany, New York.
NBu	Buffalo and Erie County Public Library, Buffalo, New York.

NCooHi	New York State Historical Association, Cooperstown, New York.
NHi	New York Historical Society, New York, New York.
NN	New York Public Library, New York, New York.
NNe	Newburgh Free Library, Newburgh, New York.
NPou	Adriance Memorial Library, Poughkeepsie, New York.
NSU	Syracuse University, Syracuse, New York.
NcD	Duke University, Durham, North Carolina.
NcU	University of North Carolina, Chapel Hill, North Carolina.
NhD	Dartmouth College, Hanover, New Hampshire.
NhHi	New Hampshire Historical Society, Concord, New Hampshire.
NjHi	The New Jersey Historical Society, Newark, New Jersey.
NjR	Rutgers–The State University, New Brunswick, New Jersey.
OCHi	The Cincinnati Historical Society, Cincinnati, Ohio.
PHi	Historical Society of Pennsylvania, Philadelphia, Pennsylvania.
PLa	Lancaster County Library, Lancaster, Pennsylvania.
PPL	Library Company of Philadelphia, Philadelphia, Pennsylvania.
PU	University of Pennsylvania, Philadelphia, Pennsylvania.
PWcHi	Chester County Historical Society, West Chester, Pennsylvania.
RNHi	Newport Historical Society, Newport, Rhode Island.
RPB	Brown University, Providence, Rhode Island.
RPHi	Rhode Island Historical Society, Providence, Rhode Island.
RPJCB	John Carter Brown Library, Brown University, Providence, Rhode Island.
ScC	Charleston Library Society, Charleston, South Carolina.
ScU	University of South Carolina, Columbia, South Carolina.
VtU	University of Vermont, Burlington, Vermont.
ViW	The College of William and Mary in Virginia, Williamsburg, Virginia.
WHi	The State Historical Society of Wisconsin, Madison, Wisconsin.
WvU	West Virginia University, Morgantown, West Virginia.

Carriers' Addresses

1720

1 Philadelphia, Pa.

Full fifty times have roul'd their changes on [First line]

No known copy

Author: Aquila Rose. Printed in his *Poems on Several Occasions* (Philadelphia, 1740), 32–33, with the explanation: 'The three following pieces, were wrote, by him, for the boys who carried the weekly newspapers to their master's customers, in Philadelphia; to whom, commonly, every New-Year's day, they present verses of this kind. Wrote in 1720.'

1721

2 Philadelphia, Pa.

How swift the weeks in various changes run [First line]

No known copy

Author: Aquila Rose. Printed in his *Poems on Several Occasions* (Philadelphia, 1740), 34–35, with the explanation: 'The three following pieces, were wrote, by him, for the boys who carried the weekly newspapers to their master's customers, in Philadelphia; to whom, commonly, every New-Year's day, they present verses of this kind. Wrote in 1721.'

1722

3 Philadelphia, Pa.

To bring New Years, revolving time makes haste [First line]

No known copy

Author: Aquila Rose. Printed in his *Poems on Sev-eral Occasions* (Philadelphia, 1740), 35–37, with the explanation: 'The three following pieces, were wrote, by him, for the boys who carried the weekly newspapers to their master's customers, in Philadelphia; to whom, commonly, every New-Year's day, they present verses of this kind. Wrote in 1722.'

1735

4 Philadelphia, Pa.
[AMERICAN WEEKLY MERCURY] ◊

There's not an ear that is not deaf [First line]

31 x 10 cm. (26.7 x 9.0 cm.) Allegorical cut at head with the words, 'Senescimus, effugit, aetas. Auson.' (Reilly 1034)

STE 40086 / MWA*

1739

5 Philadelphia, Pa.
PENNSYLVANIA GAZETTE

The yearly verses of the printer's lad, who carrieth about the Pennsylvania Gazette, to the customers thereof. Jan. 1, 1739. The spreading of news.

First line: Begin, mercurial muse, with quickest ears

32 x 11 cm. (30.8 x 8.3 cm.) Cut at right of title. (Reilly 1835)

STE 40182 / MWA* / Excerpt reproduced in Clarence W. Brigham, *Journals and Journeymen: A Contribution to the History of Early American Newspapers.* (Philadelphia, 1950), 93.

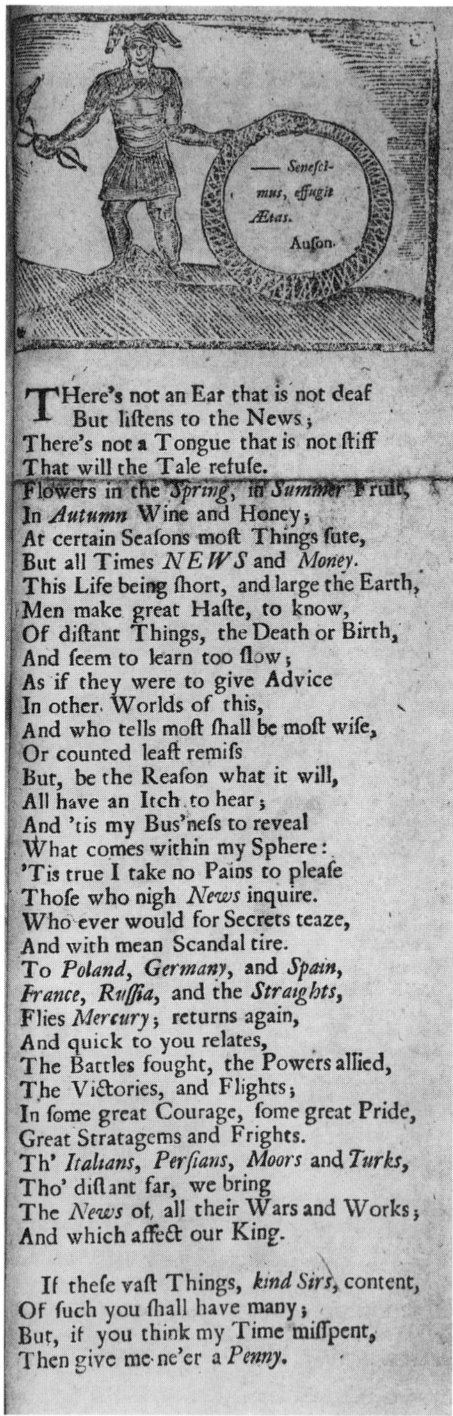

THere's not an Ear that is not deaf
    But liftens to the News;
There's not a Tongue that is not ftiff
That will the Tale refufe.
Flowers in the *Spring*, in *Summer* Fruit,
In *Autumn* Wine and Honey;
At certain Seafons moft Things fute,
But all Times *NEWS* and *Money*.
This Life being fhort, and large the Earth,
Men make great Hafte, to know,
Of diftant Things, the Death or Birth,
And feem to learn too flow;
As if they were to give Advice
In other Worlds of this,
And who tells moft fhall be moft wife,
Or counted leaft remifs
But, be the Reafon what it will,
All have an Itch to hear;
And 'tis my Bus'nefs to reveal
What comes within my Sphere:
'Tis true I take no Pains to pleafe
Thofe who nigh *News* inquire.
Who ever would for Secrets teaze,
And with mean Scandal tire.
To *Poland*, *Germany*, and *Spain*,
France, *Ruffia*, and the *Straights*,
Flies *Mercury*; returns again,
And quick to you relates,
The Battles fought, the Powers allied,
The Victories, and Flights;
In fome great Courage, fome great Pride,
Great Stratagems and Frights.
Th' *Italians*, *Perfians*, *Moors* and *Turks*,
Tho' diftant far, we bring
The *News* of, all their Wars and Works;
And which affect our King.

If thefe vaft Things, *kind Sirs*, content,
Of fuch you fhall have many;
But, if you think my Time miffpent,
Then give me ne'er a *Penny*.

Fig. 1. McDonald 4. *American Weekly Mercury*, Philadelphia, Pa., 1735. American Antiquarian Society.

1740

6　Philadelphia, Pa.
Pennsylvania Gazette

The yearly verses of the printers lad, who carrieth about the Pennsylvania Gazette, to the customer thereof. January 1, 1740.

First line: By annual services estates are held

33 x 10 cm. (31.0 x 8.2 cm.) Cut at left of title. (Reilly 1835)

STE 40269 / MWA*

1741

7　Philadelphia, Pa.
American Weekly Mercury ◊

In scenes confus'd the busy year we've past [First line]

30 x 10 cm. (27.2 x 7.8 cm.) Allegorical cut at head of text. (Reilly 1034)

STE 4666 / PHi*

8　Philadelphia, Pa.
Pennsylvania Gazette

The yearly verses of the printer's lad, who carrieth about the Pennsylvania Gazette to the customers thereof. Jan. 1, 1741.

First line: My labour's done for one unreckon'd year

33 x 10 cm. (30.3 x 8.1 cm.) Cut at right of title. (Reilly 1835)

STE 40296 / MWA* PHi / Excerpt reproduced in P. L. Ford, *Many-sided Franklin* (New York, 1899), 232.

1742

8A　Philadelphia, Pa.
American Weekly Mercury

How diff'rent are the lives of men at home, and those that over lands and oceans roam?

30 x 10.5 cm. (26 x 7 cm.) Relief cut.

STE 4877 / PHi

1743

9　Philadelphia, Pa.
American Weekly Mercury

[New-Year verses of the carriers of the American Weekly Mercury.]

Hildeburn 839 STE 5515 / No copy located.

10　Philadelphia, Pa.
Pennsylvania Gazette

The yearly verses of the printer's lads, who carry the Pennsylvania Gazette about to the customers thereof. January 1, 1743.

First line: Whilst happier brutes th' inspiring God obey | *At head of text:* On the present troubles in Europe, and the rest of the globe.

31 x 10 cm. (29.4 x 8.6 cm.) Cut, with the words, 'Post est occasio calva' at head. (Reilly 1017)

STE 5274 / MWA* PHi

1744

11　New York, N.Y.
New-York Weekly Post-Boy

[New-Year verses of the Weekly Post-Boy.]
STE 5467 / No copy located.

12　Philadelphia, Pa.
American Weekly Mercury

[New-Year verses of the carriers of the American Weekly Mercury.]

Hildeburn 889 STE 5329 / No copy located.

13　Philadelphia. Pa.
Pennsylvania Gazette

[New-Year verses of the carriers of the Pennsylvania Gazette.]

Hildeburn 890 STE 5476 / No copy located.

14   Philadelphia, Pa.
      PENNSYLVANIA JOURNAL

The verses of the printer's boy that carries about the Pennsylvania Journal, 1743–44.

First line: Time's measurer, the radiant sun

30 x 11 cm. (26.0 x 6.1 cm.) Decorated initial block.

STE 5478 / PHi*

1745

15   New York, N.Y.
      NEW-YORK WEEKLY POST-BOY ◊

The yearly verses of the printer's lad, who carrieth about the New-York Weekly Post-Boy, to the customers thereof.

First line: Two annual courses time has run | *At head of text:* Kind sirs.

22 x 14 cm. (16.5 x 8.1 cm.)

STE 40393 / NHi*

16   Philadelphia, Pa.
      AMERICAN WEEKLY MERCURY

[New-Year verses of the carriers of the American Weekly Mercury.]

Hildeburn 939 STE 5530 / No copy located.

17   Philadelphia, Pa.
      PENNSYLVANIA GAZETTE

[New-Year verses of the carriers of the Pennsylvania Gazette.]

Hildeburn 940 STE 5673 / No copy located.

18   Philadelphia, Pa.
      PENNSYLVANIA JOURNAL

[New-Year verses of the carriers of the Pennsylvania Journal.]

Hildeburn 941 STE 5675 / No copy located.

1746

19   Philadelphia, Pa.
      AMERICAN WEEKLY MERCURY

[New-Year verses of the carriers of the American Weekly Mercury.]

Hildeburn 986 STE 5730 / No copy located.

20   Philadelphia, Pa.
      PENNSYLVANIA GAZETTE

The yearly-verses of the printer's boy, who carries the Pennsylvania Gazette to the customers. January 1, 1746.

First line: Since 'tis a custom ev'ry year

30 x 20 cm. (25.6 x 17.1 cm.) Verse in two columns divided by line of type ornaments.

STE 5850 / PHi*

21   Philadelphia, Pa.
      PENNSYLVANIA JOURNAL

The New-Year's verses, of the printer's lad who carries about the Pennsylvania Journal to the customers thereof. January 1, 1746.

First line: Masters, I wish a happy year

30 x 20 cm. (24.5 x 16.2 cm.) Verse in two columns with decorated initial block.

STE 5852 / PHi*

1747

22   Philadelphia, Pa.
      PENNSYLVANIA GAZETTE

[New-Year verses of the carriers of the Pennsylvania Gazette.]

Hildeburn 1024 STE 6046 / No copy located.

23   Philadelphia, Pa.
      PENNSYLVANIA JOURNAL

[New-Year verses of the carrier of the Pennsylvania Journal.]

Hildeburn 1025 STE 6048 / No copy located.

1748

24   Philadelphia, Pa.
PENNSYLVANIA GAZETTE

The New-Year verses of the printer's boy, who carries the Pennsylvania-Gazette to the customers. 1748.

First line: Whence this tumultuous noise, these dire alarms? | *At end of text beneath line of type ornaments:* Philadelphia, January 2. By Capt. Gantony, arrived at Wilmington from St. Eustasia to his friend here, dated December 1, 1747. . . .

31 x 20 cm. (29.8 x 19.3 cm.) Verse in two columns divided by line of type ornaments. Title within mortised block. (Reilly 117)

STE 6216 / MWA*

25   Philadelphia, Pa.
PENNSYLVANIA JOURNAL

[New-Year verses of the carriers of the Pennsylvania Journal.]

Hildeburn 1087 STE 6218 / No copy located.

1749

26   Philadelphia, Pa.
PENNSYLVANIA GAZETTE

The New-Year verses of the printer's boys, who carries [*sic*] the Pennsylvania Gazette to the customers. MDCCXLIX.

First line: Since the storm's overblown, and the skies almost clear | *At end of text beneath single rule:* A list of Admiral Knowle's squadron, that fell in with a Spanish squadron. . . .

31 x 20 cm. (28.9 x 14.2 cm)

STE 6400 / MWA* PHi

27   Philadelphia, Pa.
PENNSYLVANIA JOURNAL

[New-Year verses of the carriers of the Pennsylvania Journal.]

Hildeburn 1145 STE 6402 / No copy located.

1750

28   Philadelphia, Pa.
PENNSYLVANIA GAZETTE

[New-Year verses of the carriers of the Pennsylvania Gazette.]

Hildeburn 1190 STE 6585 / No copy located.

29   Philadelphia, Pa.
PENNSYLVANIA JOURNAL

[New-Year verses of the carriers of the Pennsylvania Journal.]

Hildeburn 1191 STE 6587 / No copy located.

1751

30   New York, N.Y.
NEW-YORK GAZETTE, OR
WEEKLY POST-BOY ◊

Monday, December 31. The yearly verses of the printer's lads, who carry the New-York Gazette reviv'd, about to the customers thereof.

First line: To wish you happy thro' the coming year

31 x 18 cm. (27.1 x 11.9 cm.) Cut at head. (Reilly 936) Mortised allegorical initial block. (Reilly 440)

STE 40552 / NHi*

31   Philadelphia, Pa.
PENNSYLVANIA GAZETTE

[New-Year verses of the carriers of the Pennsylvania Gazette.]

Hildeburn 1229 STE 6750 / No copy located.

32   Philadelphia, Pa.
PENNSYLVANIA JOURNAL

[New-Year verses of the carriers of the Pennsylvania Journal.]

Hildeburn 1230 STE 6752 / No copy located.

1752

33   Philadelphia, Pa.
PENNSYLVANIA GAZETTE

The New-Year verses of the printers lad, who carries the Pennsylvania Gazette to the customers. MDCCLII. On winter.

First line: Can nature, in her brumal [*sic*] hue

32 x 24 cm. (22.6 x 16.9 cm.) Verse in two columns divided by line of type ornaments.

STE 6910 / MWA*

34   Philadelphia, Pa.
PENNSYLVANIA JOURNAL

[New-Year verses of the carriers of the Pennsylvania Journal.]

Hildeburn 1270 STE 6912 / No copy located.

1753

35   Philadelphia, Pa.
PENNSYLVANIA GAZETTE

[New-Year verses of the carriers of the Pennsylvania Gazette.]

Hildeburn 1315 STE 7088 / No copy located.

36   Philadelphia, Pa.
PENNSYLVANIA JOURNAL

[New-Year verses of the carriers of the Pennsylvania Journal.]

Hildeburn 1316 STE 7090 / No copy located.

1754

37   Philadelphia, Pa.
PENNSYLVANIA GAZETTE

[New-Year verses of the carriers of the Pennsylvania Gazette.]

Hildeburn 1375 STE 7289 / No copy located.

38   Philadelphia, Pa.
PENNSYLVANIA JOURNAL

[New-Year verses of the carriers of the Pennsylvania Journal.]

Hildeburn 1376 STE 7291 / No copy located.

1755

39   Philadelphia, Pa.
PENNSYLVANIA GAZETTE

The New-Year verses of the printers lads, who carry the Pennsylvania Gazette, to the customers. For 1755.

First line: Would you read of great battles and marvellous things

32 x 14 cm. (26.9 x 10.9 cm.)

STE 7534 / PPL*

40   Philadelphia, Pa.
PENNSYLVANIA JOURNAL

[New-Year verses of the carriers of the Pennsylvania Journal.]

Hildeburn 1427 STE 7536 / No copy located.

1756

41   Philadelphia, Pa.
PENNSYLVANIA GAZETTE

The New-Year verses of the printers lads, who carry the Pennsylvania Gazette to the customers. For 1756.

First line: Says Charon to Mercury, how goes it above?

32 x 13 cm. (25.3 x 10.5 cm.)

STE 7759 / PPL*

42   Philadelphia, Pa.
PENNSYLVANIA JOURNAL

[New-Year verses of the carriers of the Pennsylvania Journal.]

Hildeburn 1490 STE 7761 / No copy located.

1757

43   Philadelphia, Pa.
PENNSYLVANIA GAZETTE

The New-Year verses of the printers boys, who carry about the Pennsylvania Gazette to the customers. January 1, 1757

First line: How hard the hapless news-boy's fate?

30 x 19 cm. (23.8 x 14.4 cm.) Verse in two columns divided by line of type ornaments.

STE 8000 / NjHi PPL*

44   Philadelphia, Pa.
PENNSYLVANIA JOURNAL

[New-Year verses of the carriers of the Pennsylvania Journal.]

Hildeburn 1548 STE 8002 / No copy located.

1758

45   New York, N.Y.
NEW-YORK MERCURY, 1752–1768

The carriers of the New-York Mercury* (after giving their kind customers the compliments of the season) sends the following occasional piece: Greeting. Printing-office, in Hanover Square, Jan. 2, 1758.

First line: Awake, O! drooping muse and make a shift | *At end of text beneath line of type ornaments:* The word Mercury is variously applied. . . .

33 x 22 cm. (30.6 x 15.6 cm.) Verse in two columns divided by line of type ornaments. Double line of type ornaments at head of text includes two-line verse.

STE 40953 / NjHi*

46   Philadelphia, Pa.
PENNSYLVANIA GAZETTE

The New-Year verses, of the printers lads, who carry the Pennsylvania Gazette to the customers. January 1, 1758.

First line: Suppose a man's ailment admit not of cure

32 x 13 cm. (25.4 x 9.6 cm.)
STE 8232 / PPL*

47   Philadelphia, Pa.
PENNSYLVANIA JOURNAL

[New-Year verses of the carriers of the Pennsylvania Journal.]

Hildeburn 1599 STE 8234 / No copy located.

48   The news-boy's verses at the conclusion of the year 1757. Humbly addressed to the gentlemen and ladies, to whom he carries the news. ◊

First line: With heavy heart and pocket light

32 x 13 cm. (24.6 x 9.0 cm.)

MSaE* / Ms. signature on verso of Essex Institute copy: Nancy Vernon Newport Rhode Island, 1758.

1759

49   Philadelphia, Pa.
PENNSYLVANIA GAZETTE

The New-Year verses of the printers lads, who carry about the Pennsylvania Gazette to the customers. January 1, 1759.

First line: Once more my annual round has been perform'd

39 x 16 cm. (36.5 x 11.2 cm.)
STE 8462 / PPL

50   Philadelphia, Pa.
PENNSYLVANIA JOURNAL

[New-Year verses of the carriers of the Pennsylvania Journal.]

Hildeburn 1637 STE 8464 / No copy located.

1760

51   Boston, Mass.
BOSTON POST-BOY

A New Year's wish, from the lad, who carries the Post-Boy & Advertiser. . . . Boston, January 1, 1760.

First line: Led thro' a scene of blood, a dreadful year

25 x 17 cm. (25.0 x 11.0 cm.) Cut at head of text. (Reilly 1148)

STE 41232 / PHi* / Reproduced in Ola E. Winslow, *American Broadside Verse* (New Haven, 1930), 203.

52   Philadelphia, Pa.
      PENNSYLVANIA GAZETTE

The New-Year verses, of the printers lads, who carry about the Pennsylvania Gazette to the customers. January 1, 1760.

First line: Attend, my dear readers, attend to my lore

39 x 15 cm. (35.7 x 10.7 cm.)

STE 8709 / PPL*

53   Philadelphia, Pa.
      PENNSYLVANIA JOURNAL

[New-Year verses of the carriers of the Pennsylvania Journal.]

Hildeburn 1690 STE 8711 / No copy located.

1761

54   Boston, Mass.
      BOSTON NEWS-LETTER

A New-Years present from the lad that carries the Boston News-Letter, to all generous customers, January 1, 1761.

First line: Kind to my wishes till this happy day

19 x 14 cm. (18.4 x 9.7 cm.) Headband.

STE 41231 / PHi*

55   New York, N.Y.
      NEW-YORK GAZETTE, OR
      WEEKLY POST-BOY

For the New-York Gazette, Jan. 1, 1761.

First line: To all gentlefolks in town, and every, and any | *Eight lines of verse at end, signed:* Laurencius Swinney.

31 x 14 cm. (24.9 x 10.3 cm.) Cut of coat of arms at head.

STE 41248 / PHi*

56   Philadelphia, Pa.
      PENNSYLVANIA GAZETTE

[New-Year verses of the carriers of the Pennsylvania Gazette.]

Hildeburn 1754 STE 8974 / No copy located.

57   Philadelphia, Pa.
      PENNSYLVANIA JOURNAL

[New-Year verses of the carriers of the Pennsylvania Journal.]

Hildeburn 1755 STE 8976 / No copy located.

1762

58   Boston, Mass.
      BOSTON POST-BOY

A New-Year's wish, from the carrier of the Post-Boy & Advertiser. . . . Boston, January 1, 1762.

First line: The year now dawns, what tribute shall I bring?

20 x 17 cm. (18.4 x 13.5 cm.) Cut at head. (Reilly 1525)

STE 41293 / PHi*

59   Philadelphia, Pa.
      PENNSYLVANIA GAZETTE

[New-Year verses of the carriers of the Pennsylvania Gazette.]

Hildeburn 1837 STE 9234 / No copy located.

60   Philadelphia, Pa.
      PENNSYLVANIA JOURNAL

[New-year verses of the carriers of the Pennsylvania Journal.]

First line: Still as emerges from the womb of time

STE 9236 / No copy located

Author: Nathaniel Evans. Collected in his *Poems on Several Occasions, with Some other Compositions* (Philadelphia, 1772), 55–59.

1763

61   New York, N.Y.
**NEW-YORK GAZETTE, OR
WEEKLY POST-BOY**

The news-boy's verses, for New-Year's Day, 1763. Humbly address'd to his patrons, to whom he carries the Thursday's New-York Gazette.

First line: The old year now is past and gone | *At end of text:* Finis.

40 x 26 cm. (36.3 x 19.6 cm.) Verse in three columns. Stanzas numbered I–L.

STE 9217 / NN*

62   Philadelphia, Pa.
PENNSYLVANIA GAZETTE ◊

[New-Year verses of the carriers of the Pennsylvania Gazette.]

First line: Hail sacred muse! Thou harbinger of fame

Hildeburn 1912 STE 9479 / No copy located.

Author: Nathaniel Evans. Collected in his *Poems on Several Occasions, with Some other Compositions* (Philadelphia, 1772), 55, 59, 64–71.

63   Philadelphia, Pa.
PENNSYLVANIA JOURNAL

[New-Year verses of the carriers of the Pennsylvania Journal.]

Hildeburn 1913 STE 9481 / No copy located.

64   The news-carrier's verses. 1763.

First line: See honest Wiley still appear

29 x 10 cm. (21.5 x 7.2 cm.) Line of type ornaments above and below title. Tailpiece.
PHi*

**65   A valediction, for New-Year's day.
1763.**

First line: May Providence, propitious, grant my pray'r | *At end of text:* Philanthropos.

19 x 14 cm. (16.5 x 10.2 cm.) Line of type ornaments at head and end of text.
PHi*

1764

66   Boston, Mass.

A New Year's wish. A happy year to my generous customers. . . . Boston, January 1, 1764.

First line: Another memorable year is past

26 x 14 cm. (21.5 x 10.5 cm.)

STE 41474 / PHi*

67   Philadelphia, Pa.
PENNSYLVANIA GAZETTE

The New-Year verses, of the printers lads, who carry about the Pennsylvania Gazette to the customers. January 1, 1764.

First line: From Thetis' lap, thou amber sun

32 x 19 cm. (29.2 x 16.2 cm.) Verse within ornamental border in two columns divided by curvilinear decorative line. Decorated initial block.

STE 9789 / CtY DLC PPL*

68   Philadelphia, Pa.
PENNSYLVANIA JOURNAL

[New-Year verses of the carriers of the Pennsylvania Journal.]

Hildeburn 2025 STE 9791 / No copy located.

1765

69   Boston, Mass
**BOSTON EVENING-POST,
1735–1775**

The news-boy's Christmas and New-Year's verses. Humbly address'd to the gentlemen and ladies to whom he carries the Boston Evening Post, published by T. & J. Fleet. . . . December 31, 1764.

First line: The boy who weekly pads the streets

30 x 18 cm. (21.4 x 13.3 cm.) Verse in two columns with cut of heart and crown at head. (Reilly 465)

STE 41477 / DLC* PHi / Reproduced in O. E. Winslow, *American Broadside Verse* (New Haven, 1930), 205.

70   Boston, Mass.
      BOSTON GAZETTE, 1719–1798

A New-Year's address, to the customers of the Boston Gazette, &c. for January, 1765.

First line: Master, my modesty's so great | *At end of text:* J.T.

17 x 13 cm. (15.8 x 10.8 cm.) Line of type ornaments at head and end. (Reilly 726)

STE 41573 / PHi*

71   Boston, Mass.
      BOSTON NEWS-LETTER

A New-Year's addrdss [*sic*], which the carrier of the Boston News-Lettr [*sic*], &c. humbly presents to all his generous customer's. January, 1765.

First line: Come, generous patron, lend an ear

26 x 17 cm. (22.3 x 8.2 cm.) Line of type ornaments at head and end of text. Cut of Royal coat of arms at head.

STE 41574 / PHi*

72   New York, N.Y.
      NEW-YORK GAZETTE, OR
      WEEKLY POST-BOY

The news-boy's verses, for January 1, 1765. Humbly address'd to his patrons, to whom he carries the Thursday's New-York Gazette.

First line: Having labour'd to please you, by bringing you news

42 x 16 cm. (33.9 x 12.7 cm.) Verses numbered I–XI, within ornamental border.

STE 41578 / DLC*

73   New York, N.Y.
      NEW-YORK MERCURY, 1752–1768

The news-man's address to his kind and generous benefactors, the subscribers to the New-York Mercury. . . . January 1, 1765.

First line: Since now, with peace and plenty blest

42 x 15 cm. (33.2 x 9.1 cm.) Cut of Mercury at head. (Reilly 1037)

MWA* / Ms. inscription in a contemporary hand on recto of American Antiquarian Society copy: Vardillian composition; and on verso: Vardil's poem on New Year for the news man—1765. Possibly written by John Vardill, 1749–1811, who was a student at King's College in New York at that time.

74   Philadelphia, Pa.
      PENNSYLVANIA GAZETTE

The New-Year verses, of the printers lads, who carry about the Pennsylvania Gazette to the customers. January 1, 1765.

First line: Bright issuing from th' ocean stream

32 x 20 cm. (28.6 x 16.8 cm.) Verse within ornamental border divided by line of type ornaments. Decorated initial block.

STE 10126 / PHi PPL*

75   Philadelphia, Pa.
      PENNSYLVANIA JOURNAL

[New-Year verses of the carriers of the Pennsylvania Journal.]

Hildeburn 2153 STE 10128 / No copy located.

76   Philadelphia, Pa.
      WÖCHENTLICHE PHILADEL-
      PHISCHE STAATSBOTE

Des Herumträgers des Staatsboton Neujahrs-Verse, seinen resp. geehrten Kundleuten überreicht den 1ten Jenner, 1765.

First line: Wir treten jetzt, walt's Gott! ins Neue wieder ein

35 x 21 cm. (32.0 x 14.1 cm.) Single rule at head of text.

STE 10218 / PHi*

77   A New Year's wish. . . . 1765.

First line: Europa still partakes the joys of peace

18 x 12 cm. (12.8 x 9.0 cm.) Headbands at head and end

STE 41575 / PHi*

1766

78   Boston, Mass.
      BOSTON EVENING-POST,
         1735–1775 ◊

Vox populi. Liberty, property and no stamps. The news-boy who carries the Boston Evening-Post, with the greatest submission begs leave to present the following lines to the gentlemen and ladies to whom he carries the news.

First line: What time bears on his rapid wing | *At head of text:* Ode on the New Year.

33 x 14 cm. (31.5 x 9.4 cm.) Cut within title. (Reilly 434)

STE 41670 / PHi*

79   Boston, Mass.
      BOSTON GAZETTE, 1719–1798

January 1766. The carrier of the Boston-Gazette, to his customers. A New-Year's wish.

First line: 'Tis past! 'Tis gone! th' important day has fled

33 x 14 cm. (29.2 x 11.2 cm.) Single rule at head and end of text. Cut at head. (Reilly 1031)

STE 41631 / PHi* / Reproduced in O. E. Winslow, *American Broadside Verse* (New Haven, 1930), 207.

80   Boston, Mass.
      BOSTON POST-BOY ◊

New-Year's wish from the carrier of the Boston Post-Boy, &c.

First line: Generous customers, I run

19 x 14 cm. (18.2 x 11.0 cm.) Line of type ornaments at head and end.

STE 41647 / PHi*

81   New York, N.Y.
      NEW-YORK GAZETTE
         [WEYMAN'S]

Jem-mi-bul-le-ro: instead of Lillibullero. Presented by the boys that carries about the Monday's New-York Gazette, a fragment of Orpheus's ode, for the year 1766.

First line: And Jemmy is a silly dog, and Jemmy is a tool

31 x 21 cm. (30.3 x 19.4 cm.) Verse in two columns divided by line of type ornaments. Cut of Royal coat of arms at head.

STE 10426 / PPL*

Attributed to Samuel Waterhouse, 'a drunken customs officer,' in *Sibley's Harvard Graduates*, 11: 263. First published in the *Boston Evening-Post*, May 13, 1765.

82   Philadelphia, Pa.
      PENNSYLVANIA GAZETTE

The New-Year verses of the printers lads, who carry about the Pennsylvania Gazette to the customers. January 1, 1766.

First line: The sun in roseate beauty drest

33 x 21 cm. (27.3 x 16.6 cm.) Verse within ornamental border in two columns divided by line of type ornaments.

STE 10447 / MH PHi PPL*

83   Philadelphia, Pa.
      PENNSYLVANIA JOURNAL

The New-Year verses, of the printer's lads, who carry the Pennsylvania Journal to the customers. Philadelphia, January 1st, 1766.

First line: She comes! She comes!—I hear the festive sound

26 x 18 cm. (24.4 x 16.1 cm.) Verse in two columns divided by line of type ornaments with decorated initial block.

STE 10449 / PHi* / Reprinted in Joseph T. Buckingham, *Specimens of Newspaper Literature: with Personal Memoirs, Anecdotes, and Reminiscences*, 2 vols. (Boston, 1850) 1: 291–93. Wrongly dated 1776.

84   Philadelphia, Pa.
      WÖCHENTLICHE PHILADEL-
         PHISCHE STAATSBOTE

Des Herumträgers der Staatsboten Neujahrs-Verse, bey seinen resp. Geehrten Kundleuten abgelegt den 6ten Jenner, 1766.

First line: Geehrte Leser, was für Wechsel sind gewesen

26 x 19 cm. (23.8 x 14.2 cm.) Single rule at head of text.

STE 10525 / PHi*

85   New Year's ode, for the year 1766, being actually dictated by Lawrence Swinney, carrier of news, enemy to stamps, a friend to the constitution, and an Englishman every inch.

First line: I am against the Stamp Act

30 x 13 cm. (23.8 x 8.0 cm.) Cut of Mercury at head (Reilly 1037).

STE 41663 / PHi* / It is possible that this piece was not a carrier's address.

86   A New-Years wish. ◊

First line: Once more my friends I do appear

15 x 12 cm. (12.5 x 9.3 cm.) Line of type ornaments at head and end.

STE 41475 / PHi* / Pennsylvania Historical Society copy dated 1766 in a contemporary hand.

1767

87   New Haven, Conn.
      CONNECTICUT GAZETTE

New-Year's verses for the lad who carries the Connecticut Gazette to its encouragers in New-Haven. A.D. 1767.

First line: It is a point will be agreed

32 x 19 cm. (30.4 x 16.2 cm.) Verse in two columns divided by single rule.

STE 41742 / PHi*

88   Boston, Mass.
      BOSTON EVENING-POST,
         1735–1775

The boy who carries the Boston Evening Post, presents his compliments of joy on the commencement of the year 1767.

First line: Oft, gen'rous patron, to regale your taste

31 x 20 cm. (28.2 x 15.0 cm.) Verse in two columns divided by line of type ornaments. First and last stanzas centered on sheet. Cut at head. (Reilly 464)

STE 41698 / PHi*

89   Boston, Mass.
      BOSTON POST-BOY ◊

A New Year's wish from the carrier of the Post-Boy & Advertiser.

First line: Suffer my muse with soft address

19 x 14 cm. (17.6 x 10.2 cm.)

STE 41744 / PHi* / Pennsylvania Historical Society copy dated 1767 in a contemporary hand.

90   Portsmouth, N.H.
      NEW-HAMPSHIRE GAZETTE

The news-boy, who now carries the New-Hampshire Gazette, presents his compliments of joy to the customers on the commencement of the year 1767.

First line: When on the printing duties I attend

34 x 21 cm. (28.1 x 12.0 cm.)

STE 41748 / MWA*

91   New York, N.Y.
      NEW-YORK GAZETTE, OR
         WEEKLY POST-BOY ◊

New-Year's verses made and carried about to the customers of the New-York Gazette, by Lawrence Swinney, alias (for the present) Bloody-News, but on the prospect of approaching peace, for the future, Lawrence White-Flagg, alias Olive-Branch.

First line: For breaking faith, and eating frogs

41 x 14 cm. (35.2 x 8.4 cm.) Cut at head. (Reilly 864)

STE 41767 / NjHi*

92   Philadelphia, Pa.
      PENNSYLVANIA GAZETTE

The New-Year verses, of the printers lads, who carry the Pennsylvania Gazette to the customers. January 1, 1767.

First line: Let pleasure crown this smiling morn

32 x 21 cm. (26.8 x 16.5 cm.) Verse within ornamental border in two columns divided by line of type ornaments with decorated initial block.

STE 10732 / PPL*

93　Philadelphia, Pa.
PENNSYLVANIA JOURNAL

[New-Year verses of the carriers of the Pennsylvania Journal.]

Hildeburn 2313 STE 10734 / No copy located.

94　Charleston, S.C.
SOUTH-CAROLINA GAZETTE;
AND COUNTRY JOURNAL

New-Year's verses, of the printer's boys, who carry about the South Carolina Gazette, and Country Journal, addressed to the customers thereof. Thursday, January 1, 1767.

First line: My honour'd patrons, and my friends

32 x 19 cm. (28.6 x 14.9 cm.) Verse within ornamental border. Cut of Royal coat of arms at head. (Reilly 892)

STE 41743 / PHi*

95　A New-Year's address, which your obedient servant the young shaver humbly presents to all his generous customers. ◊

First line: The new-born year now usher's in

19 x 12 cm. (17.4 x 9.3 cm.) Line of type ornaments at head of text.

STE 41854 / PHi* / Pennsylvania Historical Society copy bears ms. date 1767.

1768

96　Boston, Mass.
BOSTON EVENING-POST,
1735–1775

New-Year's day, 1768. The news boy's verses who carries the Boston Evening-Post.

First line: To give his friends pleasure the new-boy [*sic*] with pain

32 x 14 cm. (30.4 x 9.7 cm.) Short rule following date.

STE 41855 / PHi*

97　Boston, Mass.
BOSTON GAZETTE, 1719–1798 ◊

A New-Year's wish.

First line: This year's begun my humble muse

19 x 13 cm. (18.0 x 8.0 cm.) Cut at head. (Reilly 1032)

STE 41859 / PHi* / Pennsylvania Historical Society copy dated 1768 in a contemporary hand.

98　Boston, Mass.
BOSTON NEWS-LETTER

An address from the carrier of the Massachusetts-Gazette, to his customers. Boston, January 1st, 1768.

First line: Encircled round with blessings far and near

18 x 14 cm. (17.5 x 11.2 cm.) Line of type ornaments at head and end of text.

STE 41782 / PHi*

99　Boston, Mass.
BOSTON POST-BOY ◊

A New Year's wish, from the carrier of the Post Boy and Advertiser.

First line: The course of time again devolves

20 x 14 cm. (18.2 x 9.0 cm.) Cut of ship at head. (Reilly 1143)

STE 41857 / PHi* / Pennsylvania Historical Society copy dated 1768 in a contemporary hand.

100　Portsmouth, N.H.
NEW-HAMPSHIRE GAZETTE

Portsmouth, January 1st, 1768. To the customers of the New-Hampshire Gazette.

First line: Gentlemen and ladies, permit a youth his compliments to pay

32 x 18 cm. (24.1 x 10.5 cm.)
STE 41821 / NHi*

1769

101   Philadelphia, Pa.
PENNSYLVANIA CHRONICLE

[New-Year verses of the carriers of the Pennsylvania Chronicle.]

Hildeburn 2378 STE 11029 / No copy located.

102   Philadelphia, Pa.
PENNSYLVANIA GAZETTE

Verses, of the printers lads, who carry the Pennsylvania Gazette to the customers. Ode on the New Year.

First line: Janus, who, with sliding pace

31 x 21 cm. (25.5 x 16.7 cm.) Verse within ornamental border in two columns divided by line of type ornaments with decorated initial block.

STE 11031 / PPL*

103   Philadelphia, Pa.
PENNSYLVANIA JOURNAL

[New-Year verses of the carriers of the Pennsylvania Journal.]

Hildeburn 2379 STE 11033 / No copy located.

104   Charleston, S.C.
SOUTH-CAROLINA AND AMERICAN GENERAL GAZETTE

To the readers of the South-Carolina & American General Gazette. January 1, 1768.

First line: Throughout the long year past, in good or in bad weather | *Signed:* Nathan B. Child. | Followed by a second anonymous verse.

32 x 20 cm. (28.4 x 15.1 cm.) Cut of Royal coat of arms at head.

STE 41897 / MWA* NHi

105   An happy New Year. ◊

First line: Revolving scenes attend revolving years

23 x 15 cm. (20.9 x 11.0 cm.) Cut of Royal coat of arms at head. Single rule beneath cut.

STE 41835 / PHi*

1769

106   Boston, Mass.
BOSTON EVENING-POST, 1735–1775

To all his kind customers, the boy who carries the Evening-Post, wishes a happy New-Year. 1769.

First line: Once more the poor boy who distributes the news

31 x 14 cm. (29.2 x 10.0 cm.) Short single rule at head of text and after sixth stanza.

STE 42010 / PHi*

107   Boston, Mass.
BOSTON GAZETTE, 1719–1798

A New-Year's wish for the public, for the year 1769. (From the carrier of the Boston-Gazette, &c.)

First line: 'Tis past, the fatal year is past

17 x 12 cm. (15.5 x 9.7 cm.) Single rule at head.
STE 41981 / PHi*

108   Boston, Mass.
BOSTON NEWS-LETTER

An happy New-Year to the worthy customers of the Massachusetts-Gazette & Boston News-Letter, Boston, January 1769.

First line: Said Ned unto Sam, what's the news of the day? | *At head of verse:* Dialogue between two lads who are news-carriers.

20 x 15 cm. (16.2 x 12.1 cm.) Woodcut of Royal coat of arms at head. (Reilly 863) Line of type ornaments at head and end of text.

STE 41942 / PHi*

109   Salem, Mass.
ESSEX GAZETTE

On the commencement of the year 1769. Job Weeden, Salem news-boy, begs leave, with profound submission and reverence, to present the following lines to the gentlemen and ladies to whom he carries the Essex Gazette.

First line: Humbly a youth begs leave to pay

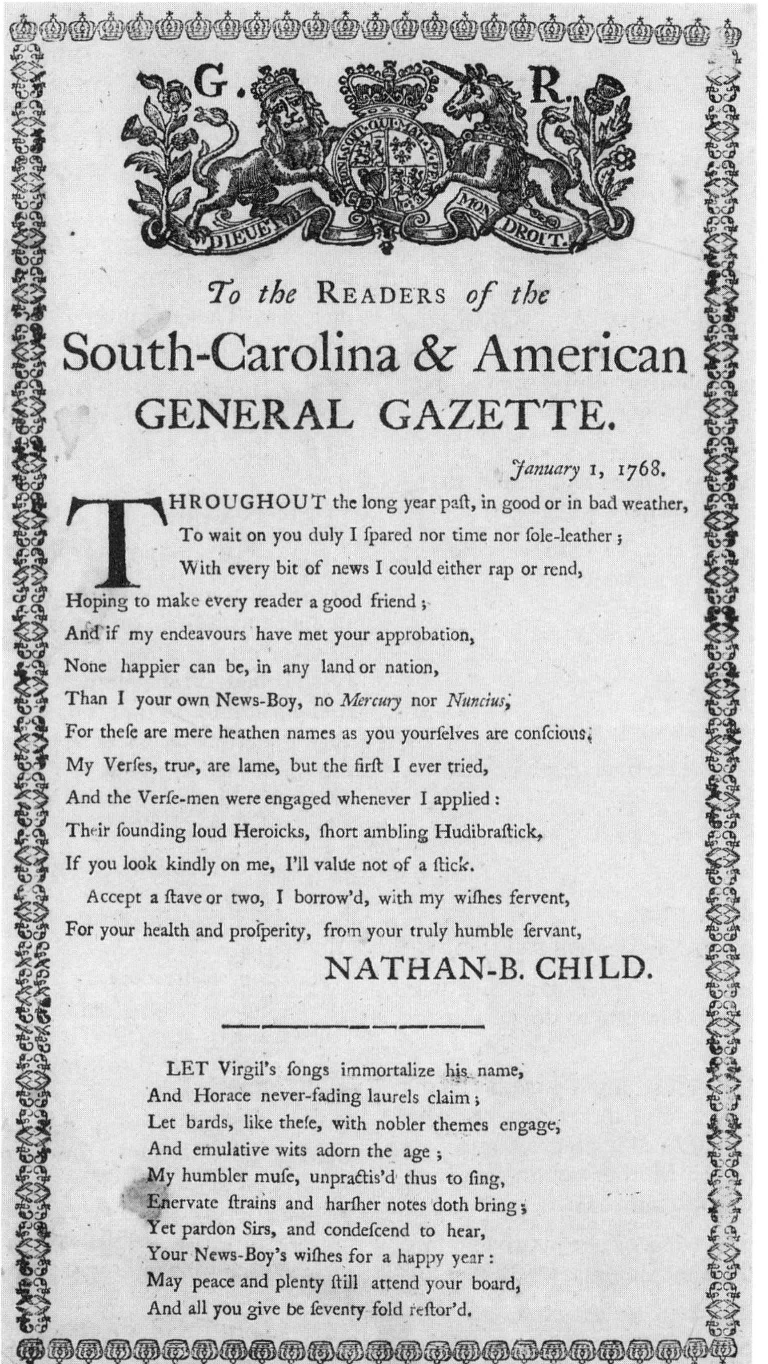

Fig. 2. McDonald 104. *South-Carolina and American General Gazette*, Charleston, S.C. January 1, 1768. American Antiquarian Society.

19 x 10 cm. (18.0 x 16.0 cm.) Line of type ornaments at head and end.

STE 42023 / PHi*

110   New York, N.Y.
NEW-YORK GAZETTE, AND WEEKLY MERCURY

Printing-Office, in Hanover Square, January 1, 1769. The printer's lads who carry about the New-York Gazette, or the Weekly Mercury, to the kind and generous customers thereof; (after giving them the compliments of the season,) beg leave to present the following verses.

First line: As on the broad Atlantic's beaten shore | *Preliminary verse with first line:* They claim attention, but be more than just!

40 x 25 cm. (35.7 x 18.2 cm.) Verse in two columns divided by line of type ornaments.

STE 41995 / MWA*

111   Philadelphia, Pa.
PENNSYLVANIA CHRONICLE

[New-Year verses of the carriers of the Pennsylvania Chronicle.]

Hildeburn 2467 STE 11405 / No copy located.

112   Philadelphia, Pa.
PENNSYLVANIA GAZETTE

The New-Year verses, of the printers lads, who carry the Pennsylvania Gazette to the customers. January, 1769.

First line: As Rome high triumph'd in the sacred bays | *At end of text:* In the above lines, we have considered the freedom and happiness—the slavery and misery of the Mother country and her colonies, as inseparably connected.

32 x 21 cm. (28.1 x 16.6 cm.) Verse in two columns divided by line of type ornaments. Decorated initial block.

STE 11407 / PPL*

113   Philadelphia, Pa.
PENNSYLVANIA JOURNAL

[New-Year verses of the carriers of the Pennsylvania Journal.]

Hildeburn 2469 STE 11409 / No copy located.

114   Newport, R.I.
NEWPORT MERCURY

New-Year's verses, addressed to the customers of the Newport Mercury: by the printer's boys who carry about the same. January 1, 1769.

First line: The joyful day returns! th' illustrious time!

25 x 21 cm. (22.0 x 12.0 cm.) Cut of Royal coat of arms at head. Line of type ornaments at end.

STE 41980 / RNHi*

115   Newport, R.I.
NEWPORT MERCURY ◊

To the customers of the Newport Mercury. Gentlemen and ladies, I once more assume the honour of presenting you with a poetical address, (if it can be so called) on the anniversary of a New-Year. If it is agreeable, I doubt not but you will confer a very generous token of approbation on, gentlemen and ladies, your very obsequious, much obliged, truly humble, and most devoted servant, Eben. Hall, N.C.

First line: Grateful and joyous once more I appear

27 x 13 cm.

Alden 414 STE 41940 / NN* RNHi / Ms. date [1769?] in a contemporary hand on Newport Historical Society copy. American Antiquarian Society states that textual references suggest that the verses were printed to commemorate the Stamp Act, which was declared on March 18, 1766. Samuel Hall, older brother of the author, printed the Newport Mercury from April 1763 to March 1768, and it is probable that the verses were printed during those years. The dated Mercury address for 1769 displayed strong loyalty to the crown. Possibly this undated one by Ebenezer Hall was offered also in 1769 in opposition to the Tory sentiments of the other.

Author: Ebenezer Hall.

1770

116　Boston, Mass.
Boston Chronicle

A New-Year's wish, for the year 1770. By the carrier of the Boston Chronicle.

First line: Neither Whig, nor Tory am I

32 x 19 cm. (26.9 x 17.2 cm.) Verse within architectural border. Line of type ornaments at head of text.

STE 42138 / PHi*

117　Boston, Mass.
Boston Evening-Post,
1735–1775

January 1, 1770. A New Year's address of the printer's boy who carries the Boston Evening-Post.

First line: Revolving time, bless'd year-renewing time

27 x 13 cm. (22.2 x 9.4 cm.) Short single rule after fourth stanza. Cut at head. (Reilly 464)

STE 42038 / PHi*

118　Boston, Mass.
Boston Gazette, 1719–1798

An ode for the year 1770. From the carrier of the Boston-Gazette &c. . . . to his customers.

First line: Still pain'd suspense awaits the lazy joy

19 x 14 cm. (17.0 x 10.6 cm.) Line of type ornaments at head and end.

STE 42142 / PHi*

119　Boston, Mass.
Boston News-Letter

An happy New-Year from the carrier of the Massachusetts and Boston News-Letter, to all his generous customers. January, 1770.

First line: Hail brave Bostonians! still we live

20 x 13 cm. (19.0 x 8.9 cm.) Line of type ornaments at head of text. Cut of Royal coat of arms at head.

STE 42105 / PHi*

120　Boston, Mass.
Boston Post-Boy

January 1, 1770. New Year's verses, from the lad who carries the Massachusetts-Gazette & Boston Post-Boy.

First line: A printer's boy (he seeks no better name)

25 x 14 cm. (20.0 x 9.0 cm.) Line of type ornaments at head and end. Cut of Royal coat of arms at head. (Reilly 910)

STE 42110 / PHi*

121　Philadelphia, Pa.
Pennsylvania Chronicle

[New-Year verses of the carriers of the Pennsylvania Chronicle.]

Hildeburn 2569 STE 11805 / No copy located.

122　Philadelphia, Pa.
Pennsylvania Gazette

The New-Year verses, of the printers lads, who carry the Pennsylvania Gazette to the customers. January, 1770.

First line: With constant pace earth rolls her seasons round

32 x 21 cm. (27.2 x 16.7 cm.) Verse in two columns divided by line of type ornaments with decorated initial block. Single rule above date.

STE 11807 / PPL*

123　Philadelphia, Pa.
Pennsylvania Journal

[New-Year verses of the carriers of the Pennsylvania Journal.]

Hildeburn 2571 STE 11809 / No copy located.

124　Newport, R.I.
Newport Mercury

New-Year's verses, addressed to the customers of the Newport Mercury: by the printer's boys, who carry about the same. January 1, 1770.

First line: Week after week, I, constant as the sun

22 x 15 cm. (20.3 x 11.7 cm.) Cut of Royal coat

of arms at head. (Reilly 921) Line of type ornaments at end.

STE 42137 / RNHi*

125   Charleston, S.C.
     SOUTH-CAROLINA GAZETTE

To the subscribers for the South-Carolina Gazette. January 1, 1770.

First line: In days of yore, when Greece the sceptre sway'd

31 x 20 cm. (27.9 x 13.8 cm.) Verse within ornamental border.

Hummel 1954 / ScC*

1771

126   Boston, Mass.
     BOSTON EVENING-POST,
       1735–1775 ◊

A New Year's wish, of the printer's boy who carries
the Boston Evening-Post.

First line: Old time again has run the circling year

20 x 13 cm. (18.1 x 8.7 cm.)

Ford 1604 / PHi*

127   Boston, Mass.
     MASSACHUSETTS SPY

The lad who carries the Massachusetts Spy, wishes
all his kind customers a Merry Christmas, and a
Happy New Year! And presents the following. . . .
Boston, January 1, 1771.

First line: May grateful omens now appear

22 x 18 cm. (19.1 x 11.6 cm.) Cut at head. (Reilly
234)

MWA*

128   Philadelphia, Pa.
     PENNSYLVANIA CHRONICLE

[New-Year verses of the carriers of the Pennsylvania Chronicle.]

Hildeburn 2683 STE 12181 / No copy located.

129   Philadelphia, Pa.
     PENNSYLVANIA GAZETTE

The New-Year verses, of the printers lads, who
carry the Pennsylvania Gazette to the customers.
January 1771.

First line: On western plains, where lofty turrets
rise

32 x 23 cm. (25.7 x 16.4 cm.) Verse in two columns
divided by line of type ornaments with decorated
initial block.

STE 12183 / PPL*

130   Philadelphia, Pa.
     PENNSYLVANIA JOURNAL

[New-Year verses of the carriers of the Pennsylvania Journal.]

Hildeburn 2685 STE 12185 / No copy located.

1772

131   Boston, Mass.
     CENSOR ◊

The carrier of the Censor, wishes all happiness to
his generous customers.

First line: What means this clamour? Why this
strife? | *At head:* Censor.

19 x 11 cm. (17.3 x 8.1 cm.)

STE 44660 / PHi*

Dated 1785 by Ford and Bristol. However, the
Censor, printed by Ezekiel Russell, was published
only from Nov. 23, 1771, to May 2, 1772. Dated
by Brigham through internal evidence.

132   Boston, Mass.
     MASSACHUSETTS SPY

The carrier of the Massachusetts Spy, wishes all
his kind customers a merry Christmas, and a
happy New Year; and presents the following, viz.
. . . . Boston, January 1, 1772.

First line: Hail happy day, important year!

32 x 12 cm. (30.7 x 8.1 cm.) Cut at head. (Reilly 234)

STE 42325 / DLC MB MWA PHi*

The LAD who carries

The MASSACHUSETTS SPY,

Wiſhes all his kind Cuſtomers

A Merry Chriſtmas, and a Happy New Year!

And preſents the following:

MAY grateful omens now appear,
To make the New a happy Year,
      And bleſs th' enſuing days :
May future peace in every mind,
Like odours wafted by the wind,
      Its ſweeteſt incenſe raiſe.

May GEORGE in his extenſive reign,
Subdue the pride of haughty SPAIN
      Submiſſive to his feet.
Thy princely ſmiles our ills appeaſe ;
Then grant that harmony and peace
      The dawning year may greet.

Kind Sirs ! your gen'rous bounty ſhow,
Few ſhillings on your Lad beſtow,
      Which will reward his pains,
Who piercing Winter's cold endures,
And to your hands the SPY ſecures,
      And ſtill his taſk mainiains.

Boſton, January 1, 1771.

Fig. 3. McDonald 127. *Massachusetts Spy*, Boston, Mass., January 1, 1771. American Antiquarian Society.

133   Salem Mass.
ESSEX GAZETTE

Job Weeden, Salem news-boy, begs leave to present the following lines to the gentlemen and ladies to whom he carries the Essex Gazette. Jan. 1, 1772.

First line: Now happily dawns the year—seventy two—

18 x 16 cm. (16.4 x 12.8 cm.) Verse within ornamental border.

STE 42389 / MWA*

134   Philadelphia, Pa.
PENNSYLVANIA CHRONICLE

[New-Year verses of the carriers of the Pennsylvania Chronicle.]

Hildeburn 2797 STE 12509 / No copy located.

135   Philadelphia, Pa.
PENNSYLVANIA GAZETTE

The New-Year verses, of the printers lads, who carry the Pennsylvania Gazette to the customers. January, 1772.

First line: Blyth Christmas, joyous season, past

35 x 22 cm. (31.2 x 15.1 cm.) Verse within ornamental border in two columns divided by line of type ornaments.

STE 12511 / MWA PPL RPB*

136   Philadelphia, Pa.
PENNSYLVANIA JOURNAL

[New-Year verses of the carriers of the Pennsylvania Journal.]

Hildeburn 2799 STE 12513 / No copy located.

137   Philadelphia, Pa.
PENNSYLVANIA PACKET

[New-Year verses of the carriers of the Pennsylvania Packet.]

Hildeburn 2800 STE 12515 / No copy located.

138   Philadelphia, Pa.

The news-boy's verses to his customers. January 1, 1772.

First line: Once the refulgent ruler of the day

27 x 22 cm. (24.2 x 11.7 cm.) Line of type ornaments at head and end.

MH*

1773

139   Boston, Mass.
BOSTON NEWS-LETTER ◊

New-Year's verses, addressed to the customers of the Massachusetts Gazette, &c.

First line: A New Year's wish is grown so common

19 x 10 cm. (17.4 x 8.5 cm.) Verse within ornamental border.

STE 42469 / CSmH* PHi

140   Salem, Mass.
ESSEX GAZETTE

The lad who carries the Essex Gazette begs leave to present the following lines to the customers thereof, on the commencement of the year 1773. January 1, 1773.

First line: Hail, happy day, propitious be the year!

26 x 14 cm. (22.1 x 10.3 cm.) Verse within ornamental border.

STE 42456 / MWA*

141   Portsmouth, N.H.
NEW-HAMPSHIRE GAZETTE

On the New-Year 1773. To all the worthy customers of the New-Hampshire Gazette, the following lines are inscribed, by their humble servants, the printers boys.

First line: While pompous players, in this happy age

36 x 13 cm. (33.2 x 9.7 cm.) Single rule underlining 'On the New-Year 1773.'

STE 42481 / NHi*

142   Philadelphia, Pa.
PENNSYLVANIA CHRONICLE

[New-Year verses of the carriers of the Pennsylvania Chronicle.]

Hildeburn 2907 STE 12926 / No copy located.

143　Philadelphia, Pa.
PENNSYLVANIA GAZETTE

The New-Year verses, of the printers lads, who carry about the Pennsylvania Gazette to the customers. January 1773.

First line: Ned Modish, when once 'mongst his friends in debate

33 x 21 cm. (27.9 x 17.3 cm.) Verse within ornamental border divided by line of type ornaments with decorated initial block.

STE 12928 / PPL*

144　Philadelphia, Pa.
PENNSYLVANIA JOURNAL

[New Year's verses of the carriers of the Pennsylvania Journal.]

Hildeburn 2908 STE 12390 / No copy located.

145　Philadelphia, Pa.
PENNSYLVANIA PACKET

[New-Year verses of the carriers of the Pennsylvania Packet.]

Hildeburn 2909 STE 12932 / No copy located.

1774

146　Boston, Mass.
BOSTON NEWS-LETTER ◊

New Year's verses, addressed to the kind customers of the Massachusetts Gazette, &c.

First line: Oft gen'rous patrons, to regale your taste

24 x 13 cm. (21.6 x 11.0 cm.) Verse within ornamental border. Cut of royal coat of arms at head. (Reilly 907)

STE 42647 / PHi*

147　Salem, Mass.
ESSEX GAZETTE

John Nurse, carrier of the Essex Gazette, humbly presents the following lines to the gentlemen and ladies to whom he carries the news, on the beginning of the year 1774.

First line: The horror of the frozen north

26 x 21 cm. (21.2 x 14.7 cm.) Verse in two columns divided by line of type ornaments. Cut of Indians at head. (Reilly 963)

STE 13271 / MSaE*

148　New York, N.Y.
RIVINGTON'S NEW-YORK GAZETTEER

Ode on the New Year 1774. Delivered by Hugh Duncan, one of the carriers of the Rivington's New-York Gazetteer.

First line: Bright sun! great source of light, of life and joy

31 x 17 cm. (25.6 x 10.9 cm.)

STE 42661 / NN*

149　Philadelphia, Pa.
PENNSYLVANIA CHRONICLE

[New-Year verses of the carriers of the Pennsylvania Chronicle.]

Hildeburn 3065 STE 13527 / No copy located.

150　Philadelphia, Pa.
PENNSYLVANIA GAZETTE

[New-Year verses of the carriers of the Pennsylvania Gazette.]

Hildeburn 3066 STE 13529 / No copy located.

151　Philadelphia, Pa.
PENNSYLVANIA JOURNAL

The New-Year's verses of those who carry the Pennsylvania Journal to the customers. Philadelphia, January 1, 1774.

First line: Ye gen'rous patrons of our annual song

35 x 22 cm. (29.0 x 17.3 cm.) Verse within ornamental border in two columns divided by line of type ornaments. Place and date set off by horizontal lines of type ornaments.

STE 13531 / DLC PHi*

152   Philadelphia, Pa.
PENNSYLVANIA PACKET

[The New-Year verses of the printer's lads, who carry the Pennsylvania Packet to the customers.]

Hildeburn 3068 STE 13262 / No copy located.

1775

153   Boston, Mass.
BOSTON NEWS-LETTER

The carrier of the Massachusetts-Gazette, and Boston Weekly News-Letter, humbly presents the following ode on the New-Year, to all his generous customers. 1775.

First line: Behold! poor Boston sore distrest

26 x 13 cm. (23.7 x 8.4 cm.) Cut of Royal coat of arms at head. (Reilly 861)

STE 42789 / PHi*

154   New York, N.Y.
RIVINGTON'S NEW-YORK GAZETTEER

Verses addressed by Joseph Cree, to the gentlemen and ladies, to whom he carries the New-York Gazetteer. January 1, 1775.

First line: Kind sirs, a young and bashful boy

26 x 18 cm. (22.3 x 14.6 cm.) Verse within ornamental border.

MWA*

155   Philadelphia, Pa.
PENNSYLVANIA GAZETTE

[The New-Year verses, of the printers lads, who carry the Pennsylvania Gazette to the customers.]

First line: While busy mortals stretch their sanguine views

Hildeburn 3247 STE 14376 / No copy located.

156   Philadelphia, Pa.
PENNSYLVANIA JOURNAL

The New-Year's verse of those who carry the Pennsylvania Journal to the customers . . . Philadelphia, January, 1775.

First line: Revolving seasons, and returning time

34 x 21 cm. (30.9 x 16.7 cm.) Verse within ornamental border in two columns divided by line of type ornaments. Place and date set off by lines of type ornaments. Preliminary verse centered at head of text. Cut centered in title. (Reilly 962)

STE 14378 / MHi MWA NHi PHi*

157   Philadelphia, Pa.
PENNSYLVANIA PACKET

The New-Year verses, of those who carry the Pennsylvania Packet to the customers. Philadelphia, January 1, 1775.

First line: Ah me! the sad minute is come

33 x 20 cm. (32.0 x 18.8 cm.) Verse within ornamental border in two columns divided by line of type ornaments. Place and date set off by lines of type ornaments.

STE 14018 / PHi*

1776

158   Philadelphia, Pa.
PENNSYLVANIA EVENING POST

New Year's verses addressed to the customers of the Pennsylvania Evening Post, by the printer's lads, who carry it. Monday, January 1, 1776.

First line: Poor Tom's a cold—God bless you, masters

26 x 21 cm. (22.1 x 18.3 cm.) Verse within ornamental border in two columns divided by line of type ornaments.

STE 15002 / MWA PHi*

159   Philadelphia, Pa.
PENNSYLVANIA GAZETTE

[New-Year verses of the carriers of the Pennsylvania Gazette.]

Hildeburn 3422 STE 15004 / No copy located.

160   Philadelphia, Pa.
PENNSYLVANIA JOURNAL

[The New-Year's verse of the carriers of the Pennsylvania Journal to the customers.]

Hildeburn 3423 STE 15006 / No copy located.

161   Philadelphia, Pa.
PENNSYLVANIA LEDGER

[New Year verses of the carriers of the Pennsylvania Ledger.]

Hildeburn 3424 STE 15008 / No copy located.

162   Philadelphia, Pa.
PENNSYLVANIA PACKET

The New-Year verses of those who carry the Pennsylvania Packet to the customers. January 1, 1776.

First line: While Whitehead signs his New-Year's ode

28 x 11 cm. (24.7 x 8.6 cm.) Verse within ornamental border.

STE 14745 / DLC* NN

1777

163   Philadelphia, Pa.
PENNSYLVANIA EVENING POST

New-Year's verses, addressed to the customers of the Pennsylvania Evening Post, by the printer's lads who carry it. Wednesday, January 1, 1777.

First line: Hail! O America!

25 x 21 cm. (22.1 x 17.2 cm.) Verse in two columns divided by line of type ornaments.

Hildeburn 3586 Wegelin 667 / MWA* PPL

164   Philadelphia, Pa.
PENNSYLVANIA PACKET

New-Year verses of the carriers of the Pennsylvania Packet.

Hildeburn 3587 / No copy located.

1778

165   Philadelphia, Pa.
PENNSYLVANIA EVENING POST

New year's verses, addressed to the kind customers of the Pennsylvania Evening Post, by the printer's lads who carry about the same. Thursday, January 1, 1778.

First line: Towne's Evening Post!—Good masters pray

34 x 20 cm. (30.7 x 16.2 cm.)

STE 15980 / MWA PPL RPB*

166   Philadelphia, Pa.
PENNSYLVANIA LEDGER

New-Year's verses of those who deliver the Pennsylvania Ledger to the subscribers. Philadelphia, January 1, 1778.

First line: 'Tis not for me to sweep the sounding strings

33 x 13 cm. (25.1 x 8.6 cm.) Place and date set off by horizontal rules.

STE 15984 / MWA NN PHi PPL*

167   Philadelphia, Pa.
PENNSYLVANIA PACKET

[New-Year verses of the carriers of the Pennsylvania Packet.]

Hildeburn 3750 STE 15987 / No copy located.

1779

168   [New Haven], Conn.

New Haven, January 1, 1779. The Post-boy's present to his customers.

First line: By the law of good nature 'tis always agreed

21 x 13 cm. (18.1 x 9.1 cm.) Line of type ornaments at head and end. Single rule at head of text.

BAL 856 / MH* / Attributed by Harvard University to Joel Barlow.

Author: Joel Barlow. See Theodore A. Zunder, *The Early Days of Joel Barlow, A Connecticut Wit* (New Haven, 1934), 64.

169 Philadelphia, Pa.
   PENNSYLVANIA EVENING POST

[New-Year verses of the carriers of the Pennsylvania Evening Post.]

Hildeburn 3915 STE 16452 / No copy located.

170 Philadelphia, Pa.
   PENNSYLVANIA GAZETTE

[New-Year verses of the carriers of the Pennsylvania Gazette.]

Hildeburn 3916 STE 16454 / No copy located.

171 Philadelphia, Pa.
   PENNSYLVANIA JOURNAL

[New-Year verses of the carriers of the Pennsylvania Journal.]

Hildeburn 3917 STE 16456 / No copy located.

172 Philadelphia, Pa.
   PENNSYLVANIA PACKET

[New-Year verses of the carriers of the Pennsylvania Packet.]

Hildeburn 3918 STE 16458 / No copy located.

1780

173 Baltimore, Md.
   MARYLAND JOURNAL

The humble address of Tobias Bond, and Benjamin Welch, flying mercuries, or news-boys, (vulgarly styled printer's devils) to the worthy customers of the Maryland Journal, and Baltimore Advertiser. January 1, 1780.

First line: Let festive mirth once more appear | *At end of text beneath line of type ornaments*: That comic genius Tom Weston. . . .

33 x 20 cm. (29.5 x 17.5 cm.) Verse within ornamental border in two columns divided by line of type ornaments.

STE 16835 / MdHi MWA*

174 Portsmouth, N.H.
   NEW-HAMPSHIRE GAZETTE

The news carrier, to the generous customers of the New Hampshire Gazette. A New Year's wish . . . Jan. 1, 1780.

First line: Around the circling year has whirl'd

35 x 22 cm. (20.7 x 7.7 cm.)
NHi*

175 Philadelphia, Pa.
   PENNSYLVANIA EVENING POST
    ◊

New Year's verses, for the lad who carries the Evening Post.

First line: Once more, my masters all, and you

34 x 13 cm. (30.4 x 10.6 cm.)
STE 16937 / MWA*

176 Philadelphia, Pa.
   PENNSYLVANIA GAZETTE

The New-Year verses of the printers lads, who carry the Pennsylvania Gazette to the customers. January 1, 1780.

First line: Let others sing in am'rous strains

36 x 22 cm. (23.3 x 14.6 cm.) Verse in two columns divided by single rule.

STE 16939 / NN*

177 Philadelphia, Pa.
   PENNSYLVANIA JOURNAL

[New-Year verses of the carriers of the Pennsylvania Journal.]

Hildeburn 4032 STE 16941 / No copy located.

178 Philadelphia, Pa.
   PENNSYLVANIA PACKET

[New-Year verses of the carriers of the Pennsylvania Packet.]

Hildeburn 4033 STE 16943 / No copy located.

1781

179   Philadelphia, Pa.
PENNSYLVANIA EVENING POST
◊

New Year's verses, for the printer's lads who carry the Evening Post to the customers.

First line: With pleading prospect we behold | *Preliminary verse with first line:* Oh pardon the faults I've committed before

26 x 15 cm. (23.5 x 8.2 cm.)

STE 17300 / MWA*

180   Philadelphia, Pa.
PENNSYLVANIA GAZETTE

The New-Year verses of the printers lads, who carry the Pennsylvania Gazette to the customers. January 1, 1781.

First line: As long as customers we find

33 x 26 cm. (15.0 x 8.7 cm.) Verse within double line border with ornamental corners.

STE 17302 / NN*

181   Philadelphia, Pa.
PENNSYLVANIA JOURNAL

[New-Year verses of the carriers of the Pennsylvania Journal.]

Hildeburn 4130 STE 17304 / No copy located.

182   Philadelphia, Pa.
PENNSYLVANIA PACKET

[New-Year verses of the carriers of the Pennsylvania Packet.]

Hildeburn 4131 STE 17306 / No copy located.

1782

183   Philadelphia, Pa.
FREEMAN'S JOURNAL, 1781–1792

[New-Year verses of the carriers of the Freeman's Journal.]

Hildeburn 4221 STE 17539 / No copy located.

184   Philadelphia, Pa.
GEMEINNÜTZIGE PHILADEL-
PHISCHE CORRESPONDENZ

Neujahrs-Verse des Herumträgers der Philadelphischen Correspondenz. Den 1sten January, 1782.

First line: Der Tag Deckt viler Herzen auf

29 x 23 cm. (23.2 x 16.5 cm.) Verse within ornamental border in two columns divided by line of type ornaments. Date set off by horizontal rules.

STE 17546 / PHi*

185   Philadelphia, Pa.
PENNSYLVANIA EVENING POST

[New-Year verses of the carriers of the Pennsylvania Evening Post.]

Hildeburn 4222 STE 17666 / No copy located.

186   Philadelphia, Pa.
PENNSYLVANIA GAZETTE

The New-Year verses of the printers lads, who carry the Pennsylvania Gazette January 1, 1782.

First line: Time was the muse could sing of peace

34 x 14 cm. (27.5 x 8.7 cm.) Verse within ornamental border.

STE 17668 / NN*

187   Philadelphia, Pa.
PENNSYLVANIA JOURNAL

[New-Year verses of the carriers of the Pennsylvania Journal.]

Hildeburn 4224 STE 17670 / No copy located.

188   Philadelphia, Pa.
PENNSYLVANIA PACKET

[New-Year verses of the carriers of the Pennsylvania Packet.]

STE 17672 / No copy located.

189   The news-carriers address, to his customers. January 1st, 1782.

First line: Once more the New Years morn returns

36 x 14 cm. (26.0 x 8.7 cm.)

STE 44241 / NHi*

1783

190   Hartford, Conn.
CONNECTICUT COURANT

The news-carriers address to his customers. Hartford, January 1, 1783

First line: In England, where the poets scribble

34 x 11 cm. (27.3 x 7.0 cm.)

STE 44430 / MWA*

Reprinted in *Independent Gazetteer* (Philadelphia), January 25, 1783, preceded by, 'The following lines, which were composed for the news-boys at Hartford, on the New-Year, are supposed to have been written by the very ingenious author of *M'Fingal*. . . .' The author of *M'Fingal* is John Trumbull.

191   Philadelphia, Pa.
FREEMAN'S JOURNAL, 1781–1792

New Year's verses addressed to the customers of the Freeman's Journal, by the lad who carries it. January 8th, 1783.

First line: Let those who will, in hackney'd rhyme

35 x 11 cm. (29.3 x 8.7 cm.)

BAL 6426 STE 17937 / DLC* / Ms. note at end of text on Library of Congress copy: Philip Freneau.

Author: Philip Freneau. Collected in his *The Poems of Philip Freneau Written Chiefly during the Late War* (Philadelphia, 1786), 385–87.

192   Philadelphia, Pa.
GEMEINNÜTZIGE PHILADELPHISCHE CORRESPONDENZ

Neujahrs-Verse des Herumträgers der Philadelphischen Correspondenz. Den 1sten Januar, 1783.

First line: So fuhlten begeisterte Dichter

27 x 21 cm. (22.2 x 16.5 cm.) Verse within ornamental border in two columns divided by line of type ornaments. Date set off by horizontal rules.

STE 17944 / PHi*

193   Philadelphia, Pa.
INDEPENDENT GAZETTEER

The compositors and distributors of the Independent Gazetteer, humbly address the following verses on the New-Year 1783, to the customers.

STE 17983 / PPL / Copy not located.

194   Philadelphia, Pa.
PENNSYLVANIA EVENING POST

[New-Year's verses, addressed to the customers of the Pennsylvania Evening Post, by the printer's lad who carries it. January 4, 1783.]

First line: Through wet and dry, and heat and cold

BAL 6425 Evans 18127 / No copy located.

Author: Philip Freneau. Collected in *The Poems of Philip Freneau* (Philadelphia, 1786), 383–85.

195   Philadelphia, Pa.
PENNSYLVANIA GAZETTE

The New-Year verses of the printers lads, who carry about the Pennsylvania Gazette to the customers. January 1, 1783.

First line: Once more the all-enliv'ning sun

36 x 15 cm. (27.2 x 9.0 cm.) Verse within ornamental border.

STE 44416 / NN*

196   Philadelphia, Pa.
PENNSYLVANIA JOURNAL

[New-Year verses of the carriers of the Pennsylvania Journal.]

Hildeburn 4328 STE 18131 / No copy located.

197   Philadelphia, Pa.
PENNSYLVANIA PACKET

[New-Year verses of the carriers of the Pennsylvania Packet.]

Hildeburn 4329 STE 18133 / No copy located.

198   [Philadelphia], Pa.

New Year verses, addressed to those gentlemen who have been pleased to favour Francis Wrigley, news carrier, with their custom. January 1, 1783.

First line: According to custom, once more I appear

27 x 19 cm. (22.8 x 12.9 cm.) Verse within ornamental border.

BAL 6424 STE 18129 / DLC*

Author: Philip Freneau. Collected in *The Poems of Philip Freneau* (Philadelphia, 1786), 381–82. Blanck and Evans wrongly assign this to the *Pennsylvania Gazette*. Francis Wrigley was a journeyman printer in Philadelphia in 1786. See the *Freeman's Journal*, June 7, 1786, 3.

1784

199 Hartford, Conn.
[CONNECTICUT COURANT]

The news-carriers address to his customers. Hartford, January 1, 1784.

First line: I'm come (you'll all expect) to express

37 x 13 cm. (25.7 x 7.4 cm.)

STE 44575 / NHi*

199A Hartford, Conn.
FREEMAN'S CHRONICLE

[The news-carriers address to his customers] to the gentlemen and ladies that he supplies with the Freeman's Chronicle. [Hartford, January 1, 1784.]

First line: The rising year, with glory bright

24 x 11 cm. (18.6 x 7.4 cm.)

BAL 20541 / MiD-B*

Attributed to John Trumbull.

200 Boston, Mass.
BOSTON EVENING-POST,
1781–1784 ◊

A New-Year's wish, from the carrier of the Post-Boy and Advertiser.

First line: To scenes of blood, and dreadful deeds of arms

19 x 16 cm. (16.0 x 10.6 cm.)

STE 44570 / PHi RPB*

201 Philadelphia, Pa.
FREEMAN'S JOURNAL,
1781–1792+

[New Year's verses, addressed to the customers of the Freeman's Journal, by the lad who carries it. January 7 (*sic*), 1784.]

First line: Blest be the man who early prov'd

BAL 6432 Evans 18484 / No copy located.

Author: Philip Freneau. Collected in *The Poems of Philip Freneau* (Philadelphia, 1786), 389–90.

202 Philadelphia, Pa.
GEMEINNUTZIGE PHILADEL-
PHISCHE CORRESPONDENZ ◊

[Neujahrs-verse des Herumtragers der Philadelphische Correspondenz den 1sten Januar, 1784.]

Hildeburn 4522 STE 18494 / No copy located.

203 Philadelphia, Pa.
INDEPENDENT GAZETTEER

[New-Year verses of the carriers of the Independent Gazetteer.]

Hildeburn 4525 STE 18536 / No copy located.

204 Philadelphia, Pa.
PENNSYLVANIA GAZETTE

New-Year verses, for those who carry the Pennsylvania Gazette to the customers. January 1, 1784.

First line: How things have changed since last New-Year

34 x 20 cm. (26.7 x 13.5 cm.) Verse within ornamental border.

BAL 6429 STE 18717 / PHi* PPL

Author: Philip Freneau. Collected in *The Poems of Philip Freneau* (Philadelphia, 1786), 387–88.

205 Philadelphia, Pa.
PENNSYLVANIA JOURNAL

[New-Year verses of the carriers of the Pennsylvania Journal.]

Hildeburn 4526 STE 18719 / No copy located.

206   Philadelphia, Pa.
PENNSYLVANIA PACKET

[New-Year verses of the carriers of the Pennsylvania Packet.]

Hildeburn 4527 STE 18723 / No copy located.

207   [A news-man's address. . . . Jan. 1, 1784.]

First line: What tempests gloom'd the by-past year—

Wegelin 163 / No copy located.

Author: Philip Freneau. Collected in *Poems Written Between the Years 1768 & 1794 by Philip Freneau of New Jersey. A new ed., rev. and corrected by the author; including a considerable number of pieces never before published.* (Monmouth, N.J., 1795).

1785

208   Hartford, Conn.
AMERICAN MERCURY ◊

The carrier of the American Mercury wishes his customers a happy New-Year, and presents the following.

First line: In the days when old Jupiter held the prime station

25 x 13 cm. (19.9 x 8.4 cm.)

STE 44646 / MH MWA*

Attributed to Joel Barlow. See Theodore A. Zunder, *The Early Days of Joel Barlow, A Connecticut Wit* (New Haven, 1934), 176–77, 285.

209   Hartford, Conn.
[CONNECTICUT COURANT]

The news-carrier's address to his customers. Hartford, January 1, 1785.

First line: Old customs teach ('tis said my [*sic*] many

39 x 14 cm. (36.7 x 37.8 cm.)

STE 44747 / NHi RPB*

210   New Haven, Conn.
NEW-HAVEN GAZETTE, AND CONNECTICUT MAGAZINE

A New-Year's present. . . . January 1, 1785

First line: Induc'd by respect and benevolent view | *At end of text:* printer's devil.

33 x 28 cm. (18.0 x 12.2 cm.)

NN*

211   Baltimore, Md.
MARYLAND JOURNAL

Caleb, the flying-Mercury, or news-boy's humble address to his good mistresses and masters, the generous supporters of the Maryland Journal and Baltimore Advertiser. January 1, 1785.

First line: As life is said a stage to be

33 x 18 cm. (22.9 x 12.5 cm.) Verse within ornamental border.

STE 19077 / MdHi*

212   Baltimore, Md.
MARYLAND JOURNAL

Martin's New-Year's salutation to his benevolent masters and mistresses, the generous supporters of the Maryland Journal, and the Baltimore Advertiser. January 1, 1785.

First line: Martin, the printer, with his humble lay

34 x 21 cm. (30.6 x 13.4 cm.) Verse within ornamental border.

PHi*

213   Boston, Mass.
AMERICAN HERALD ◊

The carrier of the American Herald's congratulation to his customers, presenting the following balloon wish! . . . Boston, January 1.

First line: In this wild, romantic age

27 x 12 cm. (24.8 x 8.2 cm.) Verse within ornamental border.

STE 44656 / PHi*

214　Boston, Mass.
INDEPENDENT LEDGER

The carrier of the Independent Ledger, &c. wishes his kind customers a merry Christmas & happy New-Year, and presents the following: . . . Boston, January 1, 1785.

First line: Joyful I see Aurora's blushing ray

25 x 11 cm. (20.3 x 7.6 cm.) Headband of type ornaments at head and end.

STE 44657 / PHi RPB*

215　Philadelphia, Pa.
FREEMAN'S JOURNAL,
1781–1792+

[New Year's verses, addressed to the customers of the Freeman's Journal, by the lad who carries it. January 1, 1785.]

First line: The constant lapse of rolling years

BAL 6433 Evans 19013 / No copy located.

Author: Philip Freneau. Collected in *Poems of Philip Freneau* (Philadelphia, 1786), 391–93.

216　Philadelphia, Pa.
PENNSYLVANIA GAZETTE

New-Year verses, for those who carry the Pennsylvania Gazette to the customers. January 1, 1785.

First line: Another year from door to door

34 x 14 cm. (28.4 x 9.3 cm.) Verse within ornamental border.

STE 44743 / MWA* NN

1786

217　Hartford, Conn.
AMERICAN MERCURY

The carrier of the American Mercury wishes his customers a happy New-Year, and presents the following. . . . January 1, 1786.

First line: I'm come, my friends, as Post-Boys use

23 x 14 cm. (19.0 x 8.3 cm.) Line of type ornaments at head and end.

BAL 863 STE 44868 / MH* NHi / Attributed by Harvard University Library to Joel Barlow.

218　Baltimore, Md.
MARYLAND GAZETTE

Verses of the printer's boy, to his good masters and mistresses, the kind encouragers of the Maryland Gazette; or the Baltimore General Advertiser. January 1, 1786.

First line: Poor Robert would invoke a muse

34 x 21 cm. (25.2 x 13.4 cm.) Verse within ornamental border.

STE 45008 / NN*

218A　Boston, Mass.
MASSACHUSETTS CENTINEL

Commerce under the influence of liberty, shall extend far & wide. The carrier of the Centinel, to the generous patrons of that publication, withing the present year may be crowned with every local and federal blessing . . . January 1, 1789.

First line: On this auspicious—happy day—

25 x 9 cm. (22.2 x 5.5 cm.) Relief cuts.

STE 21954 / DLC

219　New York, N.Y.
NEW-YORK PACKET, 1783–1792

Anniversary address of the printers carriers of the New-York Packet. For the year 1786.

First line: All hail! cry we heralds, who weekly diffuse

24 x 15 cm. (23.8 x 13.6 cm.) Verse within ornamental border.

STE 44846 / DLC*

220　Charleston, S.C.
COLUMBIAN HERALD

New Year's verses, for 1786; addressed to the customers of the Columbian Herald, by the printers lads who carry it.

First line: Old eighty-five is past and gone

32 x 17 cm. (30.7 x 11.4 cm.) Verse within ornamental border.

BAL 6434 STE 44889 / NHi*

Author: Philip Freneau. Collected in *The Miscellaneous Works of Mr. Philip Freneau containing his Essays, and Additional Poems* (Philadelphia, 1788), 142–44. Reprinted in *Poems Written Between the Years 1768 & 1794*, revised, under the title 'A Newsman's Address.'

1787

221 Hartford, Conn.
AMERICAN MERCURY

The carrier of the American Mercury presents the following to his customers, wishing them a happy New-Year. . . . Hartford, January 1, 1787.

First line: Some miles above the milky way

44 x 28 cm. (33.0 x 16.6 cm.) Verse in two columns divided by line of type ornaments. Cut of eagle at head.

STE 45049 / MSaE* NHi / Reprinted in *Independent Gazetteer* (Philadelphia), January 25, 1787; *Massachusetts Centinel* (Boston), January 10, 1787; and in *New-Haven Gazette* (New Haven, Conn.), January 25, 1787.

222 Hartford, Conn.
CONNECTICUT COURANT

The news-boys; an eclogue, for January 1, 1787. Scene-Hartford Street - Time of day; The morning.

First line: While chilly winds of cold December blow | *Printed with:* The news-boy's apology for the foregoing verses. Written by himself.

43 x 27 cm. (36.9 x 22.3 cm.) Verse within ornamental border divided by line of type ornaments.

BAL 864 STE 20295a / CtHi* MH NHi / Reprinted in *New-Haven Gazette* (New Haven, Conn.), January 11, 1787, and *Massachusetts Centinel* (Boston), January 13, 1787.

Both poems are attributed to Joel Barlow by Harvard University Library. See Zunder, *Early Days of Joel Barlow*, 200–201. 'Ira Jones and Tertius Dunning are the real names of the lads who carry the Connecticut Courant and the American Mercury.' *Connecticut Courant*, Monday, January 1, 1787, 4.

223 New Haven, Conn.

Ladies and gentlemen, the Printer's boy wishes you a happy New-Year. . . . New Haven, January 1st, 1787.

First line: According to custom, behold I appear

40 x 14 cm. (32.7 x 10.6 cm.)

NHi*/ Reprinted in Landauer

Lines 1–2, 5–8, 19–34 and 37–38 are copied from Freneau's *New Year Verses, 1783* (BAL 6424). In line 1 'behold' replaces the words 'once more' and in line 32 'newsboy' replaces 'newsman.'

224 Baltimore, Md.
MARYLAND JOURNAL

The New-Year verses, of the flying mercuries, or news-boys, who carry the Maryland Journal, and Baltimore Advertiser, to it's worthy patrons. January 1, 1787.

First line: Let gay festivity appear

(32.7 x 13.9 cm.) Verse within ornamental border.

STE 45109 / MdBE*

225 Boston, Mass.
MASSACHUSETTS CENTINEL ◊

Parks, carrier of the Centinel, begs permission to present the generous patrons of that publication the following.

First line: Time, urging on his swift career | *Signed:* Of Daniel Parks your humble servant.

25 x 12 cm. (22.6 x 8.7 cm.) Two small, oval cuts flanking title with line of border ornaments at end.

STE 45119 / MWA* / American Antiquarian Society copy dated in a contemporary hand: January 1, 1787.

226 Exeter, N.H.
FREEMAN'S ORACLE

The following verses, on the commencement of the year 1787 are addressed to the customers of the Freeman's Oracle, by the lad who carries the same.

First line: Respected public, lend an ear

16 x 12 cm. (15.3 x 11.0 cm.) Verse within ornamental border.

MH*

227　Poughkeepsie, N.Y.
COUNTRY JOURNAL

Verses of the post, to the generous subscribers of the Poughkeepsie Advertiser. . . . January 1st, 1787.

First line: Through wet and dry, and frost and snows

22 x 13 cm. (15.2 x 10.2 cm.) Verse within ornamental border.

STE 45188 / MWA* / American Antiquarian Society copy inscribed on verso: John Whitman.

Attributed to Henry Livingston, Jr. See A. P. Ver Nooy, 'The Carrier's Address—A New Year's Greeting', *Dutchess County Historical Society Yearbook* 29 (1944): 46.

228　Philadelphia, Pa.
FREEMAN'S JOURNAL, 1781–1792

Verses for New Year's day 1787. Addressed to the customers of the Freeman's Journal.

First line: [I] think you would laugh—you would smile, I am certain

25 x 20 cm. (22.3 x 18.2 cm.) Verse in two columns divided by line of type ornaments.

MiU-C*

229　Philadelphia, Pa.
INDEPENDENT GAZETTEER

Verses on the New Year, 1787 humbly addressed by the lads who distribute the Independent Gazetteer, to the customers. . . . Philadelphia, January 1, 1787.

First line: Now like a ghost has eighty-six

28 x 18 cm. (23.9 x 12.4 cm.) Verse within ornamental border.

STE 45189 / MWA* NN RPB

230　Philadelphia, Pa.
PENNSYLVANIA PACKET

Verses, for the New-Year, 1787. . . . January 1, 1787.

First line: Once more kind masters, if you can dispense

19 x 17 cm. (17.1 x 14.8 cm.) Verse within ornamental border in two columns divided by double rule.

DLC* / Library of Congress copy bears ms. note on verso: The Pennsylvania Packet and Daily Advertiser.

231　Newport, R.I.
NEWPORT MERCURY

Verses for the New-Year, 1787, by the boy who carries about the Newport Mercury.

First line: Now the fair volume of unfolding time

18 x 11 cm. (11.3 x 8.6 cm.)

STE 45187 / RPHi*

232　Charleston, S.C.
COLUMBIAN HERALD

New-Year's address, of the boys, who carry the Columbian Herald, respectfully dedicated to the subscribers to that paper, January 1, 1787.

First line: Now the Great Spirit of revolving time

41 x 17 cm. (31.0 x 14.2 cm.) Verse within ornamental border with short line of type ornaments at head of text.

NHi*

1788

233　Hartford, Conn.
AMERICAN MERCURY

The carrier of the American Mercury presents the following to his customers, wishing them a happy New-Year. . . . Hartford, January 1, 1788.

First line: From last year's mark we now aspire

44 x 28 cm. (34.8 x 15.0 cm.) Verse in two columns divided by line of type ornaments. Cut of eagle bearing words 'e pluribus unum' at head.

STE 45236 / NHi*

Reprinted in *New-Haven Gazette* (New-Haven, Conn.), Jan. 17, 1788.

234   [Hartford], Conn.

The forc'd alliance; a dialogue. Or, the news-boy's shift for January 1, 1788.

First line: Hail to my happy friends—th' accustom'd lay

43 x 27 cm. (35.0 x 20.1 cm.) Verse in two columns divided by line of type ornaments. Line of type ornaments at head and end. Short line of type ornaments at end of second column.

STE 21021 / CtHi*

235   Baltimore, Md.
MARYLAND GAZETTE

The news-boy's verses, for January 1st, 1788; respectfully inscribed to the friends and patrons of the Maryland Gazette; or, the Baltimore Advertiser.

First line: The news-boy humbly greets you all | *Printed with:* Robert's New-Year's song with first line, 'Poor Robert comes now bringing.'

39 x 32 cm. (31.0 x 9.9 cm.) Verse within ornamental border.

STE 21231 / NN*

236   Boston, Mass.
MASSACHUSETTS CENTINEL

The carrier of the Massachusetts Centinel, to its patrons, sendeth wishing. . . . The printer's lad. Printing-Office, January 1, 1788.

First line: Thanks to my stars - the unweari'd sun | *Contains three short poems:* The wish domestick. - The representation.—The wish political.

24 x 10 cm. (19.4 x 7.0 cm.) Cut at head beneath ornamental headband; headband at end.

STE 45237 / MWA*

237   New York, N.Y.
NEW YORK PACKET, 1783–1792 ◊

To the generous subscribers for the New-York Packet.

First line: We young Mercuries wish, that with all who subscribe

37 x 18 cm. (30.6 x 15.0 cm.) Verse within ornamental border.

STE 45377 / NHi*

238   Philadelphia, Pa.
FREEMAN'S JOURNAL, 1781–1792

Verses for the New Year's Day, 1788. Addressed to the customers of the Freeman's Journal, by the lad who carries it.

First line: Though past events are hourly read

20 x 16 cm. (17.1 x 12.0 cm.) Verse within ornamental border in two columns divided by line of type ornaments. Short rule at head of text.

BAL 6439 / MiU-C*

Author: Philip Freneau. Collected in *The Miscellaneous Works* (Philadelphia, 1788), 393–95.

239   Philadelphia, Pa.
PENNSYLVANIA PACKET

Verses for the New Year 1788, for the benefit of the persons who carry the Pennsylvania Packet, and Daily Advertiser. To the customers.

First line: Should I vain boy? alas! the task's too great

36 x 21 cm. (29.0 x 15.5 cm.) Verse within ornamental border.

STE 21380 / DLC*

240   Newport, R.I.
[NEWPORT HERALD] ◊

The year revolv'd;—the printer's boy on this occasion wishes joy

21 x 13 cm.

Alden 1124 STE 45270 / NJHi RHi *(photocopy) / Alden suggests that this is the New Year's Day verse for 1788 of the *Newport Herald*, printed by Peter Edes.

1789

241   Hartford, Conn.
AMERICAN MERCURY

A vision of the printer's boy. The carrier of the American Mercury, Hartford, presents the following to his customers, wishing them a happy New-Year. . . . January 1, 1789.

First line: As late soft slumber clos'd my eyes

27 x 21 cm. (17.7 x 13.1 cm.) Verse in two columns divided by line of type ornaments with short line of type ornaments at head of text.

STE 21645 / NHi*

Reprinted in *Masachusetts Centinel* (Boston), January 7, 1789.

242   Hartford, Conn.
CONNECTICUT COURANT

Verses for the New Year's day, 1789. Addressed to the customers of the Connecticut Courant, by the lad who carries it.

First line: Since now we see the Constitution

34 x 15 cm. (27.9 x 8.8 cm.) Short line of type ornaments between title and text.

STE 45733 / NHi*

243   Boston, Mass.
HERALD OF FREEDOM ◊

The carrier of the Herald of Freedom, &c. to his benevolent customers. Affectionately wishing them a happy New-Year.

First line: The modest man, it hath been said

23 x 15 cm. (20.2 x 8.8 cm.) Verse within ornamental border.

PHi*

244   New York, N.Y.
DAILY ADVERTISER, 1785–1806

Verses for the year 1789. Addressed to the subscribers for the Daily Advertiser.

First line: To fulfill the agreement I made in my last

25 x 20 cm. (21.1 x 17.4 cm.) Verse within ornamental border in two columns divided by line of type ornaments.

STE 45734 / NN*

245   New York, N.Y.
NEW-YORK JOURNAL, 1784–1793

The carrier of the New-York Journal, & Weekly Register, wishing his kind customers a Merry Christmas and happy New Year, presents the following. . . . New York, January 1, 1789.

First line: Once more my kind patrons with joy we behold

34 x 20 cm. (23.9 x 12.8 cm.) Verse within ornamental border.

NHi*

246   Philadelphia, Pa.
FEDERAL GAZETTE

[The New-Year's wish of the carrier of the Philadelphia Federal Gazette.]

STE 21817 / No copy located.

247   Newport, R.I.
NEWPORT HERALD ◊

A New-Year's address, from the carrier of the Newport Herald to the generous and kind customers.

First line: Though time retains its antient sway

24 x 13 cm. (20.9 x 11.6 cm.) Verse within ornamental border.

STE 45533 / NjHi*

248   Charleston, S.C.
CITY GAZETTE

New Year's verses for the lads that carry the Daily Advertiser, to the customers of that paper. . . . Charleston, January 1, 1789.

First line: While northern lads thro' hills of snow

30 x 15 cm. (26.4 x 9.8 cm.) Verse within ornamental border with cut at head.

STE 45534 / NN*

1790

249   Hartford, Conn.
AMERICAN MERCURY

The carrier of the American Mercury, presents the following to his customers, wishing them a happy New-Year. . . . Hartford, January 1st, 1790.

First line: The rising glory of my nation

27 x 22 cm. (18.8 x 14.4 cm.) Verse in two columns divided by line of type ornaments with short line of type ornaments at head of text.

STE 22306 / NHi* / Extracts reprinted in *Gazette of the United States* (Philadelphia), January 9, 1790; *Maryland Journal* (Baltimore), January 19, 1790; *Massachusetts Centinel* (Boston), January 20, 23, 1790; *Providence Gazette* (Providence, R.I.), February 6, 1790.

Author: Noah Webster. See E. E. Skeel and E. H. Carpenter, *A Bibliography of the Writings of Noah Webster* (New York, 1958), 335.

250   Hartford, Conn.
      [CONNECTICUT COURANT] ◊

[The news-boy's address to his customers.]

First line: Behold, another year is past

STE 2249 / No copy located. / Reprinted in *Gazette of the United States* (Philadelphia), January 13, 1790; *Salem Gazette*, February 2, 1790; *Massachusetts Centinel* (Boston), January 23, 1790.

Author: Noah Webster. See Skeel and Carpenter, *Bibliography of the Writings of Noah Webster*, 335–36.

251   Baltimore, Md.
      MARYLAND GAZETTE

The news-boys verses, for January 1, 1790; respectfully inscribed to the friends and patrons of the Maryland Gazette; or, the Baltimore Advertiser.

First line: Anxious to gain you smiles and praise | *Printed with:* Verses, on George Washington, Esquire, the illustrious President of the United States.

28 x 15 cm. (22.7 x 12.4 cm.) Verses within ornamental border.

STE 45934 / MdBE*

252   Boston, Mass.
      BOSTON GAZETTE, 1719–1798

The Boston Gazette. The news-boy: a New Year's wish. . . . Boston, January 1, 1790.

First line: Sol revolving still runs on

27 x 16 cm. (25.7 x 14.8 cm.) Verse in two columns divided by line of type ornaments; title divided horizontally by double rule; line of type orna-

ments at end. Cut at head with words in banner, 'Libertas et natale solum.'

STE 45836 / MB*

253   Albany, N.Y.
      ALBANY REGISTER

News-boy's address to the customer's of the Albany Register. January 1, 1790.

First line: Eighty-nine is now past, and ninety's begun

22 x 14 cm. (19.2 x 10.8 cm.)

Albany Institute of History and Art*

254   New York, N.Y.
      DAILY ADVERTISER, 1785–1806

The verses of the news-carrier, of the Daily Advertiser, to his customers on the New Year, 1790. . . . New-York, January 1, 1790.

First line: Poets invoke their muse for inspiration

32 x 22 cm. (28.9 x 17.4 cm.) Verse within architectural border in two columns divided by line of type ornaments.

STE 46086 / NHi* / Reproduced in Winslow, ed., *American Broadside Verse* (New Haven, 1930), 211.

255   New York, N.Y.
      GAZETTE OF THE UNITED
      STATES

The carrier of the Gazette of the United States, among the congratulations of the season, presents the following to the patrons of that publication. . . . January 1st, 1790.

First line: This day the annual wishing muse

20 x 11 cm. (15.2 x 7.2 cm.)

STE 45845 / NHi*

256   New York, N.Y.
      NEW-YORK JOURNAL, 1784–1793

New-Year's verse, for 1790, presented by the carriers of the New-York Journal and Weekly Register. News-Boy's vision. . . . January 1, 1790.

First line: While slumb'ring on bed, having scarce clos'd my eyes | *At head of left column:* block bearing letter 'U' with the word 'God' above; in block on right, the letter 'S' with the word 'save' above.

33 x 20 cm. (28.4 x 17.5 cm.) Verse within architectural border.

STE 45931 / NHi*

257   New York, N.Y.
NEW-YORK MORNING POST

Verses addressed by the carrier to the subscribers of the New-York Morning Post, and Daily Advertiser. January 1, 1790.

First line: Now hoary winter's crowned the var'ing year

24 x 14 cm. (23.1 x 11.1 cm.) Verse within ornamental border.

STE 46083 / MWA* NHi

258   New York, N.Y.
NEW YORK PACKET, 1783–1792

[Anniversary address of the carriers of the New-York Packet to their generous patrons.]

STE 22730 / No copy located.

259   New York, N.Y.
NEW-YORK WEEKLY MUSEUM

Verses for the year 1790. Addressed to the generous subscribers of the New-York Weekly Museum, wishing them a happy New Year.

First line: Once more awake the strain of grateful praise | *At end of text:* The printer's devil.

27 x 23 cm. (23.8 x 17.1 cm.) Within ornamental border in two columns divided by double rule. Cut of newsboy delivering paper at head, flanked by geometric ornamentation.

STE 46085 / MWA* NHi / Reproduced in Winslow, ed., *American Broadside Verse* (New Haven, 1930), 209.

260   Philadelphia, Pa.
FEDERAL GAZETTE

[The address of the carriers if the Federal Gazette to their customers, on the commencement of the year 1790.]

STE 22500 / No copy located.

261   Philadelphia, Pa.
PENNSYLVANIA GAZETTE

New-Year verses, of those who carry the Pennsylvania Gazette to the customers. January 1, 1790.

First line: As glides our flying hours so swift away

26 x 21 cm. (21.2 x 16.1 cm.) Verse in two columns within ornamental border divided by chained line.

STE 45925 / NHi*

1791

262   Hartford, Conn.
AMERICAN MERCURY

The carrier of the American Mercury, wishes his customers a happy New-Year, and presents the following. . . . Hartford, January 1st. 1791.

First line: Mercury, who was post of Jove

33 x 21 cm. (26.6 x 13.8 cm.) Verse in two columns with cut of eagle at head.

STE 46132 / NHi*

263   Hartford, Conn.
CONNECTICUT COURANT

The address of the lad who carries the Connecticut Courant, to his customers. Hartford, January 1, 1791.

First line: Pray gentlemen be kind and civil

35 x 22 cm. (32.4 x 17.7 cm.) Verse within ornamental border in two columns divided by curvilinear line.

STE 23287 / NHi* / Extracts reprinted in *Gazette of the United States* (Philadelphia), January 8, 1791; *Maryland Journal* (Baltimore), January 18, 1791; *Massachusetts Centinel* (Boston), January 8, 1791; *State Gazette of North Carolina* (New Bern, N.C.), January 28, 1791.

Author: Mason Fitch Cogswell. Identified by Noah Webster in his file of the *Courant*. (NN)

264   Norwich, Conn.
NORWICH PACKET

An address of the Norwich-Packet. For the year 1791. . . . December 31, 1790.

First line: Permit my friends, the printers boy

31 x 11 cm. (25.6 x 8.3 cm.)

STE 45806 / RPJCB*

265   Baltimore, Md.
MARYLAND GAZETTE

New-Year's verses for 1791; respectfully inscribed to the friends and patrons of the Maryland Gazette or, the Baltimore Advertiser.

First line: The news-boy on this festal day

34 x 12 cm. (30.5 x 7.3 cm.) Verse within ornamental border.

STE 46238 / MdBE*

266   Stockbridge, Mass.
WESTERN STAR

[The New-Year's wish of the post who carries the Western-Star.]

Ford 2640 STE 23992 / No copy located.

267   New York, N.Y.
NEW-YORK WEEKLY MUSEUM ◊

Address to the generous subscribers of the New-York Weekly Museum, wishing them a happy New-Year.

First line: To you my patrons, I present my strain

29 x 19 cm. (26.8 x 16.6 cm.) Verse within ornamental border in two columns divided by single rule.

STE 46108 / NHi*

268   Newport, R.I.
NEWPORT MERCURY

January 1, 1791. New-Year's verses humbly addressed to the customers of the Newport Mercury, by the boys who carry about the same.

First line: While storms and tempests spend their furious force

18 x 10 cm. (12.0 x 8.0 cm.)

Alden 1245 STE 46201 / NjHi*

269   Burlington, Vt.
BURLINGTON ADVERTISER

The news-carrier's address to the subscribers to the Burlington Advertiser. January 1, 1791.

First line: Bright sol has run his annual course sublime

34 x 21 cm. (29.2 x 16.3 cm.) Verse within ornamental border.

STE 23240 / NN*

1792

270   Hartford, Conn.
AMERICAN MERCURY

Addressed by the carrier of the American Mercury, to the subscribers. Hartford, January 1, 1792.

First line: Where e'er the mouth of man is found

34 x 21 cm. (31.1 x 14.2 cm.) Verse in two columns with cut of American eagle at head.

STE 46368 / MWA* NHi

Reprinted in *Massachusetts Spy* (Boston), Jan. 19, 1792.

271   Hartford, Conn.
CONNECTICUT COURANT

The news lad's address to the readers of the Connecticut Courant. . . . Hartford, January 1, 1792.

First line: My noble friends, this welcome day

35 x 21 cm. (33.0 x 14.2 cm.) Verse in two columns divided by curvilinear line.

STE 24222 / NHi*

Reprinted in *Newport Mercury* (Newport, R.I.), January 14, 1792.

272   Georgetown, D.C.
GEORGETOWN WEEKLY LEDGER

The news-carrier's address to the subscribers of the George-Town Weekly Ledger. For January 1, 1792.

First line: Kind patrons your news-boy with heart most sincere

31 x 21 cm. (27.1 x 15.8 cm.) Verse printed in two columns divided by single rule.

STE 46243 / DLC*

273   Baltimore, Md.
BALTIMORE DAILY REPOSITORY

[New-Year verses, addressed to the patrons of the Baltimore Daily Repository. . . . January 2, 1792.]
STE 24068 / No copy located.

274   Boston, Mass.
COLUMBIAN CENTINEL

The carrier of Russell's Columbian Centinel, presents the following, to his respected patrons: . . . Boston, January 1, 1792.

First line: If ever printer's boy deserv'd regard

27 x 13 cm. (24.8 x 8.2 cm.) Verse includes six lines set off by short horizontal mourning rules.

STE 46404 / MWA PHi*

275   Boston, Mass.
MASSACHUSETTS MAGAZINE

The carrier, of the Massachusetts Magazine, to his patrons and friends, presents the best wishes of a good heart. . . . Boston, Jan. 1792.

First line: Custom, the tyrant of mankind

26 x 13 cm. (22.2 x 9.5 cm.)
STE 46406 / PHi*

276   New York, N.Y.
DAILY ADVERTISER, 1785–1806

The carrier of the Daily Advertiser, presents the following lines to his customers. . . . January 1, 1792.

First line: Once more the good angel who always protects

33 x 20 cm. (29.3 x 18.7 cm.) Verse within architectural border in two columns divided by chained line. Oval of stars at head of text.

STE 46405 / NHi*

277   New York, N.Y.
NEW-YORK DAILY GAZETTE ◊

The carrier of the New-York Daily Gazette begs leave to present the following address to his respected patrons with the compliments of the season.

First line: New Year's gay morn appears

26 x 21 cm. (23.7 x 13.0 cm.) Verse within ornamental border.

STE 46407 / NHi*

278   New York, N.Y.
NEW-YORK MORNING POST

New-Year verses, humbly addressed to the patrons of the Morning Post, &c. By their most obedient servant. John Liddel. New York, January 1, 1792.

First line: At this revolving sun my masters hear

30 x 12 cm. (printed area 27.9 x 10.5 cm.) Verse within double line ornamental border.

STE 46522 / NHi*

279   New York, N.Y.
NEW-YORK WEEKLY MUSEUM

Address to the generous subscribers of the Weekly Museum. Wishing them a happy New Year. . . . New-York, January 2, 1792.

First line: Once more your humble votary must appear

28 x 25 cm. (23.4 x 18.0 cm.) Verse within ornamental border in two columns divided by double rule.

STE 46367 / NHi*

280   Lancaster, Pa.
NEUE UNPARTHEYISCHE LANCASTER ZEITUNG

Neujahrs-Verse, des Herumträgers der Neuen Unpartheyischen Lancäster Zeitung, dem 1sten Januar, 1792.

First line: Wir haben, Gott sey Dank! ein neues Jahr erleht

36 x 22 cm. (29.2 x 18.0 cm.) Verse in two columns divided by single rule. Date set off by horizontal single rules.

STE 46512 / PHi*

281   Philadelphia, Pa.
      Pennsylvania Mercury

Verses on the New-Year, January 2, 1792. Addressed to the subscribers to the Pennsylvania Mercury.

First line: Approach ye happy years! when time shall bring

27 x 25 cm. (19.7 x 17.2 cm.) Verse in two columns divided by single rule.

STE 46659 / NHi*

282   Winchester, Va.
      Virginia Centinel ◊

To the worthy patrons of the Virginia Centinel, or, the Winchester Repository.

First line: Some New-Year's rhymes your news-boy sends | *Footnote at end of text:* The lives of Goldsmith. . . .

33 x 20 cm. (18.7 x 13.3 cm.) Verse within ornamental border in two columns divided by line of type ornaments.

DLC* / Library of Congress copy bears ms. date 1792.

1793

283   Hartford, Conn.
      American Mercury

Addressed by the boy who carries the American Mercury, to the subscribers. . . . Hartford, January 1, 1793.

First line: In ancient days, in England's court

44 x 26 cm. (38.8 x 22.7 cm.) Verse in three columns with eagle at head.

STE 46684 / NHi* / Reprinted in *Columbian Centinel* (Boston), January 16, 1793, and as an extract in *American Apollo* (Boston), January 18, 1793.

Author: Richard Alsop. See K. P. Harrington, *Richard Alsop 'A Hartford Wit'* (Middletown, Conn., 1939), 60.

284   Hartford, Conn.
      Connecticut Courant

The address of the carrier of the Connecticut Courant, to his customers. Hartford, January 1, 1793.

First line: My friends I appear to give you a cheer

35 x 22 cm. (29.2 x 17.2 cm.) Verse within curvilinear line border, in two columns divided by line of type ornaments.

STE 46679 / CtHi*

285   New York, N.Y.
      Daily Advertiser, 1785–1806

The news-carrier's verses to the subscribers of the Mail or Daily Advertiser. January 1st, 1793.

First line: Once more your young news-man appears with his rhymes

30 x 14 cm. (27.4 x 11.9 cm.) Verse within ornamental border.

STE 46840 / NHi*

286   New York, N.Y.
      New-York Weekly Museum

Address to the generous subscribers of the Weekly Museum. Wishing them a happy New=Year. . . . New-York, January 1, 1793.

First line: Once more the humble carrier of your news

26 x 21 cm. (22.0 x 18.9 cm.) Verse in two columns divided by double rule within ornamental border.

NHi RPB*

287   Providence, R.I.
      [Providence Gazette]

New-Year's addresses. January 1, 1793.

First line: Now our grandame, earth has run | Verse in two columns followed by Will Honeycomb's apology to the ladies, for reminding them of the holidays.

22 x 19 cm. (19.0 x 14.0 cm.)

Alden 1321 STE 26049 / RPHi*

1794

288 Hartford, Conn.
CONNECTICUT COURANT

To all Christian people; more especially those who take the Connecticut Courant. . . . Hartford, January 1, 1794.

First line: Heaven bless the heart that loves to give

44 x 27 cm. (32.9 x 22.1 cm.) Verse in three columns divided by line of type ornaments with cut at head.

STE 47233 / NHi*

289 Baltimore, Md.
BALTIMORE DAILY INTELLI-
GENCER

New-Year's verses, addressed to the patrons of the Baltimore Daily Intelligencer, by their obedient servants, the news-carriers. January 1, 1794.

First line: Hail! gen'rous patrons! we, once more, do greet you

30 x 26 cm. (22.2 x 19.6 cm.) Verse in two columns within ornamental border.

STE 47132 / MWA* / American Antiquarian Society copy inscribed on verso: John Trimble of Isaac. United States of America.

290 Baltimore, Md.
MARYLAND JOURNAL

New-Year's verses, addressed to the friends and patrons of the Maryland Journal, &c. By the printers' boy. January 1, 1794.

First line: Again bleak winter's frosty hand

26 x 21 cm. (24.4 x 16.0 cm.) Verse within ornamental border.

STE 47133 / MdBE*

291 Boston, Mass.
AMERICAN APOLLO

The carrier of the American Apollo, wishes all his kind patrons, a happy New Year. . . . Boston, January 1, 1794.

First line: Behold another year comes on!

45 x 14 cm. (32.6 x 10.0 cm.) Allegorical cut at head with banner bearing words, 'Scientific pater musarum princeps.'

STE 47002 / MWA RPB*

292 Boston, Mass.
COLUMBIAN CENTINEL

Dedication. To the liberal and right worthy patrons of the Columbian Centinel, this tenth anniversary ode, is most humbly dedicated, by their devoted servant, the carrier. . . . January 1, 1794.

First line: The news-boy's friends, who ne'er can bear to leave

48 x 16 cm. (38.0 x 10.9 cm.)

STE 47022 / MSaE* MWA

293 Boston, Mass.
MASSACHUSETTS MAGAZINE

The carrier of the Massachusetts Magazine, to every patron, friend and customer, most sincerely wishes, the best blessings of the New Year. . . . Boston, Jan. 1, 1794.

First line: Once in a year, to bend the suppliant knee

37 x 18 cm. (33.2 x 10.2 cm.) Cut at head.

STE 47003 / PHi*

294 Boston, Mass.
MASSACHUSETTS MERCURY

The carrier of the Mercury. To his liberal and generous patrons: wishing them every happiness fancy can surmise, and hope anticipate!!. . . . January 1, 1794.

First line: Joy! joy! enlighten'd patrons! cheer! |
Poem in three parts: Exordium.—Retrospective.—Final.

43 x 15 cm. (40.0 x 8.6 cm.)

STE 47004 / MWA*

295 Newark, N.J.
WOOD'S NEWARK GAZETTE

The news-boys address to the generous subscribers of Wood's Newark Gazette and Paterson

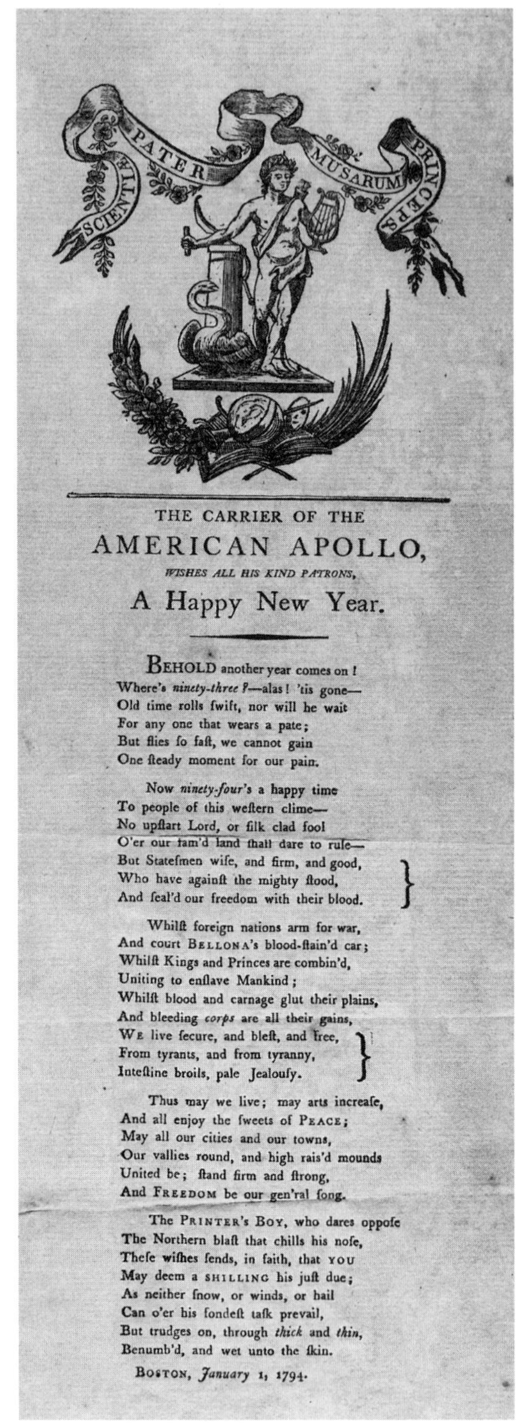

THE CARRIER OF THE

AMERICAN APOLLO,

WISHES ALL HIS KIND PATRONS,

A Happy New Year.

BEHOLD another year comes on !
Where's *ninety-three* ?—alas ! 'tis gone—
Old time rolls swift, nor will he wait
For any one that wears a pate ;
But flies so fast, we cannot gain
One steady moment for our pain.

Now *ninety-four*'s a happy time
To people of this western clime—
No upstart Lord, or silk clad fool
O'er our fam'd land shall dare to rule—
But Statesmen wise, and firm, and good,
Who have against the mighty flood,
And seal'd our freedom with their blood.

Whilst foreign nations arm for war,
And court BELLONA's blood-stain'd car ;
Whilst Kings and Princes are combin'd,
Uniting to enslave Mankind ;
Whilst blood and carnage glut their plains,
And bleeding *corps* are all their gains,
WE live secure, and blest, and free,
From tyrants, and from tyranny,
Intestine broils, pale Jealousy.

Thus may we live ; may arts increase,
And all enjoy the sweets of PEACE ;
May all our cities and our towns,
Our vallies round, and high rais'd mounds
United be ; stand firm and strong,
And FREEDOM be our gen'ral song.

The PRINTER's BOY, who dares oppose
The Northern blast that chills his nose,
These wishes sends, in faith, that YOU
May deem a SHILLING his just due ;
As neither snow, or winds, or hail
Can o'er his fondest task prevail,
But trudges on, through *thick* and *thin*,
Benumb'd, and wet unto the skin.

BOSTON, *January* 1, 1794.

Fig. 4. McDonald 291. *American Apollo*, Boston, Mass., January 1, 1794. American Antiquarian Society.

Advertiser, wishing them health, peace and prosperity, and many happy years. January 1, 1794.

First line: Most worthy citizens, accept these lays |
Signed: your humble servant.

34 x 14 cm. (28.0 x 11.3 cm.) Verse within ornamental border.

STE 47141 / NHi*

296   New York, N.Y.
        NEW-YORK WEEKLY MUSEUM ◊

Address to the generous subscribers of the Weekly Museum. Wishing them a happy New=Year.

First line: Upon the stage your news-boy comes once more

24 x 19 cm. (21.6 x 18.0 cm.) Verse within ornamental border in two columns divided by double rule with type ornaments at ends.

STE46956 / NHi*

297   Philadelphia, Pa.
        PENNSYLVANIA GAZETTE

Addressed to the customers of the Pennsylvania Gazette. . . . January 1st. 1794.

First line: Kind gentlemen, I come once more

21 x 12 cm. (16.7 x 8.2 cm.) Verse within ornamental border.

STE 46957 / MWA*

1795

298   Hartford, Conn.
        AMERICAN MERCURY

The news-boys address to the readers of the American Mercury. . . . January 1, 1795.

First line: If heroes seek for fame in fight

45 x 19 cm. (40.3 x 13.4 cm.) Verse in two columns divided by line of type ornaments.

STE 28177 / NHi* Excerpt reprinted in *Columbian Centinel* (Boston), January 17, 1795.

299   Hartford, Conn.
        CONNECTICUT COURANT

To all Christian people; more expecially [*sic*] those who take the Connecticut Courant. . . . January 1, 1795.

First line: The events of all evolving time

45 x 26 cm. (40.5 x 20.7 cm.) Verse within ornamental border in three columns divided by single rules. Cut at head.

STE 47623 / CtHi MSaE* NHi / Reprinted in *Gazette of the United States* (Philadelpia), January 13, 1795, and *Columbian Centinel* (Boston), January 14, 1795.

Author: Lemuel Hopkins. See [R. Alsop], *The Echo, with Other Poems* (New York, 1807), 210–18, 232.

300   Middletown, Conn.
        MIDDLESEX GAZETTE

[News-boy's address, or, the last words, and dying speech of citizen ninety-four; who was guillotined on the night following the 31st. of Dec. last, precisely at the hour of twelve.]

STE 29079 / No copy located.

301   New Haven, Conn.
        CONNECTICUT JOURNAL

The news-boy to the readers of the Connecticut Journal. Friends and citizens, . . . New-Haven, January 1, 1795.

First line: Perhaps it might be expected that I should

27 x 22 cm. (20.5 x 14.2 cm.) Prose in two columns divided by single rule.

CtY*

302   Norwich, Conn.
        WEEKLY REGISTER

The news-boy's address to the customers of the Weekly Register. . . . Norwich, January 1st, 1795.

First line: News! news my generous friends, and sure

34 x 20 cm. (27.5 x 16.0 cm.) Verse within ornamental border in two columns divided by line of type ornaments.

Bristol 9419 / MHi*

303   Boston, Mass.
COLUMBIAN CENTINEL

Dedication. To the ever liberal and right worthy patrons of the Columbian USA Centinel, this eleventh anniversary ode, is most humbly dedicated, by their obediant [*sic*] devoted servant, the carrier. . . . Boston Jan. 1, 1795.

First line: Joy! generous patrons!—see the day arrive

48 x 17 cm. (44.4 x 10.3 cm.)

STE 47399 / MWA RPB*

304   Boston, Mass.
FEDERAL ORRERY

[The carrier of the Federal Orrery, presents to his patrons the compliments of the season with the following New-Year apologies.]

STE 28661 / No copy located.

305   Haverhill, Mass.
GUARDIAN OF FREEDOM

A New-Year's verse. . . . Haverhill, January 1, 1795.

First line: New joys arise! new joys to cheer

13 x 14 cm. (10.8 x 10.7 cm.) Verse within ornamental border with double ornamental line at head.

STE 28780 / MHi*

306   Concord, N.H.
MIRROUR

A New Year. The carrier of the Mirrour, to his customers. . . . January 1795.

First line: Custom has, long since, made it customary | Signed: Good-News-Boy.

29 x 14 cm. (27.0 x 9.3 cm.)

STE 47510 / NHi*

307   Hanover, N.H.
EAGLE

[A New-Year's address from the Eagle-carrier to his customers.]

STE 28612 / No copy located.

308   Lansingburgh, N.Y.
LANSINGBURGH RECORDER

The news-boy's address to the subscribers of the Lansingburgh Recorder. Lansingburgh, January 1, 1795.

First line: Behold, my friends! as roll the circling spheres

31 x 18 cm. (29.0 x 14.7 cm.) Verse within architectural border in two columns with date 1795 at head, within border. Cut of dove bearing sign with word 'Recorder' at head of text.

STE 47521 / NHi*

309   New York, N.Y.
DAILY ADVERTISER, 1785–1806

Address of the carrier of the Daily Advertiser, to his customers . . . . New York, January 1, 1795.

First line: While folks of all sorts are their compliments paying

31 x 19 cm. (29.3 x 17.9 cm.) Verse within ornamental border in two columns divided by line of type ornaments.

STE 47336 / NHi*

310   New York, N.Y.
DIARY

Address presented by the carriers of the Diary, to their numerous and respectable patrons. . . . January 1st, 1795.

First line: Once more your old news-boy, appears with his rhymes

32 x 15 cm. (24.1 x 13.8 cm.) Verse within architectural border.

STE 47339 / NHi*

311   New York, N.Y.
NEW-YORK JOURNAL, 1784–1793

Address of the carrier to the patrons of the New-York Journal, and Patriotic Register, with the compliments of the season. . . . January 1, 1795.

First line: Among th' attendant of this festive time

32 x 20 cm. (26.9 x 17.6 cm.) Verse within ornamental border in two columns divided by line of

type ornaments, with line of type ornaments at head of text. Cut of two allegorical figures and eagle around shield above banner bearing word 'Excelsior' at head.

STE 47338 / NHi*

312　New York, N.Y.
NEW-YORK WEEKLY MUSEUM

Address to the generous patrons of the Weekly Museum, wishing them a happy New-Year . . . . New Year's day, 1795.

First line: While o'er the earth's expanse, the golden ray

31 x 24 cm. (23.9 x 17.5 cm.) Verse within architectural border, in two columns divided by curvilinear line with floral tailpiece. Cut of ram with garland at end of text.

STE 29858 / DLC NHi RPB*

313　Philadelphia, Pa.
DUNLAP'S AMERICAN DAILY
ADVERTISER

The carriers of the American Daily Advertiser to their customers, on the commencement of the year 1795.

First line: Though nations rage with hostile jars

23 x 18 cm. (20.5 x 16.0 cm.) Verse within ornamental border, in two columns divided by line of type ornaments. Short line of type ornaments at head of text.

STE 47373 / MWA*

314　Philadelphia, Pa.
GAZETTE OF THE UNITED
STATES

Address of the carrier of the Gazette of the United States. . . . January 1, 1795.

First line: Peace to the world! Columbia cries | *At head of text:* Peace on earth, and good will to men.

41 x 28 cm. (36.6 x 19.9 cm.) Verse within ornamental border in two columns.

STE 47337 / MWA PHi*

315　Providence, R.I.
[UNITED STATES CHRONICLE]

A New-Year's warning. . . . Providence, January 1, 1795.

First line: Another year has roll'd its round

21 x 14 cm. (15.4 x 8.4 cm.) Verse within double line border with corner and other ornaments.

STE 47511 / NHi* / Ms. inscription on New York Historical Society copy: From your humble servant J. Wheeler.

1796

316　Hartford, Conn.
AMERICAN MERCURY

The carrier of the American Mercury, wishes his customers a happy New Year, and presents them the following. . . . Hartford, January 1, 1796.

First line: Good parson, such a one (quoth I)

34 x 15 cm. (30.7 x 8.3 cm.) Verse within ornamental border.

STE 47748 / CtHi* NHi

317　Hartford, Conn.
CONNECTICUT COURANT

Guillotina; or the annual song of the tenth muse. Addressed to the readers of the Connecticut Courant. . . . Hartford, January 1, 1796.

First line: Come Guillotina, muse divine!

45 x 25 cm. (37.3 x 20.2 cm.) Verse within ornamental border in three columns.

STE 30269 / MWA* NN / Reprinted in *Massachusetts Spy* (Worcester), January 20, 1796; *Newport Mercury* (Newport), February 2, 1796; *Massachusetts Mercury* (Boston), January 5, 1796; and *Federal Orrery* (Boston), January 7, 1796.

Generally attributed to Lemuel Hopkins, the Hartford poet.

318　Middletown, Conn.
MIDDLESEX GAZETTE ◊

[The address of the lad who carries the Middlesex Gazette to his customers.]

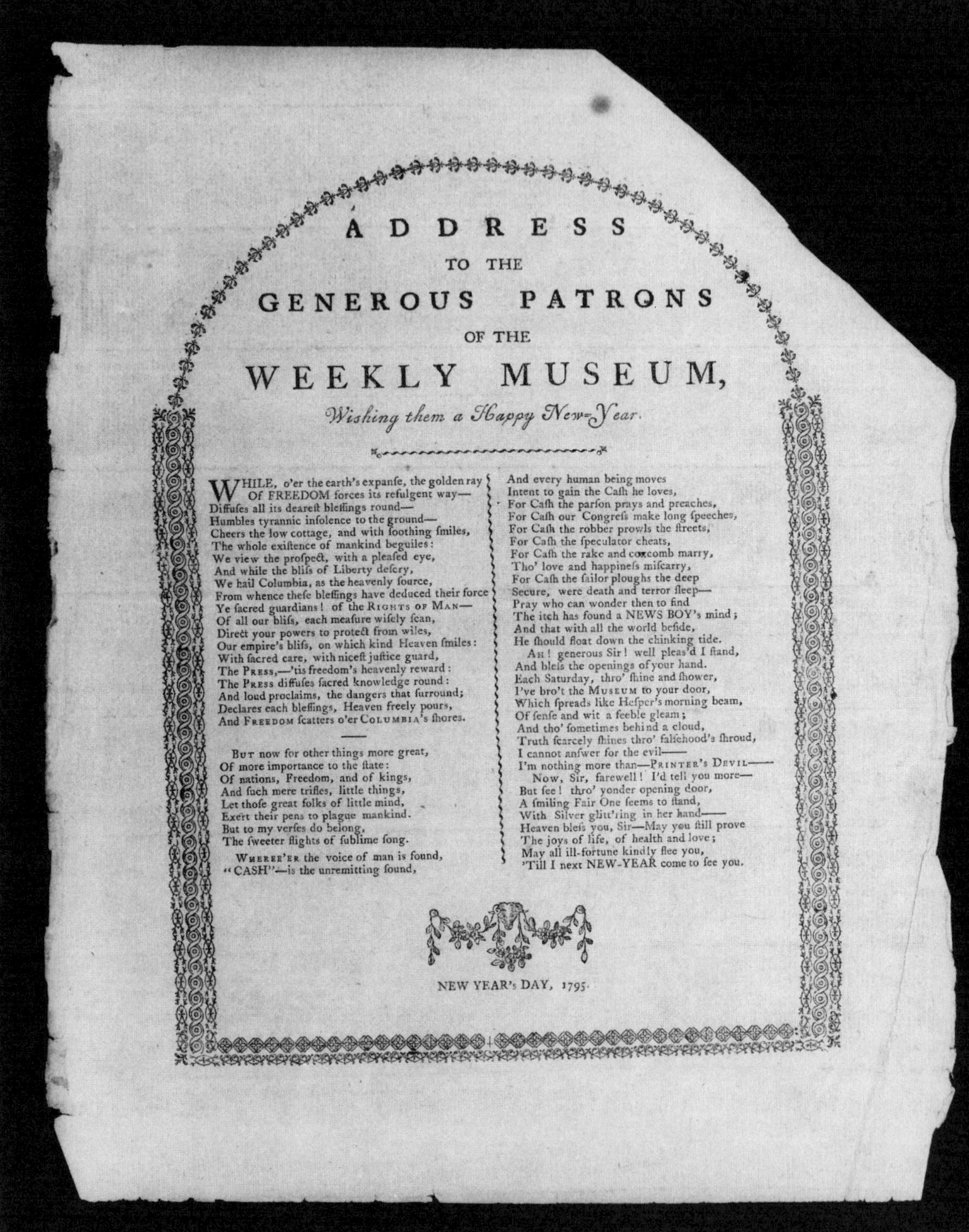

Fig. 5. McDonald 312. *New York Weekly Museum*, New York, January 1, 1795. John Hay Library.

First line: Holloa! friend time, said New-Year's day

STE 30792 / No copy located. / Reprinted in *Connecticut Courant* (Hartford, Conn.), January 11, 1796, and *Federal Orrery* (Boston), January 18, 1796.

319   Portland, Me.
EASTERN HERALD

[The carrier of the Eastern Herald, to his customers.]

STE 30378 / No copy located.

320   Boston, Mass.
COLUMBIAN CENTINEL

Address of the carrier of the Columbian Centinel, to all branches of its patrons, on the opening of the New Year, 1796.

First line: To tune his gratulary strain | *At head of text:* Gentlemen of political, and ladies of domestic, concernments: | *Signed:* The carrier.

39 x 15 cm. (38.0 x 9.3 cm.)
STE 30248 / PHi*

321   Boston, Mass.
COURIER

The carrier of the Boston Evening Courier, to his generous patrons. . . . Courier Office, January 1, 1796.

First line: The courier's lad, gent. folks, you see | *Poem in three parts:* Exordium.—Retrospect.—The wish.

38 x 14 cm. (29.1 x 10.0 cm.) Oval cut in center of title.
STE 47749 / MWA*

322   Boston, Mass.
FEDERAL ORRERY

The carrier of the Federal Orrery. Presents his kind custom-ers the following custom-ary ode, on custom. . . . January 1, 1796.

First line: 'More honor'd,' as [we newsboys preach]

25 x 21 cm. (19.9 x 16.5 cm.) Verse in two columns divided by double rules.

STE 30409 / MWA* PHi

Attributed by Evans to Thomas [i.e. Robert Treat] Paine, poet and editor of the *Federal Orrery*.

323   Boston, Mass.
INDEPENDENT CHRONICLE

The carrier of the Independent Chronicle, to his ever generous and right worthy patrons. . . . Boston, Friday, January 1, 1796.

First line: Last night December bow'd her aged head | *At head of text:* 'But once a year—and then—' Friends and patrons!

37 x 14 cm. (35.0 x 9.2 cm.)
STE 30625 / PHi*

324   Boston, Mass.
MASSACHUSETTS MERCURY

The Massachusetts Mercury carrier, to the benevolent personages, he has the superlative honor of waiting upon semi-weekly—wishing them a happy New Year, and dedicating to them, as usual, a few merry lines, to move their muscles and loosen their purse strings. . . . Boston, Jan. 1, 1796.

First line: Our old master time, a printer of fame | *Also contains:*—Review of ninety-five and America.

30 x 17 cm. (26.4 x 9.3 cm.)
STE 30776 / MWA PHi*

325   Boston, Mass.

The carrier of the Collections of the Massachusetts Historical Society, to its liberal and generous patrons! . . . Boston, January 1, 1796.

First line: The various comforts of the changeful years

29 x 15 cm. (24.0 x 9.0 cm.) Double rule at head of text. Cut of eagle with banner at head.
STE 30771 / PHi*

326   Albany, N.Y.
ALBANY REGISTER

Jan. 1, 1796. The humble address of the carriers of the Albany Register, to their generous customers, greeting them with a happy New-Year.

First line: A string of rhymes but once a year | *At head, within border:* Jan. 1, 1796. Indep. XX.

37 x 25 cm. (35.4 x 22.2 cm.) Verse within ornamental border in two columns divided by ornamental line. Two cuts at head.

STE 47817 / NN*

327   New York, N.Y.
MINERVA

New-Year verses, (or circular epistle) from the carrier, to the patrons of the Minerva. January 1, 1796.

First line: Old time the meagre elf we see

33 x 21 cm. (28.2 x 16.4 cm.) Verse in two columns divided by line of type ornaments.

STE 47855 / NHi*

328   New York, N.Y.
NEW-YORK WEEKLY MUSEUM

Address of the carrier of Weekly Museum to his patrons, with the compliments of the season. . . . January 1, 1796.

First line: While New Year's morn each breast with joy inspires

31 x 21 cm. (29.7 x 18.5 cm.) Verse within double line border of type ornaments, in two columns divided by single rule with floral tailpiece.

STE 31604 / NHi RPB*

329   Philadelphia, Pa.
GAZETTE OF THE UNITED
STATES

Address of the carrier of the Gazette of the United States. . . . January 1st, 1796.

First line: More than fill'd the poet's eye

35 x 21 cm. (20.6 x 10.3 cm.) Verse within ornamental border.

STE 47695 / MWA*

1797

330   Hartford, Conn.
CONNECTICUT COURANT

Guillotina, for 1797. Addressed to the readers of the Connecticut Courant. . . . Hartford, January 1, 1797.

First line: Sing muse the tenth, whose annual voice

48 x 29 cm. (43.9 x 25.9 cm.) Verse within ornamental border in four columns. Cut of Connecticut state seal at head.

STE 31978 / CtHi* / Reprinted in *Impartial Herald* (Newburyport), Jan. 17, 1797.

Generally attributed to Lemuel Hopkins, the Hartford poet.

331   New Haven, Conn.
FEDERAL GAZETTEER

Address, presented by the carrier of the Federal Gazetteer, to his generous and respectable patrons. January 1, 1797.

First line: Old time (if fancy told the story right

22 x 16 cm. (21.0 x 14.7 cm.) Verse in two columns with cut of eagle at head.

STE 48034 / NHi*

332   New London, Conn.
WEEKLY ORACLE

The news-carriers New-Years address to the patrons of the Weekly Oracle.

First line: I come generous patrons (how can I neglect) | *Dated at head:* New London, Monday, January 2d, 1797. | *Preliminary verse with first line:* The muse on fire spreads out her daring wing

33 x 20 cm. (29.3 x 16 cm.) Verse in two columns divided by type ornaments.

Johnson 1338 / CtSoP*

332A   Wilmington, Del.
DELAWARE GAZETTE

The news-boy's address to the subscribers.

First line: I come, your annual visitant once more

44 x 18 cm. (35.3 x 13.2 cm.)
Rink 441 / DeHi

333   Baltimore, Md.
BALTIMORE TELEGRAPHE

The news-boy to his customers. Pro bono publico. Telegraphe Office, January 2, 1797.

First line: Seventeen hundred ninety-six

29 x 19 cm. (24.2 x 12.1 cm.) Verse in two columns divided by line of type ornaments followed by twelve lines of verse.

RPB*

334   Boston, Mass.
INDEPENDENT CHRONICLE

The carrier, of the Independent Chronicle, to his ever generous and worthy patrons, wishes a happy thrice happy New-Year: . . . Chronicle-Office, Boston, Jan. 1, 1797.

First line: Begin, thou bright celestial orb | *Signed:* The carrier . . .

32 x 15 cm. (29.0 x 10.4 cm.) Type ornaments between some stanzas.

STE 32307 / PHi*

335   Greenfield, Mass.
GREENFIELD GAZETTE ◊

[New Year's address of the carriers of the Greenfield Gazette.]

STE 32209 / No copy located.

Author: Samuel Elliot. See Joseph T. Buckingham, *Personal Memoirs and Reflections of Editorial Life*, 2 vols. (Boston, 1852) 1:27. Buckingham was the carrier; he received $6.75 from his customers.

336   Newburyport, Mass.
POLITICAL GAZETTE

On the commencement of the year 1797: the grateful address of the Political Gazette post boy, to the receivers of that paper, who are served by him. . . . January 1, 1797.

First line: While Washington, with conduct sage

24 x 20 cm. (19.3 x 15.6 cm.) Verse in two columns.
MSaE*

337   Salem, Mass.
SALEM GAZETTE ◊

To the patrons of the Salem Gazette, the carrier presents the compliments of the season and the following address.

First line: Ye Louisianan nymphs begin the song

27 x 20 cm. (22.8 x 15.8 cm.) Verse on silk in two columns divided by single rule. Cut of seal of the United States at head.

Tapley p. 365 / MSaE*

338   Concord, N.H.
COURIER OF NEW-HAMPSHIRE

The news-boy's New Year's wish, to the town customers of the Courier of New-Hampshire. Concord, Tuesday, Jan. 3, 1797.

First line: Once more I have come with my compliments annual | *Signed:* The Carrier news boy.

21 x 17 cm. (15.0 x 10.0 cm.)
MeHa*

339   Newark, N.J.
CENTINEL OF FREEDOM

Address, presented by the carrier to the patrons of the Centinel of Freedom. With the compliments of the season. January 1, 1797.

First line: While in this festive season all rejoice

32 x 21 cm. (27.5 x 18.9 cm.) Verse within architectural border. Block extending from left border bearing word, 'Peace,' and one on right, 'Plenty.'

STE 48035 / NHi*

340   New York, N.Y.
ARGUS

The carrier of the Argus, presents the following address to his kind patrons, with the compliments of the season: . . . New-York, January 2, 1797.

First line: Stern winter now in pomp despotic reigns

34 x 20 cm. (30.6 x 16.7 cm.) Verse within ornamental border with cut of eagle at head.

STE 48086 / NHi*

341   New York, N.Y.
DAILY ADVERTISER, 1785–1806

Address of Robbin the carrier of the Daily Advertiser, to his kind customers. . . . Jan. 1, 1797.

First line: With withering touch, though winters hoary hands

34 x 21 cm. (20.5 x 6.6 cm.)

STE 48032 / NHi*

342   New York, N.Y.
NEW-YORK WEEKLY MUSEUM

Address of the carrier of the Weekly Museum to his patrons, with the compliments of the season . . . New-York, January 2, 1797.

First line: Lo! the fleet steps of feathery-footed time

30 x 20 cm. (29.5 x 19.4 cm.) Verse within double line border of type ornaments.

STE 33192 / NHi RPB*

343   Poughkeepsie, N.Y.
POUGHKEEPSIE JOURNAL

To the worthy supporters of the Poughkeepsie Journal. . . . January 1, 1797.

First line: Wet from the types and scarcely born | *Signed:* Godfrey Bowman | *At head of verse:* Prose, beginning, 'Good old ninety-six. . . .'

37 x 17 cm. (31.5 x 13 cm.) Verse within ornamental border.

STE 48273 / NHi*

344   Philadelphia, Pa.
GAZETTE OF THE UNITED STATES

Address of the carrier of the Gazette of the United States. January—1797.

First line: Adieu to ninety-six—eventful year!

35 x 21 cm. (27.0 x 12.0 cm.) Verse within architectural border with short double line of type ornaments at end.

STE 48033 / MWA*

345   Guillotina for January 1, 1797. Addressed to the readers of the Connecticut Courant.

First line: Sing muse, the tenth, whose annual voice

50 x 31 cm. (42.9 x 27.5 cm.) Verse within ornamental border, in four columns divided by single rules with cut at head.

Evans 31979 / MWA*

Generally attributed to Lemuel Hopkins, the Hartford poet. Reprint of Evans 31978, who suggests Philadelphia as place of publication.

346   News carrier's address to his kind customers. For January 1, 1797.

First line: As custom directs me, once more I appear

39 x 20 cm. (34.2 x 18.2 cm.) Verse within architectural border, with thick-thin rules at head of text. Triangle of stars at head.

STE 48205 / NHi*

1798

347   Hartford, Conn.
AMERICAN MERCURY

The news-boy's address, to the readers of the American Mercury. . . . Hartford, January 1, 1798.

First line: Good generous friends! as I am here | *Signed:* James McCurdy

30 x 17 cm. (25.3 x 9.7 cm.) Verse within ornamental border.

STE 48550 / NHi*

348   Hartford, Conn.
CONNECTICUT COURANT

Guillotina. For the year 1798. Addressed to the readers of the Connecticut Courant.

First line: Resume the song O! muse of fire

38 x 26 cm. (35.0 x 20.2 cm.) Verse within ornamental border in three columns divided by double rules with short thick-thin rules at head.

STE 33562 / CSmH CtY MSaE* NHi / Reprinted in *Massachusetts Mercury* (Boston), January 5, 1798, and *Columbian Centinel* (Boston), January 6, 1798.

Attributed to Lemuel Hopkins by Evans.

349 Litchfield, Conn.
LITCHFIELD MONITOR

The news-boy's New-Year's jingle, for 1798. . . . Litchfield, January 1, 1798.

First line: Scowl'd from the presence of the epic bard | *At end of text:* *Note.—All the words in this thing, mark'd in italic, are either parts of the printing-press, or printer's terms.

31 x 25 cm. (27.4 x 21.9 cm.) Verse in two columns divided by line of type ornaments.

STE 48551 / NHi*

350 New London, Conn.
CONNECTICUT GAZETTE

Bulletina. An humble imitation. The address of the lad who carries the Connecticut Gazette, to his customers. . . . New London, January 1, 1798.

First line: At Hartford, every New-Year's day

46 x 26 cm. (42.9 x 19.0 cm.) Verse in three columns. Horizontal line of type ornaments divides title after word 'imitation.'

STE 48382 / NHi*

351 Norwich, Conn.
COURIER

The news-boy's address, to the patrons of the Chelsea Courier. . . . Norwich, January 1, 1798.

First line: As rolling time, with swift career

45 x 27 cm. (42.3 x 23 cm.) Verse within ornamental border in three columns.

RPB*

352 Baltimore, Md.
FEDERAL GAZETTE

The annual address of the carriers of the Federal Gazette, & Baltimore Daily Advertiser. January 1st. 1798.

First line: The humble carriers of the Federal Print | *Preliminary verse with first line:* Does avarice gripe thee?

35 x 26 cm. (28.2 x 20.3 cm.) Verse within double line ornamental border in two columns divided by line of type ornaments.

MdHi*

353 Boston, Mass.
COLUMBIAN CENTINEL

The carrier of the Columbian Centinel, on the exit of 1797, and the entrance of one thousand seven hundred and ninety-eight most respectfully tenders to all its patrons the congratulations of the season. . . . January 1, 1798.

First line: To ask! or not to ask? That is the question.— | *At head of text:* The New-Year Pegasus, from being so often and so carelessly rode, has become lame and hipshod [sic]

30 x 17 cm. (26.2 x 11.9 cm.) Cut of sunburst bearing initials 'WA' within title.

STE 33541 / MWA PHi*

354 Boston, Mass.
INDEPENDENT CHRONICLE

The carriers, of the Independent Chronicle, to their patrons and friends! . . . Chronicle-Office, Boston, Jan. 1, 1798.

First line: Independent, dependent, depending

33 x 15 cm. (28.2 x 12.0 cm.) Thick-thin rules and cut of state seal at head.

STE 33924 / MWA PHi RPB*

355 [Dedham, Mass.]
MINERVA

Address of the carrier of the Minerva, to his patrons. . . . January 1st, 1798.

First line: Winter appears—the hoary monarch of the year

33 x 16 cm. (26.3 x 12.7 cm.) Verse within ornamental border.

STE 48329 / NHi* / Bristol assigns this to the New York *Minerva*; however, Brigham lists the last issue of that paper as September 30, 1797.

356   Newburyport, Mass.
       NEWBURYPORT HERALD ◊

To the patrons of the Newburyport Herald, &c.

First line: It is a custom to appear

28 x 15 cm. (24.6 x 11.0 cm.) Verse within ornamental border with type ornaments at head. Printed in calligraphic type.

STE 34232 / MSaE*

357   Salem, Mass.
       SALEM GAZETTE ◊

To the patrons of the Salem Gazette, the carrier presents the compliments of the season and the following address.

First line: O thou, in airy garret perch'd

36 x 24 cm. (28.8 x 12.4 cm.) Verse in two columns divided by single rule with ornamental curvilinear lines at head and end.

STE 34511 / MH MSaE* NN / Ms. inscription on Essex Institute copy: William Biglow.

358   Newark, N.J.
       CENTINEL OF FREEDOM

Address, presented by the carrier to the patrons of the Centinel of Freedom. With the compliments of the season. . . . January 1, 1798.

First line: It hath been a fashion (I can't tell how long)

34 x 29 cm. (21.0 x 18.9 cm.) Verse within arched ornamental line border in two columns divided by curvilinear line of type ornaments.

STE 33505 / NN*

359   New York, N.Y.
       NEW-YORK WEEKLY MUSEUM

Address of the carrier of the Weekly Museum to his patrons, with the compliments of the season. . . . January 1, 1798.

First line: On the pinions of time, lo! the seasons return

31 x 15 cm. (28.3 x 12.6 cm.) Verse within ornamental border.

STE 48330 / NHi*

360   New York, N.Y.
       TIME PIECE

The carrier of the Time Piece, presents the following address to his patrons, with the compliments of the season. . . . New York, January 1st, 1798.

First line: The glass has run - see ninety seven has fled

30 x 19 cm. (23.2 x 13.4 cm.) Verse within ornamental border.

BAL 6449 / NHi*

Author: Philip Freneau.

361   Troy, N.Y.
       FARMER'S ORACLE

The news-lad's address, to the readers of the Farmer's Oracle, wishing them a happy New-Year. Jan. 1, 1798.

First line: Blest be the man who early prov'd | *Signed:* [Freneau] | *Preliminary verse in two columns with first line:* Accept the address I humbly bring

31 x 21 cm. (27.9 x 19.3 cm.) Verse within architectural border in two columns divided by ornamental line.

NHi*

Author: Philip Freneau. Collected in *Poems of Philip Freneau*, 389–90. First printed as the carrier's address of the *Freeman's Journal*, January 7 [*sic*], 1784

362   Philadelphia, Pa.
       MERCHANTS DAILY
       ADVERTISER

Address of the carrier of the Merchants Daily Advertiser to its patrons. For the year 1798. . . . Philada. Printed by Thomas Pole, Junior.

First line: In vernal pride no more the woodlands bloom

49 x 32 cm. (41.0 x 26.6 cm.) Verse on silk within architectural border in two columns divided by double rule. Cut centered above border; cuts of urns at head of each column; three cuts at ends of text.

PHi*

363 Philadelphia, Pa.
PORCUPINE'S GAZETTE

The carriers of Porcupine's Gazette, to its friends; on the commencement of the year 1798.

First line: Since I the news-boy's toilsome trade profest

44 x 30 cm. (31.2 x 20.3 cm.) Verse within ornamental border in two columns divided by single rule with cut of porcupine at head.

STE 34400 / MWA RPB*

Author: William Cobbett. See Pierce W. Gaines, *William Cobbett and the United States, 1792–1835* (Worcester, 1971), 83.

364 Providence, R.I.
PROVIDENCE GAZETTE

New-Year verses of the carrier of the Gazette. . . . Providence, January 1, 1798.

First line: Once more permit the news-boy to appear

20 x 10 cm. (17.9 x 8.2 cm.)

STE 48536 / RPHi*

365 Providence, R.I.
UNITED STATES CHRONICLE

New-Year's address, for 1798. . . . January 1, 1798.

First line: Joy to my friends—The new-born year

26 x 11 cm. (23.9 x 8.8 cm.) Verse within ornamental border.

RPHi*

1799

366 Hartford, Conn.
AMERICAN MERCURY

Ode on ends; or, the boy's address, who carries the American Mercury. . . . Hartford, January 1, 1799.

First line: Of all things ends abound the freest | *At end of text:* Finis.

42 x 18 cm. (38.1 x 13.3 cm.) Verse in two columns.

STE 36004 / NHi*

367 Hartford, Conn.
CONNECTICUT COURANT

Guillotina, for the year 1799. Addressed to the readers of the Connecticut Courant.

First line: To song return ye tuneful nine

48 x 29 cm. (42.9 x 24.7 cm.) Verse within ornamental border in four columns divided by double rules.

STE48866 / CtHi MSaE*

Attributed to Lemuel Hopkins by Evans.

368 Litchfield, Conn.
LITCHFIELD MONITOR

The address of Little Jack, the carrier of the Monitor, to his old friends and customers, for the 1st. of January, 1799.

First line: Since fortune first, to 'gild my humble name,'

26 x 23 cm. (22.2 x 20.6 cm.) Verse within ornamental border in two columns divided by line of type ornaments.

STE 48767 / NHi*

369 Newfield, Conn.
AMERICAN TELEGRAPHE

Address of the carrier of the American Telegraphe to its patrons. January 1, 1799.

First line: Ye friends of good order, ye men of reflection

43 x 17 cm. (38.9 x 13.5 cm.) Preliminary verse centered followed by verse in two columns divided by double rule. Line of type ornaments at head and end of first verse. Ornamental line at head and end of all.

STE 48768 / NHi*

370 Norwich, Conn.
NORWICH PACKET

The news boys annual address to the esteemed patrons of the Norwich-Packet for the New Year. . . . Norwich, January 1, 1799.

First line: Here's Charley a good lad, and true to his word

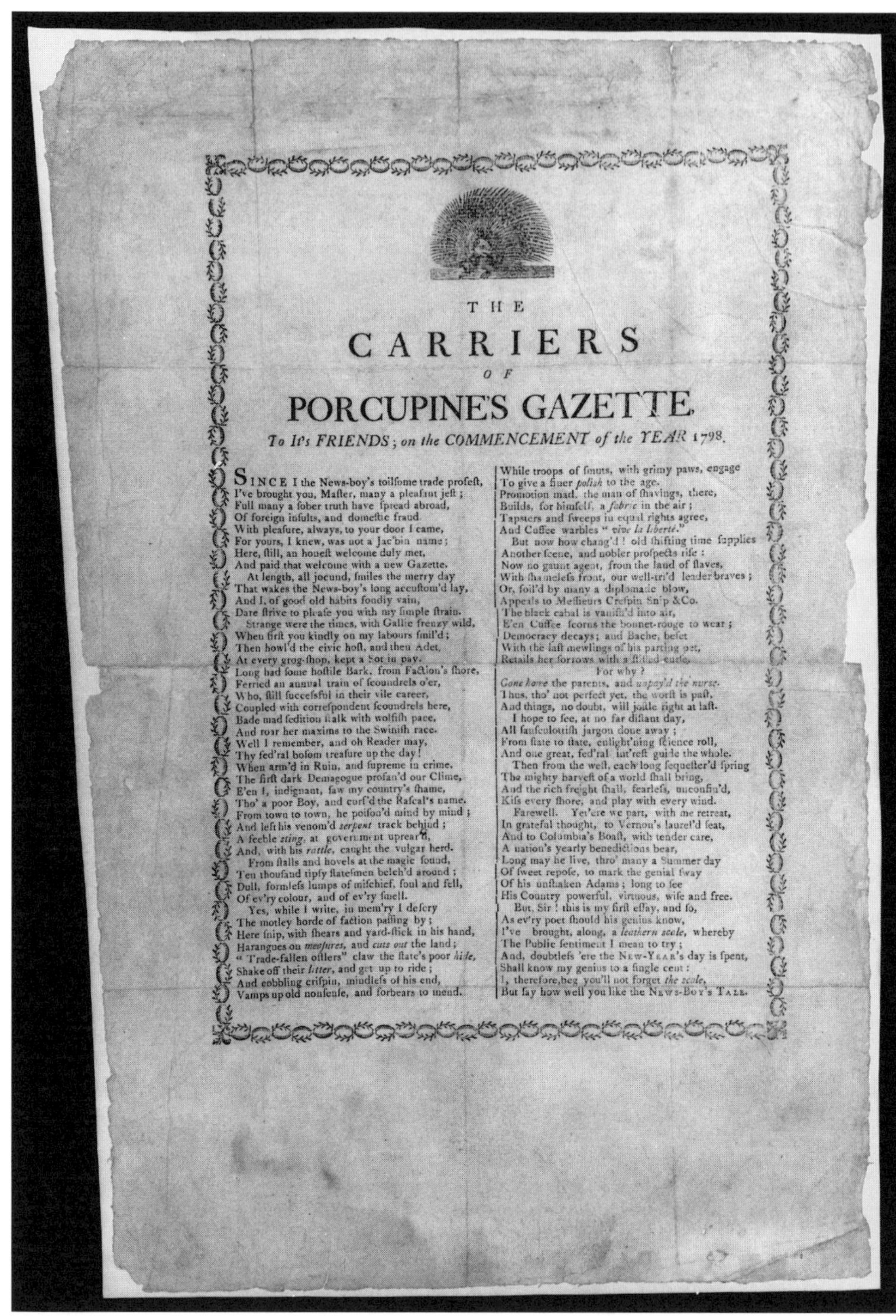

Fig. 6. McDonald 363. *Porcupine's Gazette*, Philadelphia, Pa., 1798. John Hay Library.

44 x 28 cm. (40.2 x 23.2 cm.) Verse in three columns with cut of porcupine at head.

STE 35996 / NBu*

371　Boston, Mass.
COLUMBIAN CENTINEL

January 1, 1799. A card. The carrier of the Columbian Centinel, presents his respects to its frlends [*sic*] and patrons.

First line: Midst all the gloom of winter's woe

48 x 16 cm. (37.2 x 11.2 cm.)
STE 48899 / MWA* NHi NN

372　Boston, Mass.
INDEPENDENT CHRONICLE

The carrier, of the Independent Chronicle, to his generous customers, wishes a happy New-Year. . . . Boston, January 1, 1799.

First line: Hail patrons hail!!—behold your boy appears

32 x 16 cm. (29.2 x 10.0 cm.) Triple horizontal rule and cut at head.

STE 35655 Ford 2947 / MH PHi*

373　Newburyport, Mass.
NEWBURYPORT HERALD ◊

[The New Year. From the carrier of the Newburyport Herald, &c. to his generous customers.]

First line: Around successive years have pass'd
STE 35965 Ford 2948 / No copy located.

374　Concord, N.H.
MIRROUR

New-Year's address, from the news-boy, to the patrons of the Mirrour. . . . Concord, January 1, 1799.

First line: Lo! on the wings of time, sugacious [*sic*] borne

41 x 25 cm. (34.5 x 14.6 cm.) Verse in two columns divided by single rule.

STE 35824 / NhHi*

375　Newark, N.J.
CENTINEL OF FREEDOM

Address presented by the carrier to the patrons of the Centinel of Freedom. With the compliments of the season. January 1, 1799.

First line: Hail, festive morn! hail, dear auspicious day

34 x 20 cm. (31.6 x 18.9 cm.) Verse within architectural border in two columns divided by single rule.

Evans 35961 / NHi*

376　Trenton, N.J.
NEW-JERSEY STATE GAZETTE

The news-boy's address to the patrons of the New-Jersey State Gazette. January 1, 1799.

First line: Again, with steady pace, our rolling sphere

33 x 20 cm. (25.8 x 17.8 cm.) Verse within ornamental border in two columns divided by ornamental line.

STE 35909 / NHi*

377　Albany, N.Y.
ALBANY CENTINEL

The news-boy's address, to the patrons of the Albany Centinel. Albany, January 1, 1799.

First line: To day a new year opes to view

32 x 14 cm. (29.1 x 10.5 cm.) Verse within ornamental border.

STE 35089 / DLC*

378　New York, N.Y.
ARGUS ◊

The carrier of the Argus most respectfully presents the following address to his patrons.

First line: Attir'd in storms and drifting snows

26 x 15 cm. (23.3 x 11.7 cm.) Verse within ornamental border.

STE 35956 / NHi* / Ms. note on New York Historical Society copy: January 1799.

379   New York, N.Y.
DAILY ADVERTISER, 1785–1806

Address of the carrier of the Daily Advertiser: To his kind customers and patrons. . . . January 1, 1799.

First line: Whilst genial friendship on this festive day

28 x 20 cm. (27.3 x 16.8 cm.) Verse within ornamental border in two columns divided by line of type ornaments.

STE 35958 / NHi*

380   New York, N.Y.
NEW-YORK WEEKLY MUSEUM

Address of the carrier of the Weekly Museum to his patrons, with the compliments of the season. . . . New-York, January 1, 1799.

First line: Gay from the east the bright'ning hours appear

27 x 22 cm. (23.7 x 19.0 cm.) Verse within ornamental border in two columns divided by double rule.

Evans 36693 / NHi* NN

381   Philadelphia, Pa.
TRUE AMERICAN

Address of the carrier of the Dessert to the True American to his patrons. For the year 1799.

First line: Lo! winter's come, with all his hoary train

30 x 20 cm. (25.2 x 18.0 cm.) Verse within ornamental border in two columns divided by double rule.

STE 48769 / NHi*

1800

382   Hartford, Conn.
AMERICAN MERCURY

Progress of truth and genius, through the eighteenth century: Or the boy's address who carries the American Mercury. . . . Hartford, January 1, 1800.

First line: Let faction's little-minded boys rehearse

44 x 21 cm. (41.2 x 16.0 cm.) Verse within double line ornamental border in two columns divided by ornamental line.

STE 36818 / NHi*

383   Hartford, Conn.
CONNECTICUT COURANT

The death of General Washington having filled the hearts of all the virtuous people in the United States with the sincerest affliction, we presume our readers will pardon us for presenting them, instead of the common New-Year's address, with the following tribute to the memory of that great, and illustrious friend and father of his country. . . . Hartford, Jan. 1, 1800.

First line: Far, far from hence be satire's aspect rude

43 x 35 cm. (31.5 x 20.6 cm.) Verse within ornamental border, in two columns divided by mourning rule, with short mourning rule at head.

STE 37235 / CSmH ICHi RPB*

384   New Haven, Conn.
CONNECTICUT JOURNAL

'The trial of time' presented by the carrier of the Connecticut Journal to his customers. New-Haven, January 1, 1800.

First line: Old time was charg'd with manners rude

34 x 10 cm. (30.0 x 6.7 cm.) Headbands of type ornaments at head and end.

STE 37240 / CtY DLC*

385   Boston, Mass.
BOSTON GAZETTE, 1800–1820+

Boston, January 1st, 1800. The carriers' of the Boston Commercial Gazette, as custom dictates, thus addresses its readers and patrons.

First line: Thou New-Year's muse, who condescends to sing | *At end of text:* Poem 'Postscript,' within ornamental border with first line, 'But hark what solemn sound salutes the ear,'

42 x 17 cm. (36.0 x 9.0 cm.)

STE 37026 / MiU-C*

386   Boston, Mass.
COLUMBIAN CENTINEL

The carriers of the Columbian Centinel, present their respects to its patrons, on the reputed exit of a century, and th [*sic*] real entrance of a New-Year.

First line: Patrons, and friends, whose soften'd smile | *At head:* Boston, January 1, 1800.

51 x 17 cm. (39.5 x 11.5 cm.) Within heavy line border.

STE 37208 / MSaE*

387   Boston, Mass.
INDEPENDENT CHRONICLE

To the patrons of the Independent Chronicle, their news carrier presents the compliments of the season. . . . Boston, January 2, 1800.

First line: Tho' winter bends the floods in chains | Verse includes elegy on the death of George Washington.

26 x 15 cm. (23.7 x 8.7 cm.) Cut within title.

STE 37686 / MWA PHi*

388   Boston, Mass.
MASSACHUSETTS MERCURY ◊

The carriers of the Massachusetts Mercury, to each of their beneficent customers.

First line: Old time, sir, by his process queer

35 x 22 cm. (26.4 x 17.3 cm.) Verse within ornamental border, in two columns divided by line of type ornaments. Cut of Mercury with banner at head.

STE 37933 / MWA*

389   Newark, N.J.
CENTINEL OF FREEDOM

The news-carrier's address to the patrons of the Centinel. . . . January 1, 1800.

First line: The New's-Man comes with hat in hand | *Also contains:* A New-Year's view of important political events with first line, 'When onward Time's resistless current bears.'

42 x 27 cm. (41.8 x 23.6 cm.) Verse within ornamental border in three columns divided by single rule. Swag of type ornaments at head within border.

STE 37114 / NHi*

390   New York, N.Y.
COMMERCIAL ADVERTISER

The Embassina, addressed to the patrons of the Commercial Advertiser, by the carriers—with the compliments of the season—January 1, 1800.

First line: Oh, gen'rous patrons of the news

41 x 25 cm. (37.6 x 20.3 cm.) Verse within ornamental border in three columns divided by single lines of type ornaments.

STE 37217 / NNe* / Reprinted in *Spectator* (New York), January 4, 1800, and *Commercial Advertiser* (New York), January 2, 1800.

391   New York, N.Y.
NEW-YORK WEEKLY MUSEUM ◊

The carrier of the Weekly Museum, begs leave to present the following New Year's address to his kind customers, with the compliments of the season.

First line: Hail to the New-born Year!—hail, festive day! | Last stanza, centered within mourning border, contains elegy to George Washington.

35 x 22 cm. (31.5 x 19.3 cm.) Verse within ornamental border in two columns divided by double rule.

STE 39059 / DLC MHi MWA NHi*

392   Lancaster, Pa.
INTELLIGENCER

Address of the news-boys, to the patrons of the Intelligencer, & Weekly Advertiser, on the commencement of the year, 1800.

First line: Good mercy! how I tore my shoes

PLa (microfilm) Verse in two columns divided by single rule.

393   Philadelphia, Pa.
TRUE AMERICAN

An elegiac poem on the death of General George Washington, Commander in Chief of the Armies

The *DEATH* of GENERAL WASHINGTON having filled the hearts of all the virtuous people in the *United States* with the sincerest affliction, we presume our Readers will pardon us for presenting them, instead of the common New-Year's Address, with the following tribute to the memory of that GREAT, AND ILLUSTRIOUS FRIEND AND FATHER OF HIS COUNTRY.

FAR, far from hence be Satire's aspect rude,
No more let Laughter's frolic-face intrude,
But every heart be fill'd with deepest gloom,
Each form be clad with vestments of the tomb.
From VERNON'S SACRED HILL dark sorrows flow,
Spread o'er the land, and shroud the world in woe.
From Missisippi's proud, majestic flood,
To where St. Croix meanders thro' the wood,
Let business cease, let vain amusements fly,
Let parties mingle, and let Faction die,
The Realm perform, by warm affection led,
Funereal honours to the MIGHTY DEAD.

Where shall the heart for consolation turn,
Where end its grief, or how forget to mourn!
Beyond these clouds appears no cheering ray,
No morning Star proclaims the approach of day.
Ask hoary Age from whence his sorrows come,
His voice is silent, and his sorrow dumb;
Enquire of Infancy why droops his head,
The prattler lisps—" great WASHINGTON is dead."
Why bend yon Statesmen o'er their task severe?
Why drops yon Chief the unavailing tear?
What sullen grief hangs o'er yon Martial Band?
What deep distress pervades the extended land?
In sad responses sounds from shore to shore—
" Our FRIEND, our GUIDE, our FATHER is no more."

Let fond Remembrance turn her aching sight,
Survey the past, dispel Oblivion's night,
By Glory led pursue the mazy road,
Which leads the traveller to her high abode,
There view that great, that venerated NAME,
Inscrib'd in sun-beams on the roll of Fame.
No lapse of years shall soil the sacred spot,
No future age its memory shall blot;
Millions unborn shall mark its sacred fire,
And latest Time behold it, and admire.

O widow'd Country! what protecting Form,
Shall ope thy pathway thro' the gathering storm!

What mighty hand thy trembling barque shall guide
Thro' Faction's rough, and overwhelming tide!
The hour is past—thy WASHINGTON no more
Descries, with Angel-ken, the peaceful shore.
Freed from the terrors of his awful eye,
No more fell Treason seeks a midnight sky,
But, crawling forth, on deadliest mischief bent,
Rears her black front, and toils with curst intent.
Behold! arrang'd in long, and black array,
Prepar'd for conflict, thirsting for their prey,
Our foes advance,—nor force, nor danger dread,
Their fears all vanish'd when his Spirit fled.
Oft, when our bosoms, fill'd with dire dismay,
Saw mischief gather round our country's way;
When furious Discord seiz'd her flaming brand,
And threaten'd ruin to our infant land;
When Faction's Imps sow'd thick the seeds of strife,
And aim'd destruction at the bliss of life;
When War with bloody hand her flag unfurl'd,
And her loud trump alarm'd the Western World;
His awful voice bade all contention cease,
At his command the storms were hush'd to peace.

But who can speak, what accents can relate,
The solemn scenes which mark'd the GREAT MAN's
        fate!
Ye ancient Sages, who so loudly claim,
The highest station on the list of Fame,
At his approach with diffidence retire,
His higher worth acknowledge, and admire.
When keenest anguish rack'd his mighty mind,
And the fond heart the joys of life resign'd,
No guilt, nor terror stretch'd its hard controul,
No doubt obscur'd the sunshine of the Soul.
Prepar'd for death, his calm, and steady eye,
Look'd fearless upward to a peaceful Sky;
While wondering Angels point the airy road,
Which leads the CHRISTIAN to the THRONE of GOD.

HARTFORD, Jan. 1, 1800.

Fig. 7. McDonald 383. *Connecticut Courant*, Hartford, Conn., January 1, 1800. John Hay Library.

of the United States. Dedicated to the patrons of the True American. At the commencement of the year 1800.

First line: His worth! His death, whose heaven-directed hand

55 x 34 cm. (44.0 x 24.5 cm.) Verse within architectural border in three columns with urn at head of each column. Cut at head of border.

STE 36453 / NHi* / Ms. inscription at end on New York Historical Society copy: By Charles Caldwell.

394   Providence, R.I.
PROVIDENCE GAZETTE

New-Year verses, by the carrier of the Gazette. . . . January 1, 1800.

First line: Ladies and gentlemen, here comes the news-boy, faithful, true, sincere

24 x 15 cm. (20.6 x 7.7 cm.)

STE 38346 / MWA RPHi*

Author suggested by last line, 'Your very humble servant, William Gerrish.'

395   Addr[ess] ◊

First line: How war rides forth on wheels of thunder

19 x 20 cm. (16.6 x 12.5 cm.) Top portion torn off. Verse in two columns divided by chained line. Elegy to Washington follows address.

MeHa*

1801

396   Hartford, Conn.
CONNECTICUT COURANT

Addressed to the readers of the Connecticut Courant. . . . Hartford, January 1, 1801.

First line: Precisely twelve o'clock, last night

34 x 26 cm. (33.6 x 25.3 cm.) Verse within ornamental border in four columns divided by single rules.

MiD-B*

397   Augusta, Me.
KENNEBEC GAZETTE

The carrier of the Kennebec Gazette to his generous and liberal patrons.

First line: It's an old saying, and perhaps 'tis wise | *At head:* Hallowell, January 1, 1801.

30 x 18 cm.

MeHi*

398   Baltimore, Md.
FEDERAL GAZETTE

The carrriers of the Federal Gazette & Baltimore Daily Advertiser, with due humility and proper respect, wish their customers a happy New Year; and as is usual on such occasions, with the compliments of the season, present them their dabblings of poetry. . . . Baltimore, January 1, 1801.

First line: 'O time!' exclaims the happy lover

44 x 25 cm. (27.6 x 16.1 cm.) Verse within ornamental border in two columns divided by line of type ornaments.

MdHi*

399   Boston, Mass.
INDEPENDENT CHRONICLE

Address to the patrons of the Independent Chronicle by their humble servant the carrier. . . . Thursday, January 1, 1801.

First line: Once in a year, O! 'tis a day of joy

32 x 18 cm. (27.0 x 8.6 cm.)

MWA PHi*

400   Boston, Mass.
MASSACHUSETTS MERCURY

The carriers of the Mercury present the following address to their generous customers, wishing them a prosperous and happy year! . . . Mercury-Office, January 2, 1801.

First line: Kind sirs, you've lived another year

32 x 17 cm. (28.5 x 11.0 cm.) Verse within ornamental border. Cut of state seal at head.

Sh 922 / MWA*

401   Salem, Mass.
      SALEM GAZETTE ◊

To the patrons of the Salem Gazette, the carriers present the compliments of the season and the following address.

First line: Ye patrons kind, whatever name

38 x 23 cm. (26.2 x 14.8 cm.) Verse in two columns divided by line of type ornaments.

MH*

402   New York, N.Y.
      MERCANTILE ADVERTISER

Address from the carriers of the Mercantile Advertiser, to the subscribers. . . . January 1, 1801.

First line: In ages past, when not the typic art

33 x 14 cm. (23.2 x 9.0 cm.) Verse within ornamental border.

MWA*

403   New York, N.Y.
      TEMPLE OF REASON

The carrier's address to the patrons of the Temple of Reason. January 1, 1801.

First line: From reason's sacred altar fir'd

31 x 12 cm. (27.6 x 8.2 cm.) Verse within ornamental border.

MWA*

404   New York, N.Y.
      NEW-YORK WEEKLY MUSEUM ◊

A New-Year's address, respectfully presented by the carrier of the Weekly Museum, to his much esteemed patrons.

First line: Blest be this morn! Hail, patrons, dear!

28 x 23 cm. (24.8 x 18.8 cm.) Verse within ornamental border in two columns divided by double rule.

Sh 1048 / MWA* / American Antiquarian Society copy dated 1801 on recto in a contemporary hand.

405   Troy, N.Y.
      NORTHERN BUDGET ◊

The news-boy's address to the patrons of the Northern Budget.

First line: Once more revolving Earth has run |
Preliminary verse with first line: A new song, for a new century.

46 x 28 cm. (43.3 x 20.0 cm.) Verse within architectural border.

RPB*

406   Lancaster, Pa.
      INTELLIGENCER ◊

Address of the news-boy to the patrons of the Intelligencer & Weekly Advertiser, on the commencement of a new century.

First line: Old time, the porter of our years

PLa (microfilm)

407   Philadelphia, Pa.
      AURORA ◊

The carrier of the Aurora, to his customers.

First line: The constant lapse of rolling years

23 x 15 cm. (21.0 x 19.0 cm.) Verse within ornamental border.

MWA* / Imprint date suggested from typographical evidence.

408   Philadelphia, Pa.
      POULSON'S AMERICAN DAILY ADVERTISER

The carriers of Poulson's American Daily Advertiser respectfully present to its patrons the following address on the commencement of the year 1801.

First line: Whilst innovation, with destructive rage

45 x 13 cm. (39.8 x 10.8 cm.) Verse within double line ornamental border.

PPL*

409   Charleston, S.C.
      CITY GAZETTE

New-Year's address. From the carriers of the City Gazette, to their generous customers. January 1, 1801.

First line: Kind friends and patrons of our daily page

45 x 20 cm. (38.0 x 14.5 cm.) Verse within ornamental border with corner blocks. Cut of tree in each upper block.

NN ScC*

1802

410 Hartford, Conn.
AMERICAN MERCURY

Genius of Liberty. The newsboy's address to the patrons of the American Mercury. Hartford, January 1, 1802.

First line: Ye viewless sylphs and elves and fairy trains

51 x 32 cm. (47.1 x 23.6 cm.) Verse within ornamental border, in three columns divided by line of type ornaments. The first twenty-four lines of column three within mourning border.

MWA* NHi

411 Hartford, Conn.
CONNECTICUT COURANT

Symptoms of the millennium. Addressed to the readers of the Connecticut Courant. Hartford, January 1, 1802.

First line: Oft has the period been foretold

44 x 27 cm. (37.8 x 19.9 cm.) Verse within ornamental border in three columns divided by single rules.

Sh 3131 / MWA*

Author: [John Ellsworth] supplied from footnote, 'e,' in third column.

412 Boston, Mass.
COLUMBIAN CENTINEL

Annual address of the carrier of the Columbian Centinel, to his generous patrons: wishing them a happier New Year than they expect to realize. . . . Boston, January 1, 1802.

First line: Another year is gone! and past—that bourn | *Signed:* The carrier | *Poem in five parts:*

Preface.—Retrospective-Domestic.—Retrospective-Foreign.—The hint-oblique.—The close.

51 x 21 cm. (48.0 x 17.7 cm.) Verse within double line border in two columns divided by double rule. Cut of eagle within title.

MWA* NN / Reprinted in *Independent Chronicle* (Boston), January 7, 1802.

413 Boston, Mass.
CONSTITUTIONAL TELEGRAPH

The carrier to the worthy and respected patrons of the Constitutional Telegraphe. . . . Boston, January 1, 1802.

First line: Revolving time has roll'd another year

25 x 21 cm. (19.5 x 14.2 cm.) Verse within ornamental border in two columns divided by single rule with thick-thin rules at head of text.

MB*

414 Boston, Mass.
INDEPENDENT CHRONICLE

The carrier of the Independent Chronicle, respectfully presents to our Republican friends, those who patronise the 'Good Old Cause' and 'Advocate the Rights of Man;'—the following—as a memento of real esteem, and a 'New-Year's gift'. . . . Boston Jan. 1, 1802.

First line: No more - to meditate on scenes of war

34 x 20 cm. (31.5 x 15.2 cm.) Verse within ornamental border in two columns divided by line of type ornaments. Cut of eagle and Indian within title.

MB*

415 Salem, Mass.
SALEM GAZETTE

To the patrons of the Salem Gazette, the carrier presents the compliments of the season and the following address. . . . January 1, 1802.

First line: Descend, ye powers of rhyme and reason

32 x 23 cm. (29.4 x 14.6 cm.) Verse on silk in two columns divided by line of type ornaments.

Sh 3089 / MSaE* MWA RPB (paper)

416   Salem, Mass.
SALEM REGISTER

To the Republican patrons of the Salem Register, the carrier presents the compliments of the season, and the following song: . . . January 1, 1802.

First line: Republican patrons, attend to my song

21 x 15 cm. (18.5 x 11.6 cm.) Verse within ornamental border.

NHi*

417   Concord, N.H.
COURIER OF NEW HAMPSHIRE

The news-boy's 'message' to the readers of the Courier of New Hampshire, addressed more particularly to those customers whom he serves in Concord. January 1st, 1802.

First line: Good customers, since 'tis the fashion

45 x 28 cm. (38.4 x 19.2 cm.) Verse in three columns.

MeHa*

418   New York, N.Y.
LADY'S MONITOR

An address, respectfully inscribed to the patrons of the Lady's Monitor. By their humble servant, the carrier. . . . January 1, 1802.

First line: While others sing, in harsher strains

32 x 18 cm. (26.1 x 15.9 cm.) Verse within ornamental border in two columns divided by curvilinear line.

NHi*

419   New York, N.Y.
NEW-YORK WEEKLY MUSEUM

New Year's address, presented by the carrier of the Weekly Museum, to his patrons. . . . New-York, January 1, 1802.

First line: From the regions of day, when fair science first came

29 x 15 cm. (27.5 x 11.3 cm.) Verse within ornamental border.

MWA* NHi

420   Poughkeepsie, N.Y.
POUGHKEEPSIE JOURNAL

The carrier's address, to the patrons of the Poughkeepsie Journal. January 1, 1802.

First line: Huzza my good patrons! once more I am here

44 x 25 cm. (40.5 x 21.3 cm.) Verse within architectural border in two columns divided by single rule.

NNe*

421   Philadelphia, Pa.
PHILADELPHIA REPOSITORY ◊

Address of the carrier, to the patrons of the Philadelphia Repository.

First line: Since mankind had rather, on ev'ry occasion

27 x 21 cm. (25.6 x 18.5 cm.) Verse within ornamental border in two columns divided by lines of type ornaments.

MWA*

422   New-Year's address, for 1802.

First line: While in a chilly winter night

20 x 12 cm. (18.5 x 8.3 cm.) Headband of type ornaments.

RPB*

1803

423   Baltimore, Md.
FEDERAL GAZETTE

Address of the carriers of the Federal Gazette & Baltimore Daily Advertiser, to their patrons. January 1, 1803.

First line: Inspiring nine, ye virgins fair!

33 x 27 cm. (28.4 x 20.6 cm.) Verse within ornamental border in three columns divided by line of type ornaments.

MdHi*

424   Boston, Mass.
BOSTON GAZETTE, 1800–1820+

The news-carriers' address, to the patrons of the Boston Gazette. January 1st, 1803.

First line: Scarce had this morn gleam'd faint along

32 x 18 cm. (27.3 x 11.8 cm.) Verse within ornamental border.

MWA* NHi

425 Boston, Mass.
COLUMBIAN CENTINEL

Hudibrastic effusion. Being the nineteenth since the publication of the Columbian Centinel: respectfully dedicated, with the compliments of the day, to the patrons thereof, by the public's humble servant, at all times, and in all weathers, The carrier. Boston, January 1, 1803.

First line: Howe'er the car of state may go—

37 x 22 cm. (35.2 x 15.5 cm.) Verse within curvilinear border in two columns divided by double rule.

PHi*

426 Boston, Mass.
INDEPENDENT CHRONICLE

The carrier of the Independent Chronicle, to his customers. . . . Boston, January 1, 1803.

First line: Happy the man, who cheers the paths of life | *At head of text:* The 'Union of honest men,' on the principles of honest friendship - are recommended to all. . . .'

36 x 20 cm. (33.0 x 13.6 cm.) Verse in two columns divided by line of type ornaments.

PHi*

427 Boston, Mass.
NEW-ENGLAND PALLADIUM

Poetical justice: or the New-Year's message of the carrier of the Palladium to its patrons; Boston, January 1, 1803.

First line: What shall the muse of western climes | *At head of text:* Poetical justice. | *Preliminary verse with first line:* And while their fees his purse enrich

45 x 16 cm. (35.6 x 12.0 cm.) Verse in two columns divided by single rule.

NHi*

428 Newburyport, Mass.
NEWBURYPORT HERALD

To the generous patrons of the Newburyport Herald, the carrier presents the compliments of the season, wishing them, and others, all the pleasures and blessings of a happy New-Year. . . . January 1st, 1803.

First line: In mammoth times, when wit is bought and sold

30 x 22 cm. (25.0 x 16.5 cm.) Verse within ornamental border in two columns divided by single rule.

MSaE*

429 Salem, Mass.
SALEM GAZETTE ◊

To the patrons of the Salem Gazette, the carrier presents the compliments of the season and the following 'message.'

First line: Long has it been, you know, our way

35 x 23 cm. (30.9 x 13.7 cm.) Verse within ornamental border.

Tapley p. 389 / MSaE*

430 Salem, Mass.
SALEM REGISTER

To the patrons of the Salem Register, the carrier tenders the compliments of the season with the following address. . . . January 1, 1803.

First line: Patrons and friends whose glowing smile

28 x 18 cm. (26.2 x 15.3 cm.) Verse within ornamental border in two columns divided by line of type ornaments. Cut of eagle at head.

Tapley p. 390 / MSaE*

431 Trenton, N.J.
TRUE AMERICAN

An address from the carrier of the True American to his patrons. . . . January 1, 1803.

First line: Patrons, again you see me here

35 x 22 cm. (28.4 x 16.2 cm.) Verse within ornamental border in two columns divided by single rules.

MWA*

432 New York, N.Y.
AMERICAN CITIZEN

A New Year's address to the subscribers for the American Citizen. By the news-carrier. . . . New-York, January 1, 1803.

First line: On this auspicious, festive day | 'By the news-carrier' within short horizontal double rule.

30 x 21 cm. (25.1 x 17.8 cm.) Verse within ornamental border in two columns divided by line of type ornaments.

NHi*

433 New York, N.Y.
MERCANTILE ADVERTISER

The carrier of the Mercantile Advertiser presents the following address to his respectable patrons, with the compliments of the season. . . . January 1, 1803.

First line: Now summer with her wanton court is gone

30 x 20 cm. (27.9 x 13.3 cm.) Verse within ornamental border with cut of eagle at head.

NHi*

434 New York, N.Y.
NEW-YORK EVENING POST,
1801–1820+

A New-Year's address from the carriers of the Evening Post, to their patrons. . . . New York, January 1, 1803.

First line: Full thirteen moons are gone and wasted

39 x 27 cm. (30 x 19 cm.) Verse in three columns divided by single rules.

NSU* / Reprinted in *New York Herald*, January 1, 1803.

435 New York, N.Y.
NEW-YORK WEEKLY MUSEUM

New-Year's address of the carrier of the Weekly Museum, to his patrons. . . . New York, Jan. 1, 1803.

First line: The onward rolling waves of time

30 x 21 cm. (28.1 x 17.3 cm.) Verse within orna-mental border in two columns divided by double rule.

MWA* NHi

436 Poughkeepsie, N.Y.
POLITICAL BAROMETER

The news-boy's address to the patrons of the Political Barometer. January 1, 1803.

First line: All hail to the season so jovial and gay

34 x 20 cm. (27.8 x 18.4 cm.) Verse within architectural border of type ornaments with words 'Twenty-seventh year of American Independence' beneath upper arch.

NN* (photocopy)

Author: Henry Livingston, Jr. Ms. inscription on verso of New York Public Library copy: . . . Attributed to Henry Livingston, Jr.

437 Lancaster, Pa.
LANCASTER JOURNAL

News-boy's address to the patrons of the Lancaster Journal, for the year 1803.

First line: With merry heel, and heart full light

19 x 15 cm. (17.7 x 13.2 cm.) Verse in two columns divided by single rule.

Sh 50381 / PU* RPB

438 Philadelphia, Pa.
PHILADELPHIA REPOSITORY ◊

Address of the carrier, to the patrons of the Philadelphia Repository.

First line: Good news, another year is past

27 x 22 cm. (23.4 x 17.2 cm.) Verse within ornamental border in two columns divided by line of type ornaments.

MWA*

439 Philadelphia, Pa.
POULSON'S AMERICAN DAILY
ADVERTISER

The carriers of Poulson's American Daily Advertiser respectfully present to its patrons the following address on the commencement of the year 1803.

First line: That rolling planet called the sun

45 x 15 cm. (39.5 x 11.5 cm.) Verse within triple line ornamental border.

NHi PPL*

440   Newport, R.I.
      NEWPORT MERCURY

New-Year's address. . . . Office of the Newport Mercury, Jan. 1, 1803.

First line: Too long has discord, bath'd the earth in gore

40 x 25 cm. (35.1 x 23.7 cm.) Verse within ornamental border in two columns divided by line of type ornaments. Cut of eagle flanked by urns at head.

RPB*

441   Providence, R.I.
      PROVIDENCE GAZETTE

New-Year verses. By the carrier of the Gazette. Providence, January 1, 1803.

First line: Joy to my friends; another year

23 x 16 cm. (19.2 x 8.1 cm.) Line of type ornaments at head and end.

RPHi*

442   Alexandria, Va.
      ALEXANDRIA ADVERTISER

New-Year's verses. The carrier's compliments to the patrons of the Alexanrdia [*sic*] Advertiser. . . . January 1, 1803.

First line: All have their hobbies;-this I'm bold t'assert

23 x 12 cm. (22.3 x 10.7 cm.) Verse within ornamental border.

DLC*

1804

443   Hartford, Conn.
      CONNECTICUT COURANT

Sketches of the times; addressed to the inhabitants of New-England, from the office of the Connecticut Courant. . . . Hartford, January 1, 1804.

First line: What vast advantages we find

47 x 28 cm. (43.8 x 25.2 cm.) Verse within ornamental line border in four columns divided by single rules.

NHi*

Reprinted in *The Echo*, 295–312. Sabin 21778 says, 'the authors [of the Echo] were Alsop, Dwight, Cogswell, Hopkins and Trumbull.' The Houghton Library catalogue states, 'written principally by Richard Alsop and Theodore Dwight.'

444   Baltimore, Md.
      AMERICAN

The carriers' address to the patrons of the American, for the year 1804. . . . January 1st, 1804.

First line: Come, sisters of the tuneful nine

46 x 27 cm. (37.2 x 23.1 cm.) Verse within architectural border. Cut at head and cut of eagle with word 'American' centered within border at head.

PPL*

445   Baltimore, Md.
      FEDERAL GAZETTE

The respectful address of the carriers of the Federal Gazette and Baltimore Daily Advertiser, to their numerous patrons. . . . Baltimore, January 1, 1804.

First line: Time, whose unwearied pinions bear

34 x 21 cm. (28.3 x 14.1 cm.) Verse within ornamental border in two columns divided by line of type ornaments.

MdHi*

446   Boston, Mass.
      BOSTON WEEKLY MAGAZINE

Address to the patronesses & patrons of the Boston Weekly Magazine, by their humble servant, the carrier. . . . Magazine Office, Jan. 2, 1804.

First line: Fair ladies, your servants, in hot, cold or dry | *At head of text between horizontal lines:* Generosity needs few arguments.

29 x 16 cm. (25.9 x 10.4 cm.)

MWA*

NEW-YEAR'S ADDRESS.

TOO long has Discord, bath'd the Earth in Gore,
Too long has Europe bled, thro' ev'ry Pore;
Too long has War, his fatal Flag unfurl'd,
And shook his Thunders o'er a prostrate World.
Lo! Peace asserts her Majesty divine,
All Nations bow before her sovereign Shrine!
War hears her Voice, and, struck by magic Spell,
Back with his writhing Furies, sinks to Hell.
Lighted by Polar Fires, see *Commerce* smiles,
Ev'n mid the rigors of the Zembleian Isles;—
Or mid the Climes of Equatorial Day,
Tho' Thunders round her roll, and Lightnings play,
Undaunted loosens, her advent'rous Sail,
To catch the Favors of the spicy Gale.
See *Agriculture*, with alluring Charms,
Tempt smiling Plenty to her fost'ring Arms,
Reclaim from Blood her Fields, new dress her Bowers,
And smile enchanted mid unfolding Flowers.
Religion's Domes with new-born Splendor rise,
And vocal Piety ascends the Skies:
Rous'd to Reflection, see repentant France
Awak'd to *Reason*, from her drunken Trance;
Again, the God of Christians to adore,
With Zeal to praise, with Penitence implore:
But still some Trace of Misery appears,
And Patriot-Sorrows claim indignant Tears.
The Friend of Man, the honest Swiss behold,
Tho' rough, humane, tho' hospitable, bold,
Tho' poor, yet free; whose unproductive Soil,
Might claim Exemption from invading Spoil:
But Pride, grown envious of a Scene like this,
Goes Hell-commissioned to destroy his Bliss,
Invasion's Myrmidons surround the Land,
With Myriad Hosts, o'erwhelm that faithful Band,
Who fall, brave Martyrs, to their Country's Cause,
Its sacred Freedom, and its equal Laws.
As swift as sure, their fell Destruction came,
The Hour of Combat, and of Death the same.
Some Brother, as thro' Climes remote he goes,
Beyond his Iceclad Cliffs, his Mountain Snows,
Rous'd by his *Country's sacred Voice*, returns
While patriot Ardor in his Bosom burns;
His *native Music* fires to fierce Alarms,
Home rushes onward, with resistless Charms,
And all his lab'ring Soul is up in Arms.
With patriot Hope inflamed, behold him fly,
The Fire of Combat, Lightning in his Eye;
But what can Zeal, or honest Warmth avail,
When countless Legions, one poor Band assail?
Already is his Country lost—with Blood defil'd;
His Mountain Snows, with festring Dead uppil'd;
His Rocks, his Pastures, all he held most dear,
His Hills, his Home, one dreary Waste appear.
What shall he do! or frantic where retire?
Here springs an Ambush, and there sweeps a Fire;

On all Sides frowns, irremed'able Grief,
And Death alone administers Relief.
Still may that Flame in Freedom's holy Urn,
Which has for Ages burnt, for Ages burn;
Till fann'd by Fortune, and by Science nurst,
Thro' every dull Incumbrance it shall burst,
O'er the wide World its living Justres play,
And bless the Nations with perennial Day.
Why does the Muse incline, with fond Delay,
Amid these scenes, with Sympathy to stay,
O! why not turn, impatient to descry,
The bounteous Blessings of *our* Western Sky.
Yet even here ferment the Seeds of Ill,
And sweets, with Bitter's mixt, our Chalice fill.
What tho' no Despot crush, beneath his Throne,
Contented Slaves, who bear its Weight, and groan;
Nor Cæsar, careless of an honest Fame,
Erect his Glory, on his Country's Shame;
Nor Cromwell, while a mad Ambition fires,
O'er humbled Man to sovereign Sway aspires;
Nor yet the Corsican, whose Upstart Sway,
Five Nations own, and tremble and obey.
But where the easy Mind, the soft Repose,
The tranquil Bliss, that mild Contentment knows?
All fled! on that auspicious Day,
When *Virtue* call'd her WASHINGTON away.
See now a Chief, with Flattery's glozing Art,
Delicious Poison pours, and lulls the Heart,
Persuades the People, with seductive Song,
He's ever right, for they are never wrong.
See NATIVE WORTH, by Calumny depress'd,
While foreign Miscreants only are caress'd;
'Tis *out-cast* Merit, claims the Sages Tear,
" All that the Gibbet 'scape, find Friendship here."
The Hosts of Slanderers see, absurdly base,
Essay, all former Merit, to efface;
All branded with the Name of Freedom's Foe,
Receive alike, the deep-envenom'd Blow.
Even He, who nobly, every Peril brav'd,
And from a Tyrant's Grasp, our Country sav'd,
Whose Death we mourn, with unaffected Tears,
One gen'ral Grief, and strange forboding Fears,
Even He, by Factions Instinct lead,
They tear, vindictive, from the hallow'd Dead.
Illustrious Shade, their weak Attempt forgive,
They feed on Malice, and Detraction live,
What tho' this reptile Crew, to thee deny,
The generous Sympathy, the Patriot Sigh,
Still shall Posterity, with Rapture see,
The Hero, Patriot, Statesman, all in Thee.
Nation's shall glory in thy well-earn'd Fame,
And after-ages consecrate thy Name;
Time with unfading Wreaths thy Brows shall crown,
While fresher bloom the Laurels of Renown.

Office of the Newport Mercury, Jan. 1, 1803.

Fig. 8. McDonald 440. *Newport Mercury*, Newport, R.I., January 1, 1803. Brown University.

447 Boston, Mass.
INDEPENDENT CHRONICLE

The carrier of the Independent Chronicle, to his customers: presenting the best wishes of a republican heart for their private and public prosperity. . . . January 2, 1804.

First line: The times, in ever variable display

41 x 20 cm. (35.8 x 13.5 cm.) Verse in two columns divided by ornamental line with line of type ornaments at head.

MWA*

448 Newburyport, Mass.
NEWBURYPORT HERALD

Address to the patrons of the Newburyport Herald, by the carriers. . . . January 1, 1804.

First line: Twelve toilsome months have slowly pass'd | *Preliminary verse with first line:* In vain we search'd the town around

30 x 22 cm. (27.5 x 16.5 cm.) Verse within architectural border in two columns divided by line of type ornaments.

MSaE* NHi

449 Hanover, N.H.
DARTMOUTH GAZETTE

The news boy's 'memorial' to the patrons of the Dartmouth Gazette, January 1, 1804.

First line: Old time, who eats, nor drinks, nor sleeps

47 x 15 cm. (41.0 x 12.2 cm.) Verse in two columns.

NhHD*

450 Lansingburgh, N.Y.
FARMER'S REGISTER

The news boy's address to the patrons of the Farmers' Register. . . . Lansingburgh, January 3d, 1804.

First line: This chilly morn I take my stand

40 x 15 cm. (38.7 x 13.2 cm.) Headband of type ornaments. Verse in two columns divided by line of type ornaments.

RPB*

451 New York, N.Y.
MORNING CHRONICLE

Address of the carriers of the Morning Chronicle, to their patrons. . . . January 1, 1804.

First line: At this season of mirth, when the full tide of pleasure

39 x 15 cm. (32.2 x 10.5 cm.) Verse within ornamental border.

NHi*

452 New York, N.Y.
NEW-YORK EVENING POST,
1801–1820+

The carrier of the New-York Evening Post to his patrons. . . . January 1, 1804.

First line: Prince of the months, in youthful prime

38 x 26 cm. (29.7 x 18.2 cm.) Verse in three columns.

NSU*

453 New York, N.Y.
NEW-YORK WEEKLY MUSEUM

New-Year's address of the carrier of the Weekly Museum, to his patrons. . . . January 1, 1804.

First line: Another year is gone—and yet frail man

31 x 21 cm. (26.3 x 16.7 cm.) Verse within ornamental border in two columns divided by line of type ornaments.

MWA*

454 Newburgh, N.Y.
RECORDER OF THE TIMES ◊

The address of the carriers of the Recorder of the Times, to his patrons; with the compliments of the season. . . . Printed by Dennis Coles.

First line: New-Year once more, comes hast'ning o'er | *At head of text:* Newburgh, January 1, 1804.

46 x 30 cm. (41.9 x 28.7 cm.) Verse within architectural border in three columns divided by single rules.

NNe* MWA

455   Lancaster, Pa.
INTELLIGENCER ◊

The newsboy of the Intelligencer, & Weekly Advertiser, to his customers, greeting.

First line: True to my trust, as is old Father Time

PLa (microfilm) Verse in two columns.

456   Lancaster, Pa.
LANCASTER JOURNAL

News-boy's address to the patrons of the Lancaster Journal, for the year 1804.

First line: With joyful heart I now appear

28 x 22 cm. (24.0 x 18.3 cm.) Verse in two columns divided by line of type ornaments.

RPB*

457   Philadelphia, Pa.
PHILADELPHIA REPOSITORY

The carrier of the Philadelphia Repository, to its patrons, of the commencement of the New-Year, January, 1804.

First line: The night was dark, loud roar'd the storm

28 x 21 cm. (26.7 x 20.0 cm.) Verse within architectural border in two columns divided by curvilinear line.

MWA*

458   Philadelphia, Pa.
POULSON'S AMERICAN DAILY ADVERTISER

Address of the carriers of Poulson's American Daily Advertiser, to its patrons, on the commencement of the year 1804.

First line: Kind patrons will you hear your news boy's song?

24 x 16 cm. (21.4 x 12.6 cm.) Verse within chained line border.

NHi* / Ms. inscription on verso of New York Historical Society copy: Written by the Reverend John Blair Linn, D.D.

459   [Philadelphia], Pa.
TRUE AMERICAN

New-Year address of the carrier of the True American to his customers. . . . January 2, 1804.

First line: Custom, whom all mankind obey

39 x 22 cm. (32.7 x 16.4 cm.) Verse within ornamental border in two columns divided by line of type ornaments.

NN* / Ms. note on verso of New York Public Library copy: Philadelphia.

460   Newport, R.I.
RHODE-ISLAND REPUBLICAN

Address of the carrier of the Rhode-Island Republican, to its patrons, for January 1st, 1804.

First line: Another year is past and gone

33 x 20 cm. (29.9 x 17.4 cm.) Verse within ornamental border in two columns divided by chained line.

NHi*

461   Providence, R.I.
UNITED STATES CHRONICLE

An address, from the carrier of the U.S. Chronicle, for 1804.

First line: Full thirteen moons are gone and wasted

23 x 15 cm. (19.1 x 9.0 cm.) Verse within ornamental border.

RPHi*

462   Bennington, Vt.
VERMONT GAZETTE

The carrier of the Vermont Gazette, presents the following, with sincere respect, and wishes all his customers a happy New-Year. . . . Bennington, January 1st, 1804.

First line: Kind friends, once more on New-Year's Day

42 x 34 cm. (36.0 x 21.5 cm.) Eight lines of verse, followed by verse in two columns.

VtU*

463   Richmond, Va.
ENQUIRER

The news-carriers' address to the patrons of the Enquirer. For the year 1804.

First line: As sol diffuseth his enliv'ning ray

20 x 11 cm. (17.4 x 9.0 cm.) Verse within double line ornamental border.

NHi*

1805

464 Georgetown, D.C.
WASHINTON FEDERALIST

To the patrons of the Washington Federalist. . . . December 25th, 1804.

First line: From custom since 'tis wrong to vary | *Signed:* The carrier.

32 x 22 cm. (28.9 x 15.8 cm.) Verse within ornamental border in two columns divided by ornamental rule.

MWA* / American Antiquarian Society copy contains manuscript annotations.

465 Portland, Me.
EASTERN ARGUS

A New Year's poesy, presented to the patrons of the Eastern Argus, by their humble servant, the carrier. . . . Argus Office, January 1, 1805.

First line: Old time's industrious charioteer | *Signed:* Selah! | 'Postscript' follows and footnotes in two columns divided by single rule.

33 x 16 cm. (30.3 x 14.2 cm.) Verse within ornamental border in two columns divided by single rule.

MWA*

466 Boston, Mass.
BOSTON GAZETTE, 1800–1820+

The carriers of the Boston Gazette, respectfully present to its patrons and friends, the compliments of the season, and according to antient usage, request their acceptance of the following address. . . . January 1, 1805.

First line: The Muse, who notes all changes here

32 x 22 cm. (27.2 x 15.2 cm.) Verse within orna-

mental border in two columns divided by line of type ornaments.

MWA PHi*

467 Boston, Mass.
BOSTON WEEKLY MAGAZINE

Address to the patrons & patronesses of the Boston Weekly Magazine, by their humble servant, the carrier. . . . Magazine-office, Jan. 1, 1805.

First line: The wind it was cold, and the fast falling snow

32 x 27 cm. (23.5 x 21.6 cm.) Verse in two columns divided by line of type ornaments; all within architectural border bearing words at head, 'Here comes the annual greeting.'

RPB*

468 Boston, Mass.
COLUMBIAN CENTINEL

Something for something: or, An address of the carrier of the Columbian Centinel. To its friends and patrons:—Wishing them a happy New Year. . . . Centinel-Office, Jan. 1, 1805.

First line: The gorgeous palaces, and towers | *At head of text:* Address, &c. | *Signed:* The carrier.

50 x 33 cm. (46.9 x 27.2 cm.) Verse in four columns with cut of eagle within title.

MWA*

469 Boston, Mass.
INDEPENDENT CHRONICLE

Address of the patrons of the Independent Chronicle by the carrier. . . . Boston, January 1, 1805.

First line: 'Tis New Year's Day again! Your new's-boy comes!

35 x 20 cm. (32.5 x 15.8 cm.) Verse within ornamental border in two columns divided by chained line.

MWA PHi*

470 Boston, Mass.
NEW-ENGLAND PALLADIUM

L'Expose; a New Year's message from the carriers of the Palladium to its patrons, with the compliments of the season. . . . Palladium-office, January 1, 1805.

First line: Ladies and gents, with vast humility

36 x 28 cm. (31.1 x 24.6 cm.) Verse in four columns divided by single rules.

MWA*

471   Boston, Mass.
       REPERTORY

Address of the carriers, to the patrons of the Repertory. . . . Jan. 1, 1805.

First line: May't please your Honour's pow'r and glory-

32 x 18 cm. (29.1 x 9.2 cm.) Verse within ornamental border.

MWA*

472   Newburyport, Mass.
       NEWBURYPORT HERALD ◊

Address to the patrons of the Newburyport Herald, by the carriers.

First line: No more the stream meanders through the vale

27 x 15 cm. (17.2 x 8.9 cm.)

MSaE* MWA NHi

473   Northampton, Mass.
       HIVE

The news carrier's address to the patrons of the Hive. . . . January 1 - 1805.

First line: You, friend and patron of the Hive | *Preliminary verse with first line:* I weekly bring the Hive and all the honey

47 x 29 cm. (27.3 x 16.1 cm.) Verse in two columns divided by double rule.

MWA*

474   Salem, Mass.
       SALEM GAZETTE ◊

To the patrons of the Salem Gazette, the carrier presents the compliments of the season and the following address.

First line: Money's the centre of attraction

28 x 23 cm. (26.7 x 15.1 cm.) Verse in two columns divided by double rules. Cut of U.S. Seal at head.

Tapley p. 400 / MSaE*

475   Salem, Mass.
       SALEM REGISTER

The carrier of the Salem Register presents its patrons with the compliments of the season, and the following address: . . . January 1st, 1805.

First line: Still as the circling seasons roll

31 x 19 cm. (27.8 x 15.7 cm.) Verse on silk, within ornamental border in two columns divided by double curvilinear line, with cut of eagle within title.

Tapley p. 400 / MSaE RPB* MWA

476   Amherst, N.H.
       FARMER'S CABINET

From the carrier of the Farmer's Cabinet: a New-Year's address, attempted in rhyme. [Amherst, N.H., 1805.]

First line: Though in my teens, unskill'd in learned lore

8 p.   23 cm.

Sh 8426 / DLC NhHi* NHi

Author: David Everett.

477   Hudson, N.Y.
       BEE

Address of the carrier of the Bee to his patrons. . . . Hudson, January 1, 1805.

First line: Well, Christmas and New-Year, these holiday times

31 x 14 cm. (25.1 x 9.6 cm.) Verse within border of type ornaments.

NN*

478   Lancaster, Pa.
       LANCASTER JOURNAL

The news-boy's ode to the patrons of the Lancaster Journal for the year, 1805.

First line: Tune the harp and fiddle-string

28 x 23 cm. (24.8 x 18.8 cm.) Verse within orna-

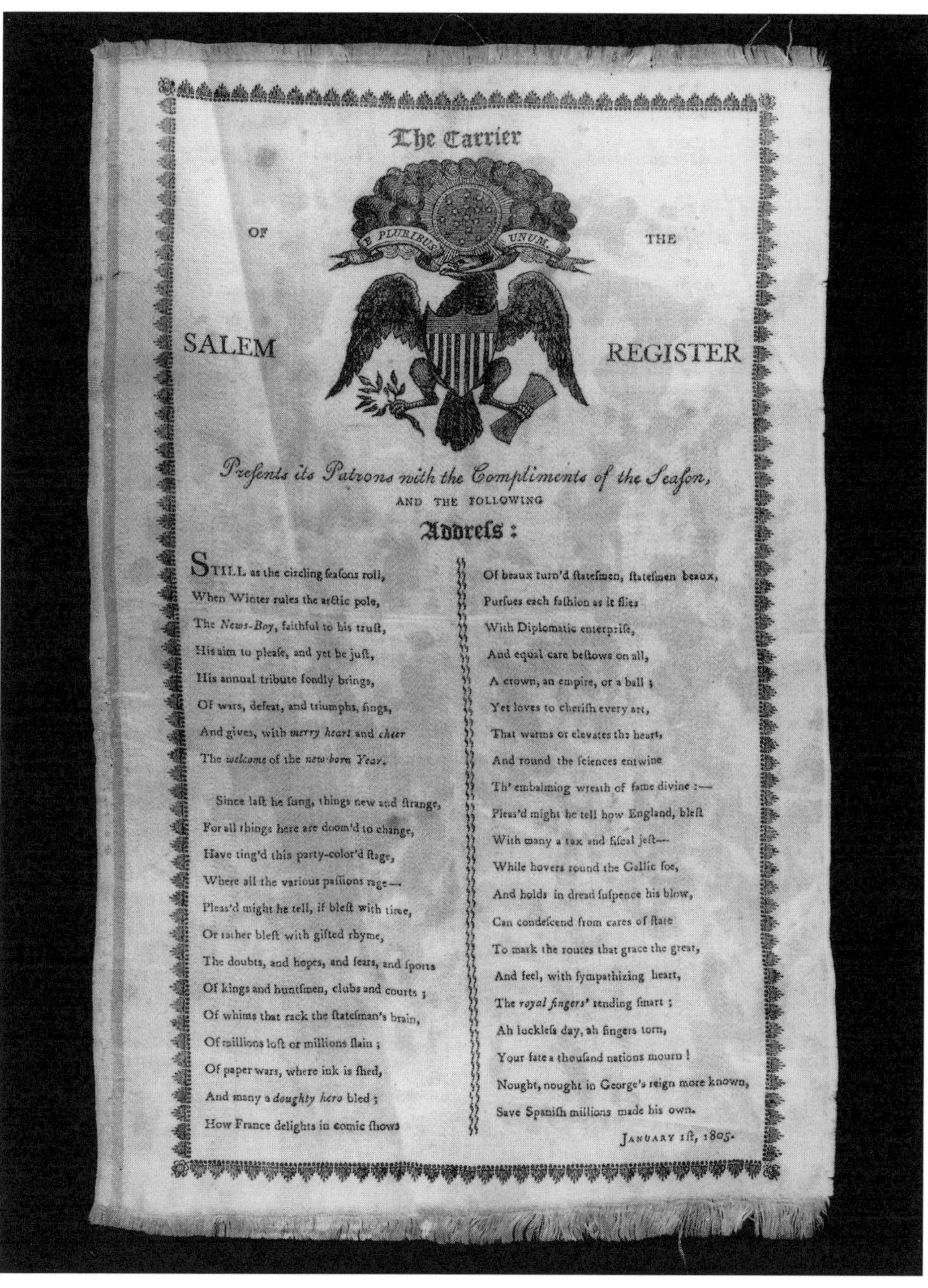

Fig. 9. McDonald 475. *Salem Register*, Salem, Mass., January 1, 1805. John Hay Library.

mental border in two columns divided by curvilinear line with thick-thin rules at head of text.
RPB*

479   Philadelphia, Pa.
AURORA

Address of the carriers of the Aurora, to their customers, on the commencement of the year 1805.

First line: On the first of the year, 'tis a natural case

46 x 27 cm. (34.8 x 21.5 cm.) Verse within ornamental border in two columns divided by double rule.

MWA*

480   Philadelphia, Pa.
POLITICAL AND COMMERCIAL REGISTER

Address of the carriers of the Political and Commercial Register, to their patrons, on the commencement of the year, 1805.

First line: Revolving seasons usher in the year

32 x 21 cm. (29.0 x 15.2 cm.) Verse within ornamental border in two columns divided by single rule.

NHi*

481   Philadelphia, Pa.
POULSON'S AMERICAN DAILY ADVERTISER

Address of the carriers of Poulson's American Daily Advertiser, to its patrons, on the commencement of the year 1805.

First line: True as the rising sun, thro' wet and dry | *At end of text:* There is a certain class of people in France.

34 x 21 cm. (30.5 x 17.3 cm.) Verse within ornamental border in two columns divided by woven line.

DLC NHi PHi*

482   [Philadelphia], Pa.
TRUE AMERICAN

The carrier of the True American to his patrons. . . . January 1. 1805.

First line: Loud let our songs of praise ascend

31 x 13 cm. (29.2 x 9.2 cm.) Verse within ornamental border.

NN* / Ms. note on verso of New York Public Library copy: Philadelphia.

483   Reading, Pa.
READINGER ADLER

Neu-Jahr-Wunsch des Herumträgers des Readinger Adlers, an seine Kunden. Reading, Dienstags, den 1 sten Januar, 1805.

First line: Ja, wieder, wieder schwand ein Jahr-

28 x 23 cm. (22.5 x 19.0 cm.) Verse within ornamental border in two columns.

MWA*

484   Middlebury, Vt.
MIDDLEBURY MERCURY

New-Year's address. The carrier of the Middlebury Mercury, to his customers. . . . January 1, 1805.

First line: The year of our Lord, eighteen hundred and four

27 x 23 cm. (23.5 x 18.2 cm.) Verse in two columns divided by curvilinear line with ornamental lines at head and end.

McCorison 799A / MWA*

485   Alexandria, Va.
ALEXANDRIA EXPOSITOR

The address of the carrier of the Alexandria Expositor, to its patrons. . . . January 1st, 1805.

First line: Inspir'd with respect, and a prospect of meeting

26 x 10 cm. (25.1 x 9.8 cm.) Verse within ornamental border, with cut of a rose in each upper corner.

DLC*

1806

486 Wilmington, Del.
MIRROR OF THE TIMES

Address from the carrier of the Mirror to its patrons. . . . Mirror Office, January 1, 1806.

First line: Old time, who moves with steady pace | *Signed:* John M'Bride

31 x 21 cm. (29.1 x 19.0 cm.) Verse in two columns divided by curvilinear line.

MWA*

487 Fredericktown, Md.
HORNET

New-Year's verses, addressed to the friends and patrons of the Gazette and Hornet, by the carrier. . . . January 1, 1806.

First line: The old year's past, time ushers in the new

36 x 22 cm. (22.8 x 17.2 cm.) Verse in two columns divided by line of type ornaments.

Sh 50679 / PPL*

488 Boston, Mass.
BOSTON MAGAZINE

Address, for the New-Year, 1806: Respectfully presented (with the compliments of the season,) by the carrier of the Boston Magazine, to its patrons.

First line: Ladies and gentlemen! Old father time, with scythe upheld

28 x 22 cm. (26.5 x 16.0 cm.) Verse within ornamental border in two columns divided by curvilinear line.

NHi*

489 Boston, Mass.
INDEPENDENT CHRONICLE

New Year's address of the carrier of the Independent Chronicle, respectfully presented to its patrons. . . . Boston, January 1, 1806.

First line: Ye friends of truth and freedom's reign

35 x 17 cm. (32.1 x 13.8 cm.) Verse in two columns divided by single rule.

CSmH MWA* WHi

490 Boston, Mass.
NEW-ENGLAND PALLADIUM

The carriers of the New-England Palladium, to its generous patrons. . . . Palladium-Office, January 1, 1806.

First line: For many years, the carrier's muse

36 x 28 cm. (23.5 x 20.3 cm.) Verse within ornamental border in two columns divided by ornamental line.

NHi*

491 Boston, Mass.
REPERTORY

New Year's address, of the carriers of the Repertory to its patrons. . . . Boston, January 1st, 1806.

First line: What here again?—Why sure it is not Tuesday-

46 x 29 cm. (36.6 x 22.5 cm.) Verse in three columns divided by single rules.

RPB*

492 Newburyport, Mass.
NEWBURYPORT HERALD

The news-carrier's address to the patrons of the Newburyport Herald. January 1st, 1806.

First line: Old earth, my dear patrons, once more has whirl'd round

30 x 25 cm. (21.0 x 18.2 cm.) Verse within architectural border in two columns divided by line of type ornaments.

MSaE* NHi

493 Northampton, Mass.
REPUBLICAN SPY

The news-boy's address to the readers of the Republican Spy. January 1, 1806.

First line: As 'tis the custom now a days | *Signed:* The 'Printers Devil'

46 x 28 cm. (39.4 x 25.5 cm.) Verse in four columns divided by line of type ornaments with short curvilinear line at head of text.

DLC*

494   Salem, Mass.
SALEM GAZETTE ◊

To the patrons of the Salem Gazette, the carrier presents the compliments of the season, and the following address.

First line: Had we the powers of G. + D.

27 x 22 cm. (20.2 x 14.6 cm.) Verse on silk in two columns divided by single rule.

Sh 11452 / MH MSaE* / Harvard University copy bears ms. date 1806.

495   Salem, Mass.
SALEM REGISTER

The news-boy's address to the patrons of the Salem Register, on the commencement of the year eighteen hundred and six. . . . January 1st, 1806.

First line: A New-Year's ode, the newsboy sighs-

37 x 24 cm. (31.1 x 15.8 cm.) Verse within ornamental border in two columns divided by curvilinear line.

MWA*

496   Trenton, N.J.
TRUE AMERICAN

To the patrons of the True American. January 1, 1806

First line: What scripture pronounces, experience proves true

38 x 26 cm. (31.2 x 19.3 cm.) Verse within ornamental border in two columns divided by chained line.

NjHi*

497   Lansingburgh, N.Y.
FARMER'S REGISTER

. . . to the patrons of the Farmer's Register. . . . Lansingburgh, January 1, 1806.

First line: O, nature! 'inexhaustive' pow'r

Fragments

RPB*

498   New York, N.Y.
AMERICAN CITIZEN

The New Year's address of the carriers of the American Citizen, for 1806, respectfully dedicated to their employers.

First line: Borne on the rapid wings of time

32 x 22 cm. (27.4 x 18.9 cm.) Verse within ornamental border in two columns divided by curvilinear line.

MH*

499   Newburgh, N.Y.
RECORDER OF THE TIMES

The canticle of the carrier of the Recorder, to his patrons. January 1, 1806.

First line: Readers, good morn

45 x 28 cm. (35.8 x 17.1 cm.) Verse within ornamental border in three columns divided by single rules.

NNe* MWA

500   Philadelphia, Pa.
POULSON'S AMERICAN DAILY ADVERTISER

Address of the carriers of Poulson's American Daily Advertiser, to its patrons, on the commencement of the year 1806.

First line: Since last I pass'd the threshold of your door

35 x 21 cm. (29.5 x 17.0 cm.) Verse within ornamental border in two columns divided by line of type ornaments with thick-thin rules at head and end.

DLC PHi PPL RPB*

501   Philadelphia, Pa.
RELF'S PHILADELPHIA GAZETTE

The carriers of Relf's Philadelphia Gazette, to their patrons, on the commencement of the year 1806. . . . 1st January, 1806.

First line: O Yes! O yes! O yes!—On you, good friends | Trumpeting angel at head of border bearing words 'To Eaton.'

46 x 29 cm. (41.4 x 24.7 cm.) Verse within architectural border framed by line of type ornaments.

Sh 50725 / PPL*

502   Newport, R.I.
RHODE-ISLAND REPUBLICAN

The carrier of the Rhode-Island Republican, respectfully presents to the public, the following address. . . . Newport, January 1, 1806.

First line: In those insipid barren times

32 x 20 cm. (28.6 x 16.1 cm.) Verse within ornamental border in two columns divided by line of type ornaments.

RPHi*

503   Alexandria, Va.
ALEXANDRIA ADVERTISER

Address. The carrier of the Alexandria Daily Advertiser to his patrons. . . . January 1st, 1806.

First line: Blest be the man, the world has said

33 x 16 cm. (29.9 x 15.7 cm.) Verse within ornamental border in two columns divided by single rule.

DLC*

1807

504   Portland, Me.
[EASTERN ARGUS]

New Year.

First line: Swift and perpetual is the lapse of years | Address followed by 'Postscript. The carrier's hint!,' dated January 1, 1807.

31 x 18 cm. (30.4 x 17.1 cm.) Verse within ornamental border in two columns divided by curvilinear line.

Sh 13215 / MWA* / American Antiquarian Society copy inscribed in a contemporary hand: Carriers epistle by D-W-L. [and] Mr. Daniel W. Lincoln.

Author: Daniel Waldo Lincoln.

505   Boston, Mass.
NEW-ENGLAND PALLADIUM

The carriers of the New-England Palladium, to their patrons, greeting. . . . Palladium-Office, Jan. 1, 1807.

First line: Our good friend, Time, still on his way

32 x 27 cm. (26.2 x 18.1 cm.) Verse in two columns divided by curvilinear line with ornamental borders at head and end and cut at head.

MHi*

506   Boston, Mass.
REPERTORY

New Year's address, of the carriers of the Repertory to its patrons. . . . Repertory Office - Boston, January 1, 1807.

First line: Pythagoras, that learned wight

35 x 27 cm. (27.8 x 20.6 cm.) Verse in three columns divided by single rules.

MWA*

507   Salem, Mass.
SALEM REGISTER

To the patrons of the Salem Register the carrier presents the compliments of the season and the following address. January 1st, 1807.

First line: Once more the carrier brings addresses

37 x 23 cm. (33.0 x 16.0 cm.) On silk.

MSaE*

508   Newark, N.J.
CENTINEL OF FREEDOM

The news-boy's address, to the patrons of the Centinel of Freedom. . . . January 1, 1807.

First line: Subscrirer [*sic*] (By the fireside, with his waiter by him.) See who knocks at the door?

45 x 28 cm. (33.5 x 19.4 cm.) Verse within ornamental border divided by line of type ornaments.

NCooHi* NjR

509   Albany, N.Y.
REPUBLICAN CRISIS

The carrier's New-Year's address to the patrons of the Republican Crisis. . . . January 1st, 1807.

First line: A plague on the practice (some pendant's invention

38 x 24 cm. (35.1 x 22.4 cm.) Verse within ornamental border in two columns divided by curvilinear line.

NHi*

510　　Hudson, N.Y.
　　　BEE

Address of the carrier of the Bee, to its patrons. For 1807. . . . Hudson, January 1, 1807.

First line: It's hard, confounded hard, this freezing weather

34 x 21 cm. (28.7 x 14.7 cm.) Verse in two columns divided by single rule, with ornamental line at head and end.

NHi*

511　　Lansingburgh, N.Y.
　　　LANSINGBURGH GAZETTE

The news-boy's address, to the patrons of the Lansingburgh Gazette. January 1, 1807.

First line: Again, my patrons dear, behold | *Preliminary verse with first line:* Necessity, though I am no wit

42 x 17 cm. (35.9 x 13.9 cm.) Verse within ornamental border in two columns divided by line of type ornaments with thick-thin rules at head of text.

MiD-B*

512　　New York, N.Y.
　　　INDEPENDENT REPUBLICAN

The news carriers' address to the patrons of the Independent Republican. For the year 1807.

First line: Attend ye patrons of the printing art

32 x 13 cm. (29.2 x 9.8 cm.) Verse within ornamental border with five type ornaments at head of text.

NHi*

513　　New York, N.Y.
　　　MORNING CHRONICLE

New-Year's address from the carrier of the Morning Chronicle. . . . January 1, 1807.

First line: The smiling muse, on rosy wings

25 x 21 cm. (21.0 x 18.1 cm.) Verse within ornamental border in two columns divided by curvilinear line, with thick-thin rules at head of text.

NHi*

514　　New York, N.Y.
　　　NEW-YORK GAZETTE,
　　　　1795–1820+

Address of the carriers of the New-York Gazette to their subscribers. January 1, 1807.

First line: Old surly winter frowns again

32 x 20 cm. (30.6 x 17.8 cm.) Verse within ornamental border in two columns divided by line of type ornaments with thick-thin rules at head of text.

NHi*

515　　New York, N.Y.
　　　NEW YORK SPY

Address of the carrier of the New York Spy, to his generous patrons, wishing them a happy New-Year. . . . January 1, 1807.

First line: Once every week our Spy comes out

34 x 19 cm. (29.6 x 14.5 cm.) Verse in two columns divided by curvilinear line.

NHi*

516　　New York, N.Y.
　　　NEW-YORK WEEKLY MUSEUM

New-Year's address of the carrier of the Weekly Museum. To his patrons. . . . January 1, 1807.

First line: Stern winter now with all her gloomy train

30 x 19 cm. (23.2 x 17.2 cm.) Verse within ornamental border in two columns divided by line of type ornaments.

NHi*

517　　New York, N.Y.
　　　PEOPLE'S FRIEND

The carrier of the People's Friend and Daily Advertiser to his customers. January 1, 1807.

First line: As bridegroom joys on wedding morn

33 x 18 cm. (28.5 x 11.7 cm.) Verse in two columns divided by curvilinear line with thick-thin rules at head of text.

NHi* MWA

518 Newburgh, N.Y.
POLITICAL INDEX

The carrier of the Political Index, to his patrons, with the compliments of the season. Newburgh, January 1, 1807.

First line: Revolving time, in his career

35 x 20 cm. (29.9 x 17.1 cm.) Verse within ornamental border in two columns divided by line of type ornaments.

NNe* MWA

519 Wardsbridge, N.Y.
ORANGE COUNTY REPUBLICAN

The news-carrier's address, to the generous patrons of the Orange County Republican. Wardsbridge, January 1st, 1807.

First line: Another year's past—'tis gone!

48 x 31 cm. (38.2 x 20.2 cm.) Verse in two columns divided by curvilinear line.

NNe* MWA

520 Philadelphia, Pa.
AURORA

The carriers of the Aurora, to their patrons, on the commencement of the New Year. January 1, 1807.

First line: Aurora ushers in the year

53 x 38 cm. (47.9 x 33.6 cm.) Verse within architectural border in two columns divided by double rule. Cut of Mercury in cloud at head of border.

PHi*

521 Philadelphia, Pa.
POULSON'S AMERICAN DAILY
ADVERTISER

The address of the carriers of Poulson's American Daily Advertiser, to its patrons, on the commencement of the year 1807.

First line: Joy to my patron—may his face

46 x 28 cm. (41.8 x 26.3 cm.) Verse within architectural border in two columns divided by line of type ornaments. Cut of trumpeting angel at head above border. Cut of ship at head of each column.

PHi RPB*

522 Philadelphia, Pa.
RELF'S PHILADELPHIA
GAZETTE

1807. To the patrons of Relf's Philadelphia Gazette, by the carriers. . . . January 1, 1807.

First line: Cold blows the blast: The snow and hail descend

52 x 44 cm. (46.8 x 37.4 cm.) Verse within architectural border in two columns. Cut of ship at head of and between columns.

PPL*

523 Reading, Pa.
READINGER ADLER

Neu-Jahrs-Wunsch des Herumträgers des Readinger Adlers, an seine Werthen Kunden. . . . Reading, den 1 sten Januar, 1807.

First line: Ich wünsch' Euch Frieden, auf daß weit

22 x 14 cm. (20.2 x 11.0 cm.) Verse within ornamental border.

MWA*

524 Newport, R.I.
NEWPORT MERCURY

New-year's address. . . . Office of the Newport Mercury, Jan. 1, 1807.

First line: Again, revolving in his swift career

35 x 31 cm. (28.3 x 20.8 cm.) Verse within ornamental border in two columns divided by line of type ornaments.

MWA RPHi*

Neu-Jahrs-Wunsch

des Herumträgers des Readinger Adlers, an seine werthen
Kunden.

Ich wünsch' Euch Frieden, auf daß weit
  Von des Krieges Ungewittern,
Ruhe und Zufriedenheit
  Jezt und niemals möge zittern;
Daß der Freyheit güt'ge Hand
Ferner schüze unser Land.

Ich wünsch' Euch Eintracht, daß die Wuth
  Des Partheygeist schnell entfliehet;
Bruderliebe nur im Blut
  Und in jeder Nerve glühet,
Daß der Freyheit ächter Sinn
Mög' in jedes Herze ziehn.

Auch wünsch' ich, daß mit ihrem Glück
  Die Gesundheit stets Euch kröne;
Daß ein freundliches Geschick
  Jeden Segen stets Euch gönne;
Daß mit Freuden ohne Zahl
Ihr durchwallt dies Pilgerthal.

Das heißt gewünscht! Wüßt ich nur mehr
  So wär mein Wunsch noch nicht zu Ende.
Zwar sinn' ich hin und sinne her,
  Ob ich vielleicht noch etwas fände;
Allein mit allem meinem Sinnen
Vermag ich nichts mehr zu gewinnen.

Allein ich zweifle nicht wenn Ihr
  Die Hälfte nur von jenen Gaben,
Die ich gewünschet nach Gebühr,
  Gesichert für Euch werdet haben,
Daß Ihr damit zufrieden wärt
Und ferner nicht viel mehr begehrt.

Wißt Ihr indeßen etwas mehr,
  So wünsch ich's Euch von Herzen gerne,
Sey's feder-leicht, sey's zentner-schwer,
  Sey's in der Nähe oder Ferne;
Nur keinen Scepter, keine Kron',
Keinen Purpur-Mantel oder Thron.
Reading, den 1sten Januar, 1807.

Fig. 10. McDonald 523. *Readinger Adler*, Reading, Pa., January 1, 1807. American Antiquarian Society.

525　Providence, R.I.
PROVIDENCE GAZETTE

New-Year address from the carrier of the Providence Gazette, to his friends. January 1, 1807.

First line: While gladsome notes of joy resound

33 x 20 cm. (28.1 x 17.0 cm.) Verse within ornamental border in two columns divided by line of type ornaments.

RPB*

1808

526　Middletown, Conn.
MIDDLESEX GAZETTE

News-boy's address. To the patrons of the Middlesex Gazette. . . . Middletown (Ct.) January [sic] 1, 1808.

First line: Blest be th' indulgent hand of Heav'n

40 x 18 cm. (39.2 x 17.3 cm.) Verse within ornamental border in two columns divided by curvilinear line.

MWA*

527　Portland, Me.
EASTERN ARGUS

To the esteemed patrons of the Eastern Argus, the petition of their humble servant, the carrier, respectfully sheweth: . . . Portland, January 1, 1808.

First line: Wet, shivering, cold, the sport of every blast

35 x 13 cm. (30.8 x 10.4 cm.) Verse within ornamental border.

MWA*

528　Boston, Mass.
EMERALD

The annual address of the carriers of the Emerald, to their highly respected patrons. . . . Emerald Office, January 1, 1808.

First line: With ever steady and unerring pace |
Signed: The printer's boy.

40 x 20 cm. (33.1 x 12.2 cm.) Verse within ornamental border.

MWA*

529　Boston, Mass.
INDEPENDENT CHRONICLE

The carriers of the Independent Chronicle, to its patrons; with the compliments of the season. . . . Boston, January 1, 1808.

First line: The never-erring book of fate

32 x 18 cm. (26.6 x 11.5 cm.) Verse in two columns.

PHi*

530　Boston, Mass.
REPERTORY

New Year's address, presented by the carrier, to the patrons of the Repertory. . . . Boston, Jan. 1, 1808.

First line: Kind patron - patron! aye the noun is common

32 x 17 cm. (28.1 x 9.7 cm.) Verse within ornamental border.

MWA*

531　Salem, Mass.
ESSEX REGISTER

To the patrons of the Essex Register, the carrier presents the New Year's compliments, with the following address. . . . Salem, January 1, 1808.

First line: Insatiate time, who nothing spares

34 x 19 cm. (28.5 x 16.3 cm.) Verse on silk within ornamental border in two columns divided by curvilinear ornamental line. Paper copy: 30 x 26 cm. (27.8 x 16.5 cm.)

Tapley p. 411 / MSaE*

532　Salem, Mass.
SALEM GAZETTE

To the patrons of the Salem Gazette, the carrier presents the compliments of the season, and the following proclamation. . . . January 1, 1808.

First line: Whereas by use, time out of mind

25 x 17 cm. (20.5 x 11.9 cm.) On silk.

MSaE*

533   Albany, N.Y.
ALBANY REGISTER

New-Year's address of the carrier of the Albany Register, to his generous patrons. . . . January 1, 1808.

First line: A few short months have quickly roll'd away

45 x 19 cm. (37.5 x 13.5 cm.) Verse within ornamental border.

N*

534   Albany, N.Y.
GUARDIAN

The carrier of the Guardian presents its patrons with the following hasty and imperfect 'effusion from the Muse,'—accompanied by an ardent prayer for their happiness . . . the happiness of America, and of the Universe . . . that the horrors of War may be averted from our land, and that Peace, with the commencement of a New-Year, may not be interrupted till 'time shall be no more'. . . . January 1st, 1808.

First line: A little infant (scarcely two months old)

28 x 21 cm. (23.8 x 18.1 cm.) Verse in two columns divided by curvilinear line with headbands at head and end.

MWA*

535   Kingston, N.Y.
ULSTER GAZETTE

1808. The carrier's address to the patrons of the Ulster Gazette. Kingston, January 1, 1808.

First line: Be it known to all the folks

39 x 17 cm. (34.5 x 13.4 cm.) Verse within architectural border.

NHi*

536   Lansingburgh, N.Y.
LANSINGBURGH GAZETTE

New-Year's reflections, for January 1, 1808. Lansingburg: Printed by Tracy & Bliss.

First line: Hail, aged time! thou mother of all years!

19 p.   19 cm.

Sh 15744, 16339 Stoddard 171 / MiD-B RPB*

Attributed by Shaw and Shoemaker and Stoddard to Joseph W. Tracey, whose signature, spelled Tracy, appears twice in the MiD-B copy according to Stodddard.

537   New York, N.Y.
NEW-YORK GAZETTE,
1795–1820+

Gazette Marine List, for the New Year 1808. With the carrier's remarks.

First line: Arrived this morning, full of freight

27 x 14 cm. (26.3 x 13.7 cm.) Verse within ornamental border in two columns divided by single rule, with cut of ship at head.

MWA* NHi

538   New York, N.Y.
NEW-YORK WEEKLY MUSEUM

New Year's address of the carrier of the Weekly Museum, to his patrons. . . . January 1, 1808.

First line: Among the fine New-Year's addresses

28 x 23 cm. (27.4 x 16.9 cm.) Verse within architectural border.

NHi NN RPB*

539   New York, N.Y.
WEEKLY VISITOR, 1802–1807(?)

New Year's address, to the patrons of The Lady's Weekly Miscellany. . . . New York, January 1, 1808.

First line: Old time's rapid stream has put out, like a dream

30 x 18 cm. (27.1 x 16.2 cm.) Verse within ornamental double line border in two columns divided by line of type ornaments.

NN*

Brigham lists last issue of this paper as October 24, 1807. After this date the periodical became more like a magazine.

540   Newburgh, N.Y.
POLITICAL INDEX

The carrier, of the Political Index, to his patrons.

First line: Hail! all hail! th' auspicious day

44 x 28 cm. (38.7 x 18.5 cm.) Verse within ornamental border in two columns divided by line of type ornaments.

NNe*

541   Philadelphia, Pa.
       POULSON'S AMERICAN DAILY
          ADVERTISER

Address of the carriers of Poulson's American Daily Advertiser to its patrons, on the commencement of the year 1808.

First line: When princes, arm'd with power

26 x 19 cm. (23.7 x 17.9 cm.) Verse within ornamental border in two columns divided by line of type ornaments.

PHi RPB*

542   Philadelphia, Pa.
       RELF'S PHILADELPHIA
          GAZETTE

To the patrons of Relf's Philadelphia Gazette, on the commencement of the year 1808. By the carriers. . . . 1st January, 1808.

First line: Of all employments in this world of strife | *At head of text:* Whatever measures have a tendency to dissolve the Union, . . . Washington.

50 x 29 cm. (40.0 x 25.8 cm.)

PPL*

543   Philadelphia, Pa.
       TRUE AMERICAN

An address of the carriers of 'True American and Commercial Advertiser,' to its patrons, on the commencement of the year 1808.

First line: Good patrons, gentlemen, and ladies

41 x 33 cm. (38.8 x 23.5 cm.) Verse within ornamental border in two columns divided by curvilinear line, with cut above border.

PPL*

544   Philadelphia, Pa.
       UNITED STATES GAZETTE

Address of the carriers of the United States Gazette to their patrons, on the commencement of the New Year, 1808.

First line: Good masters, gentle and genteel

50 x 32 cm. (44.5 x 27.7 cm.) Verse within architectural border in two columns divided by line of type ornaments.

PPL*

545   Reading, Pa.
       READINGER ADLER ◊

Neu-jahrs-wünsch des herumträgers des Readinger Adlers an seine Kunden. . . . Reading, den 1sten Januar, 1808.

First line: Bey diesem und bey jedem Scheiden.

28 x 11 cm. (20.8 x 9.0 cm.) Verse within ornamental border.

MWA* PRHi

546   Newport, R.I.
       NEWPORT MERCURY

New-year's address. . . . Office of Newport Mercury. January 1, 1808.

First line: The new-born year, with rising lustre crown'd

36 x 30 cm. (30.6 x 21.0 cm.) Verse within ornamental border in two columns divided by curvilinear line.

RNHi*

547   Middlebury, Vt.
       MIDDLEBURY MERCURY

New-Year's address. The carrier of the Middlebury Mercury, to his patrons. . . . January 1, 1808.

First line: Old time, since when this crazy earth

41 x 27 cm. (32.9 x 19.4 cm.) Verse in three columns with double line of type ornaments at head and end.

NHi* / Ms. inscription within title on New York Historical Society copy: John Kellogg.

1809

548   Hartford, Conn.
AMERICAN MERCURY

The New Year. . . . Mercury office, Hartford, January 1, 1809.

First line: Come muse, I invoke thee, light up thy fire-

48 x 30 cm. (42.0 x 21.3 cm.) Verse within ornamental border in two columns divided by double rule, with thick-thin rules at head of text.

MWA RPB*

549   New Haven, Conn.
CONNECTICUT JOURNAL

The newsman's New-Year address, for 1809, to those whom he supplies weekly with the Connecticut Journal.

First line: Joy to the morn, and gladness to the day

40 x 22 cm. (30.5 x 16.9 cm.) Verse in two columns.

CtY*

550   New London, Conn.
CONNECTICUT GAZETTE

New Year's verses by the carrier of the Connecticut Gazette: addressed to his patrons. . . . New London, January 1, 1809.

First line: Time like a quick stage rushes on

41 x 34 cm. (36.0 x 20.8 cm.) Verse within ornamental border in three columns.

MWA*

551   Augusta, Ga.
AUGUSTA HERALD

The news-boys' address, to the patrons of the Augusta Herald. Augusta, 1st January, 1809.

First line: Old time who still his course pursues

46 x 29 cm. (33.1 x 26.5 cm.) Verse within architectural border in two columns divided by line of type ornaments, with cut of eagle at head.

RPB*

552   Portland, Me.
EASTERN ARGUS

Address, from the carrier of the Eastern Argus to its generous patrons.

First line: When first by freedom fired our sires began | *At head:* Argus-Office, January 1, 1809.

32 x 14 cm. (28.1 x 10.5 cm.)

MH MWA*

553   Portland, Me.
FREEMAN'S FRIEND

The carrier of the Freeman's Friend, to his friends and patrons respectfully tenders the compliments of the New Year and the homage of his high respect. . . . January 1, 1809.

First line: Old Time, (whom none can check in race)

35 x 21 cm. (31.0 x 15.0 cm.) Verse within ornamental border in two columns divided by curvilinear line.

MeHi*

554   Baltimore, Md.
NORTH AMERICAN

Address of the carriers of the North American, to their patrons for the year 1809.

First line: By your leave, gents and ladies all

33 x 26 cm. (28.6 x 19.7 cm.) Verse within ornamental border in two columns.

MdHi*

555   Boston, Mass.
INDEPENDENT CHRONICLE

The carrier of the Independent Chronicle, to his numerous patrons, with the congratulations of the season. . . . Boston, January 1, 1809.

First line: With humble hope—a heart with zeal

35 x 23 cm. (29.0 x 12.3 cm.) Verse in two columns.

DLC PHi RPB*

556　Boston, Mass.
NEW-ENGLAND PALLADIUM

The humble memorial of the carriers to their respected patrons. . . . Palladium-Office, Jan. 1, 1809.

First line: Since last the sun his southern visit paid | *At head of text:* May it please your honours! | *Signed:* The Carriers.

36 x 17 cm. (34.2 x 14.8 cm.) Verse within ornamental border with short thick-thin rules at head.

MWA PHi*

557　Boston, Mass.
REPERTORY

Address of the carrier of the Repertory, to his patrons. . . . Boston, January 1st, 1809.

First line: The times are hard and money scarce

45 x 28 cm. (36.9 x 20.5 cm.) Verse within ornamental border in two columns divided by curvilinear line.

MWA*

558　Newburyport, Mass.
NEWBURYPORT HERALD

The [New Year's] address to all the [patrons of the] Newburyport [Herald]. . . . January 2d, 1809.

First line: Fashion, that little flat'ring jade

41 x 19 cm. (29.5 x 14.1 cm.) Verse in two columns divided by curvilinear line.

MWA*

559　Salem, Mass.
ESSEX REGISTER

The carrier of the Essex Register, presents his patrons with the following address. . . . January 1st, 1809.

First line: Old time, who listens to no pray'r

36 x 12 cm. (25.0 x 9.0 cm.) On silk.

Tapley p. 415 / MH MSaE*

560　Salem, Mass.
SALEM GAZETTE

New-Year address of the carriers of the Salem Gazette, to its patrons. 1809.

First line: Embargo! What a new year's theme!

32 x 22 cm. (26.8 x 14.0 cm.) Verse in two columns divided by single rule with thick-thin rules at head of text. Elegiac verse within ornamental border in center of right column.

DLC MH RPB*

561　Concord, N.H.
CONCORD GAZETTE

Reflections on the New Year. . . . Gazette Office, Concord, Jan. 1, 1809.

First line: How short is time! and canst thou well complain

24 x 21 cm. (18.7 x 13.1 cm.) Verse in two columns divided by curvilinear line.

RPB*

562　Albany, N.Y.
ALBANY REGISTER

Address of the carrier of the Albany Register, to his generous patrons. For January 1, 1809.

First line: Again the earth, in rapid flight, has run

29 x 23 cm. (24.0 x 20.0 cm.) Verse within ornamental border in two columns divided by curvilinear line.

N*

563　New York, N.Y.
AMERICAN CITIZEN

New Year's address of the carriers of the American Citizen to their patrons. 1809.

First line: Before the morning ray shines bright

34 x 21 cm. (31.0 x 17.4 cm.) Verse within ornamental border in two columns divided by single rule. Cut of eagle at head above horizontal double rule.

N*

564　New York, N.Y.
COMMERCIAL ADVERTISER

The carrier of the Commercial Advertiser to his patrons. . . . January 1, 1809.

First line: Old time, commander of the sun

34 x 25 cm. (31.5 x 19.8 cm.) Verse in three columns divided by single rules.

N*

565   New York, N.Y.
     DAILY ADVERTISER, 1808–1809

The carriers of the Daily Advertiser, to their patrons.... New York, January 1, 1809.

First line: Kind patrons, with a New-Year's face

39 x 24 cm. (28.1 x 18.7 cm.) Verse within ornamental border in two columns divided by single rule.

N*

566   New York, N.Y.
     NEW-YORK GAZETTE,
         1795–1820+

New-York Gazette Marine List, New-Year, 1809. The carriers to their customers.... New York, January 1, 1809.

First line: Arrived, from climes beyond the line

33 x 20 cm. (28.1 x 16.1 cm.) Verse within ornamental border in two columns divided by curvilinear line.

N*

567   New York, N.Y.
     NEW-YORK WEEKLY MUSEUM

New-Year's address. The carriers of the New-York Weekly Museum, to their patrons. January 1, 1809.

First line: Now from the dreary north bleak blows the wind

30 x 22 cm. (25.9 x 17.2 cm.) Verse within ornamental border in two columns divided by curvilinear line.

NN*

568   Philadelphia, Pa.
     HOPE'S PHILADELPHIA PRICE-
         CURRENT

Address from the carrier of Hope's Philadelphia Price-Current, and Commercial Record, to its patrons, on the commencement of the year one thousand eight hundred and nine.

First line: Night's gloom departs, the shadows disappear

46 x 29 cm. (40.6 x 23.2 cm.) Verse within architectural border in two columns divided by double rule.

PHi*

569   Philadelphia, Pa.
     POULSON'S AMERICAN DAILY
         ADVERTISER

The address of the carriers of Poulson's American Daily Advertiser, to its patrons, on the commencement of the year 1809.

First line: We hunted up the man of rhyme

29 x 16 cm. (28.2 x 14.9 cm.) Verse in two columns divided by line of type ornaments.

RPB*

570   Philadelphia, Pa.
     TICKLER

The carrier of the Tickler to his patrons.... January 2, 1809.

First line: Another year has roll'd around

43 x 27 cm. (38.8 x 22.9 cm.) Verse within architectural border in two columns divided by line of type ornaments. Cut of trumpeting angel at head with scroll bearing date 1809.

NHi*

571   Providence, R.I.
     PROVIDENCE GAZETTE

The Gazette carrier's New-Year address to his old friends. Providence, January 1, 1809.

First line: While all the wise heads of the nation

30 x 14 cm. (27.0 x 8.2 cm.) Line of type ornaments at head and end.

RPHi*

572 Providence, R.I.
RHODE-ISLAND AMERICAN

New-Year's address of the carrier of the American to his patrons. Providence, January 1, 1809.

First line: O would the present year commence

37 x 26 cm. (33.2 x 21.0 cm.) Verse within ornamental border in two columns divided by double curvilinear line.

RPB*

1810

573 Hartford, Conn.
CONNECTICUT MIRROR

Reflections, from the Connecticut Mirror. . . . Hartford, January 1, 1810.

First line: What bold, adventurous, tuneful sprite

45 x 30 cm. (38.1 x 25.0 cm.) Verse within ornamental border in four columns divided by single rules.

MWA*

574 Portland, Me.
EASTERN ARGUS

Annual tribute of respect, from the carrier to the patrons of the Eastern Argus. . . . Argus-Office, January 1, 1810.

First line: Revolving time, that ever steady friend

43 x 15 cm. (39.5 x 12.6 cm.) Verse within ornamental border.

MH* NHi

575 Portland, Me.
FREEMAN'S FRIEND

From the carrier of the Freeman's Friend to the patrons of the paper, with the compliments of the morning—New Year's day, A.D. 1810.

First line: Mankind have been too apt to cherish

29 x 24 cm. (24.3 x 20.1 cm.) Verse in three columns divided by single rules.

MWA NHi NN RPB*

576 Baltimore, Md.
FEDERAL REPUBLICAN

Address of the carriers of the 'Federal Republican,' to their patrons. Jan. 1, 1810.

First line: We, heralds, sirs, of Father Time

35 x 27 cm. (20.6 x 20.5 cm.) Verse within ornamental border in two columns divided by curvilinear line.

MdHi*

577 Boston, Mass.
BOSTON GAZETTE, 1800–1820+

The annual address of the carriers of the Boston Gazette, to their respected and liberal patrons. Illustrissimo Christophoro Gore, &c. College Theses. . . . Gazette Office, January 1st, 1810.

First line: To our illustrious Gore

35 x 22 cm. (30.3 x 20.0 cm.) Verse within ornamental border in two columns divided by line of type ornaments. Also contains nine short verses in three columns at end.

MWA PHi RPB*

578 Boston, Mass.
BOSTON MIRROR

The carrier of the Boston Mirror, proud of the honour of 'exchanging' the compliments of the season, wishes you health, wealth, and a happy New Year. . . . January, 1. 1810.

First line: Pity the pockets of a poor young man |
Preliminary verse with first line: Is this a dollar that I see before me

33 x 14 cm. (26.8 x 9.6 cm.) Verse within ornamental border.

MHi*

579 Boston, Mass.
BOSTON PATRIOT

The carrier to the patrons of the Boston Patriot. . . . Patriot Office, Jan. 1, 1810.

First line: An ancient people, taught on freedom's plan

45 x 18 cm. (36.2 x 12.9 cm.) Verse within ornamental border.

NHi*

580   Boston, Mass.
COLUMBIAN CENTINEL

The carriers, of the Columbian Centinel, offer their congratulations, not only on the birth of a New-Year; but on the completion of the twenty-fifth anniversary since the first publication of this paper. . . . Centinel-Office, Jan. 1, 1810.

First line: Time shakes his plumes, and from December's night | *At end of text:* The carriers . . .

33 x 16 cm. (31.9 x 14.8 cm.) Verse within ornamental border in two columns.

MWA* NHi

581   Boston, Mass.
INDEPENDENT CHRONICLE

The carriers of the Independent Chronicle, to their liberal patrons. . . . Chronicle Office, Jan. 1, 1810.

First line: The muse, to whom the talk belongs

45 x 18 cm. (37.3 x 12.7 cm.) Verse in two columns.

MWA*

582   Northampton, Mass.
HAMPSHIRE GAZETTE

A New-Year's ode, addressed to the readers of the Hampshire Gazette. . . . January 1, 1810. . . . Northampton, Jan. 1, 1810.

First line: To all his patrons, sage divines

43 x 26 cm. (38.4 x 21.6 cm.) Verse in three columns with short double rule at head of text.

DLC*

583   Salem, Mass.
ESSEX REGISTER

The carrier presents the compliments of the season to the patrons of the 'Essex Register,' and respectfully submits the following address. . . . Salem, January 1, 1810.

First line: Ye sons of Freedom's peaceful soil

38 x 21 cm. (28.4 x 15.4 cm.) Verse within ornamental border in two columns divided by line of type ornaments.

MH*

584   Salem, Mass.
SALEM GAZETTE

New Year address of the carriers of the Salem Gazette, to its patrons. 1810.

First line: Patrons and friends, your printer's boys

33 x 23 cm. (27.3 x 18.6 cm.) Verse in three columns.

Sh 21268 / NHi MSaE MWA RPB*

585   Portsmouth, N.H.
NEW-HAMPSHIRE GAZETTE

The news-boy's annual address, to the patrons of the New-Hampshire Gazette. . . . Portsmouth, January 1, 1810.

First line: As another New-Year begins its career

51 x 34 cm. (46.1 x 30.3 cm.) Verse in three columns divided by line of type ornaments.

MBAt MHi MWA* NHi

586   Brooklyn, N.Y.
LONG ISLAND STAR

New-Year's address of the carrier of the Long Island Star, to his patrons. . . . Brooklyn, January 1, 1810.

First line: With rapid speed, the swift wing'd flight of time

34 x 22 cm. (30.0 x 18.5 cm.) Verse within ornamental border in two columns divided by curvilinear line.

NHi*

587   Lansingburgh, N.Y.
LANSINGBURGH GAZETTE

The news-boy's address, to the patrons of the Lansingburgh Gazette. Janaury 1, 1810.

First line: On New-Year's day, by custom old

45 x 28 cm. (36.6 x 21.8 cm.) Verse within ornamental border in three columns divided by curvilinear lines.

NHi*

588   New York, N.Y.
AMERICAN CITIZEN

The New-Year's address of the carrier of the American Citizen to his patrons. January 1, 1810.

First line: Though cheerless winter closes round

33 x 19 cm. (28.8 x 16.1 cm.) Verse within ornamental border in two columns divided by line of type ornaments.

NHi*

589   New York, N.Y.
       COLUMBIAN

The critic: respectfully presented, with the best compliments of the season, to the patrons of the Columbian, by their humble servant, the carrier. . . . January 1, 1810.

First line: Mankind, in every clime and age |
Signed: The carrier.

40 x 28 cm. (36.0 x 19.7 cm.) Verse within curvilinear line border in two columns divided by curvilinear line.

NHi*

590   New York, N.Y.
       COMMERCIAL ADVERTISER

The carrier of the Commercial Advertiser, to his patrons. . . . January 1, 1810.

First line: See winter, with forbidding brow

35 x 26 cm. (29.2 x 19.1 cm.) Verse in three columns divided by single rules.

NHi*

591   New York, N.Y.
       MERCANTILE ADVERTISER

New-Year's address of the carrier of the Mercantile Advertiser, for January 1st, 1810.

First line: At school I've heard my master say

32 x 17 cm. (30.3 x 14.7 cm.) Verse within ornamental border in two columns divided by line of type ornaments.

NHi RPB*

592   New York, N.Y.
       NEW-YORK EVENING POST,
       1801–1820+

New-York Evening Post, January 1, 1810. Farewell to the old year; with the carrier's New-Year address to his customers.

First line: Good bye t'ye, eighteen hundred nine

35 x 26 cm. (25.9 x 18.6 cm.) Verse in three columns.

NHi*

593   New York, N.Y.
       NEW-YORK GAZETTE,
       1795–1820+

The year 1810. Annual marine list addressed by the carriers of the New-York Gazette, to their patrons.

First line: Arrived from ancient Chaos' den

33 x 17 cm. (27.4 x 15.3 cm.) Verse within double line ornamental border in two columns divided by single rule.

NHi RPB*

594   New York, N.Y.
       NEW-YORK PRICE-CURRENT,
       1796–1817+

From the office of the New-York Price-Current, January, 1810.

First line: Well, now my lad, what brings you here? | *At head of text:* All the world's a stage. . . . Scene, between a subscriber and the printer's devil,—. . .

29 x 16 cm. (19.8 x 10.9 cm.) Verse within double line ornamental border.

NHi*

595   New York, N.Y.
       PUBLIC ADVERTISER

Address of the carriers of the Public Advertiser, to their patrons. On New Year's Day, 1810.

First line: Old Father Time, once more has gone his round

40 x 17 cm. (35.0 x 10.7 cm.) Verse within ornamental border.

NHi*

596   Troy, N.Y.
TROY GAZETTE

New-Year's address, from the carrier of the Troy Gazette to its patrons. January 1, 1810.

First line: Old time, with his scythe, in the midst of last night | *At head:* ISL in rectangular block. | *At head within border ornament:* IND 34.

46 x 27 cm. (40.1 x 24.5 cm.) Verse within architectural border in two columns divided by curvilinear line.

PPL*

597   Carlisle, Pa.
CUMBERLAND REGISTER ◊

The carrier's address to the patrons of the Cumberland Register.

First line: Once more the steady wheel of time has wound

33 x 11 cm. (edges trimmed to border) Verse within ornamental border.

ICHi*

598   Lancaster, Pa.
INTELLIGENCER

Newsboy's address, to the patrons of the Intelligencer & Weekly Advertiser. January 1, 1810.

First line: The newsboy comes - prepare the way -

29 x 12 cm. (24.2 x 6.9 cm.)

NN*

599   Lancaster, Pa.
LANCASTER JOURNAL

The newsboy's address to the patrons of the Lancaster Journal. 1810.

First line: In heat and in cold, through rain and thro' snow | '1810' within horizontal double rule.

28 x 14 cm. (25.9 x 10.9 cm.) Verse within ornamental double line border.

NHi* NN

600   Philadelphia, Pa.
AURORA

The carriers of the Aurora, to their patrons, on the commencement of the New Year. January 1, 1810.

First line: Another year has passed before our view

56 x 44 cm. (48.8 x 37.7 cm.) Verse within architectural border in two columns divided by line of type ornaments.

PPL*

601   Philadelphia, Pa.
DEMOCRATIC PRESS

Address from the carriers of the Democratic Press, to their patrons, on the commencement of the year, 1810.

First line: When winter with his raging winds

46 x 29 cm. (41.8 x 24.6 cm.) Verse within architectural border in two columns divided by single rule.

PPL*

602   Philadelphia, Pa.
FREEMAN'S JOURNAL,
1804–1820+

The carriers of the Freeman's Journal and Philadelphia Mercantile Advertiser, to their patrons, on the commencement of the New Year. January 1, 1810.

First line: Once more old Time, with never-ceasing haste

50 x 35 cm. (42.7 x 32.4 cm.) Verse within architectural border in two columns divided by chained line. Cut of ship at head of border.

PPL*

603   Philadelphia. Pa.
POULSON'S AMERICAN DAILY
ADVERTISER

The address of the carriers of Poulson's American Daily Advertiser, to its patrons on the commencement of the year 1810.

First line: Time, who as every poet sings

45 x 27 cm. (41.6 x 23.2 cm.) Verse within architectural border in two columns divided by line of

type ornaments. Cuts of eagle and two ships above border. Cut of farming scene at end.

PPL*

604 Philadelphia, Pa.
RELF'S PHILADELPHIA GAZETTE

The carriers of Relf's Philadelphia Gazette, to its patrons. January 1st, 1810.

First line: To patrons, num'rous and so kind

48 x 33 cm. (45.3 x 31.5 cm.) Verse within architectural border in two columns divided by lines of type ornaments.

PPL RPB*

605 Philadelphia, Pa.
TICKLER

The carriers' address to the patrons of the Tickler, on the commencement of the New Year, January 1, 1810.

First line: And now the car of bright Phoebus once more

55 x 44 cm. (47.2 x 32.8 cm.) Verse within architectural border in two columns divided by curvilinear line. Cut of arm and hand holding whip above dog at head.

PPL RPB*

606 Philadelphia, Pa.
TRUE AMERICAN

Address of the carriers of the True American & Commercial Advertiser, to their patrons, on the commencement of the New Year, 1810.

First line: Come, sisters of the tuneful nine

50 x 33 cm. (40.5 x 28.5 cm.) Verse within architectural border in two columns divided by line of type ornaments.

PPL*

607 Philadelphia, Pa.
UNITED STATES GAZETTE

Address of the carriers of the United States Gazette to their patrons, on the commencement of the New Year, January 1, 1810.

First line: With congee, bending to right angle

45 x 29 cm. (41.5 x 24.1 cm.) Verse within architectural border in three columns divided by single rules.

PPL*

608 Reading, Pa.
READINGER ADLER

Neu-Jahrs-Wunsch des Herumträgers des Readinger Adlers, an seine Kunden. Reading, den 1sten Januar, 1810.

First line: Schon wieder sinket uns ein Jahr

26 x 22 cm. (23.0 x 17.1 cm.) Verse within ornamental border in two columns.

MWA*

609 Newport, R.I.
NEWPORT MERCURY

To the patrons of the Newport Mercury, the carrier presents the compliments of the season, and the following address. . . . January 1, 1810.

First line: 'Tis strange, but true, that in this isle

52 x 27 cm. (46.0 x 16.9 cm.) Verse within ornamental border in two columns divided by single rule.

RPB*

610 Providence, R.I.
COLUMBIAN PHENIX

The carriers' address to the patrons of the Columbian Phenix. Providence, January 1, 1810.

First line: Such is the fashion of the time

27 x 21 cm. (23.6 x 13.5 cm.) Verse in two columns divided by line of type ornaments with headband of type ornaments at head and end.

RPB*

611 Richmond, Va.
ENQUIRER

The address of the carriers, to the patrons of the Enquirer. Christmas, 1809.

First line: Twelve fleeting months their course have run

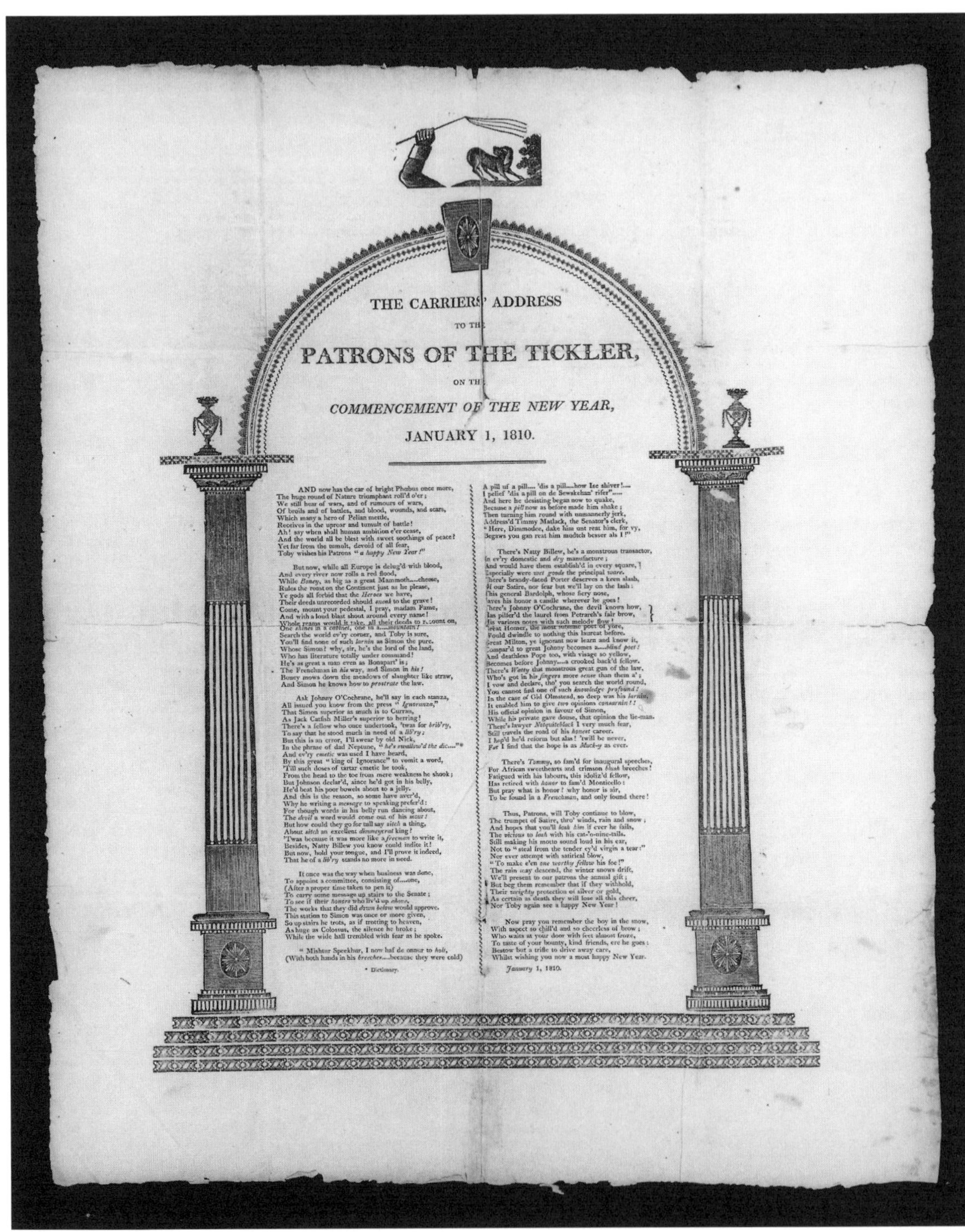

Fig. 11. McDonald 605. *Tickler*, Philadelphia, Pa., January 1, 1810. John Hay Library.

44 x 27 cm. (37.8 x 22.4 cm.) Verse within architectural border in two columns divided by curvilinear line.

PPL*

1811

612　Hartford, Conn.
CONNECTICUT COURANT

The New-Years address, of the carrier of the Connecticut Courant, to his patrons. . . . January 1st, 1811.

First line: Good gentlemen, and ladies all

37 x 26 cm. (31.9 x 18.8 cm.) Verse within ornamental border in two columns divided by curvilinear line.

NN*

613　Hartford, Conn.
CONNECTICUT MIRROR

The close of the year. Addressed to the readers of the Connecticut Mirror. . . . Hartford, January 1, 1811.

First line: Another year has pass'd away—

53 x 31 cm. (48.2 x 27.2 cm.) Verse within ornamental border in four columns divided by single rules; three woodcuts within text.

NCooHi* NHi

614　Savannnah, Ga.
REPUBLICAN

Republican and Evening Ledger. The news-boy to his patrons. Savannah January 1. 1811.

First line: Kind patrons and friends, of every clime | *At head of text:* Scroll bearing words, 'Republican & Evening Ledger.' | '1811' in squares at ends of arch.

49 x 21 cm. (43.6 x 18.2 cm.) Verse within architectural border.

DLC*

615　Portland, Me.
HERALD OF GOSPEL LIBERTY

Address to the patrons of the Herald of Gospel Liberty.　Herald-Office, Portland, January 1, 1811.

First line: The glorious day by prophets long foretold | *Signed:* Epenetus

41 x 19 cm. (34.4 x 12.9 cm.) Verse in two columns divided by line of type ornaments.

MWA*

616　Baltimore, Md.
AMERICAN

Address to the patrons of the American and Commercial Daily Advertiser, by the carriers. . . . Jan. 1, 1811.

First line: On frosty wings with rapid flight

34 x 20 cm. (30.5 x 16.3 cm.) Verse within ornamental border in two columns divided by double rule. Cuts of ship, eagle and plow at head.

PPL*

617　Baltimore, Md.
BALTIMORE EVENING POST, 1805–1811

Carrier's address to the patrons of the Baltimore Evening Post. For the year 1811.

First line: Hard is his lot who's strictly bound

35 x 21 cm. (31.5 x 17.5 cm.) Verse within ornamental border in two columns divided by line of type ornaments.

MdHi*

618　Baltimore, Md.
FEDERAL GAZETTE

Address of the carriers of the Federal Gazette & Baltimore Daily Advertiser to their patrons. . . . January 1, 1811.

First line: With hope elate, with heart sincere

34 x 21 cm. (20.7 x 17.2 cm.) Verse within ornamental border. Cut of ship at head of border with cuts of eagle at left and right.

MdHi*

619   Fredericktown, Md.
       HORNET

The News-boy's address, to the patrons of the Hornet. . . . January 1, 1811.

First line: Whilst old Time presents another year

33 x 21 cm. (28.8 x 18.0 cm.) Verse within architectural border.

PPL*

620   Boston, Mass.
       BOSTON GAZETTE, 1800–1820+

Address of the carriers of the Boston Gazette, to their liberal and enlightened customers. . . . Boston, January 1st, 1811.

First line: A claim prescriptive, who will dare deny?

35 x 18 cm. (29.9 x 14.1 cm.) Verse within ornamental border.

DLC MWA*

621   Boston, Mass.
       INDEPENDENT CHRONICLE

The carriers of the Independent Chronicle, to their liberal patrons. . . . January 1, 1811.

First line: Once more in these eventful times

36 x 22 cm. (28.5 x 14.9 cm.) Verse within ornamental border in two columns divided by curvilinear line.

MWA* WHi RPB

622   Boston, Mass.
       REPERTORY

Address of the carrier of the Repertory, to his patrons. . . . Boston, January 1, 1811.

First line: All hail the glorious New-Year's day

35 x 27 cm. (30.6 x 19.3 cm.) Verse within triple line ornamental border in two columns divided by single rule.

MWA*

623   Newburyport, Mass.
       NEWBURYPORT HERALD

The carrier's address, to the kind patrons of the Newburyport Herald. . . . January 1, 1811.

First line: Hail first-born offspring of the year!

42 x 28 cm. (33.4 x 17.0 cm.) Verse within ornamental border in two columns divided by curvilinear line.

MWA*

624   Salem, Mass.
       ESSEX REGISTER

The carrier respectfully presents to the patrons of the Essex Register, the compliments of the season, and the following address. . . . January 1, 1811.

First line: Hail natal day! you usher from the skies

39 x 23 cm. (34.6 x 17.5 cm.) Verse on silk within ornamental border in two columns divided by curvilinear line. Paper copy: 39 x 25 cm. (34.6 x 17.5 cm.)

Tapley, 422 / MSaE* MWA

625   Salem, Mass.
       SALEM GAZETTE

New Year address of the carriers of the Salem Gazette, to its patrons. 1811.

First line: Again, kind patrons as we meet you

28 x 14 cm. (22.0 x 10.1 cm.) Verse on silk within ornamental curvilinear line border with thick-thin rules at head.

RPB*

626   Concord, N.H.
       NEW-HAMPSHIRE PATRIOT

New-Year's gift, addressed to the patrons of the New-Hampshire Patriot. . . . January 1, 1811.

First line: Our eagle shall soar till time is no more

51 x 32 cm. (48.6 x 29.0 cm.) Verse in three columns divided by single rules.

MWA RPB*

627   Portsmouth, N.H.
       NEW-HAMPSHIRE GAZETTE

The New-Hampshire Gazette news-boy's address, to his patrons—for 1811. . . . Portsmouth, January 1.

First line: The wheel of time

46 x 29 cm. (41.3 x 21.8 cm.) Verse within ornamental border in three columns divided by line of type ornaments.

MWA*

628   Newark, N.J.
        CENTINEL OF FREEDOM

The news carrier's address to the patrons of the Centinel. . . . Newark, January 1, 1811.

First line: Tho' Borea's chill blasts curls the hair of my head

36 x 25 cm. (27.6 x 19.2 cm.) Verse within ornamental border in two columns divided by curvilinear line.

NHi* NjR

629   Brooklyn, N.Y.
        LONG ISLAND STAR

New-Year's address of the carrier of the Long-Island Star to his patrons. Brooklyn, January 1, 1811.

First line: Now eighteen hundred ten is gone

32 x 20 cm. (29.0 x 18.3 cm.) Verse within ornamental border in two columns divided by curvilinear line.

NHi*

630   New York, N.Y.
        COMMERCIAL ADVERTISER

The carrier of the Commercial Advertiser to his patrons. . . . January 1st, 1811.

First line: Winter, again, like pilgrim old

37 x 27 cm. (25.9 x 19.0 cm.) Verse in three columns.

NHi*

631   New York, N.Y.
        NEW-YORK GAZETTE,
        1795–1820+

The carriers of the New-York Gazette, to their customers. January 1, 1811.

First line: Hard a lee, see the breakers! ahoi! all hands ahoi!

40 x 27 cm. (33.1 x 14.5 cm.) Verse in two columns divided by single rule.

NHi*

632   New York, N.Y.
        NEW-YORK MORNING POST

Address of the carriers of the New-York Morning Post, to their patrons. . . . January 1, 1811.

First line: The season's circling round is past

27 x 19 cm. (22.0 x 14.6 cm.) Verse within ornamental border in two columns divided by woven line.

NHi*

633   New York, N.Y.
        OBSERVER

Address of the carrier of the Observer, to his patrons. . . . New-York, January 1, 1811.

First line: May my infantine muse your attention arrest

27 x 14 cm. (25.4 x 11.3 cm.) Verse within ornamental line border.

NHi*

634   New York, N.Y.
        PUBLIC ADVERTISER

Address of the carriers of the Public Advertiser to their patrons. . . . January 1, 1811.

First line: By old earth's journey round the heav'n

33 x 21 cm. (25.1 x 12.4 cm.) Verse in two columns.

NHi*

635   Poughkeepsie, N.Y.
        POUGHKEEPSIE JOURNAL

The carrier's New-Year's address, to the patrons of the Poughkeepsie Journal, and Constitutional Republican. . . . January 1st, 1811.

First line: Young misses have their valentine | *At head of text:* The patrons of Mr. Potter's Journal in the village of Poughkeepsie, will please to accept the following address from their ever obedient Stephen Marshall, youngest assistant and faithful carrier.

48 x 25 cm. (38.8 x 21.0 cm.) Verse within architectural border in two columns divided by curvilinear line. Words 'New-Hampshire, Massachusetts . . . Thirty-fifth year of American Independence;' at head within border.

DLC* / NPou

636   Cincinnati, Ohio
WESTERN SPY

New-Year's address, submitted to the patrons of the Western Spy, by the carrier. . . . January 1, 1811.

First line: Rejoice, Columbia's sons rejoice

39 x 32 cm. (33.5 x 23.6 cm.) Verse within architectural border in two columns divided by curvilinear line.

PHi*

637   Carlisle, Pa.
CARLISLE GAZETTE

New-Year's address, January 1st, 1811. By the carrier of the Carlisle Gazette, to his patrons.

First line: Clad in her icy robes the New-Year comes

28 x 22 cm. (24.9 x 20.1 cm.) Verse within ornamental border in two columns divided by line of type ornaments.

ICHi*

638   Carlisle, Pa.
CARLISLE HERALD

Address, of the carrier, to the patrons of the Carlisle Herald, January 1, 1811.

First line: Old time his constant motion keeps

20 x 18 cm. (edges trimmed to border) Verse within ornamental border in two columns divided by line of type ornaments.

ICHi*

639   Carlisle, Pa.
CUMBERLAND REGISTER

The carrier's address to the patrons of the Cumberland Register. January 1, 1811.

First line: With silent step another year

37 x 9 cm. (edges trimmed to border) Verse within ornamental border.

ICHi*

640   Philadelphia, Pa.
AURORA

The carriers of the Aurora, to their patrons, on the commencement of the New Year. January 1, 1811.

First line: Patrons we hail you! Time's impetuous sway

55 x 42 cm. (43.0 x 35.6 cm.) Verse within architectural border in two columns divided by line of type ornaments. At head of border, banner bearing word 'Aurora' above words 'Surgo ut prosim.'

PPL*

641   Philadelphia, Pa.
EVENING STAR

Address of the carriers of the Evening Star, to their patrons, on the commencement of the year 1811. . . . Philadelphia, Jan. 1, 1811.

First line: Borne on the wings of time another year

32 x 20 cm. (28.6 x 16.4 cm.) Verse within ornamental border in two columns divided by curvilinear line. Cut of eagle with vine garlands at head.

PPL*

642   Philadelphia, Pa.
POLITICAL AND COMMERCIAL REGISTER

Address of the carriers of the Political and Commercial Register, to their patrons, on the commencement of the New Year. . . . January 1, 1811.

First line: This festal morn once more your carrier brings

40 x 33 cm. (31.0 x 22.4 cm.) Verse within ornamental border in two columns divided by curvilinear line. Cut of ship above newspaper name.

PPL*

643　Philadelphia, Pa.
PHILADELPHIA REPERTORY

Address of the carriers of the Philadelphia Repertory to their patrons, on the commencement of the year 1811.

First line: Once more round the monarch of light has earth roll'd her

34 x 23 cm. (30.2 x 20.1 cm.) Verse within ornamental border in two columns divided by curvilinear line.

MWA RPB*

Author: Joseph Hutton. Collected in his *Leisure Hours; or Poetic Effusions* (Philadelphia: Hellings and Atkins, 1812), 72–76.

644　Philadelphia, Pa.
POULSON'S AMERICAN DAILY ADVERTISER

Address of the carriers of Poulson's American Daily Advertiser, to its patrons, on the commencement of the year 1811.

First line: As the bold merchant watches every gale

35 x 20 cm. (26.2 x 17.2 cm.) Verse within ornamental border in two columns divided by line of type ornaments.

MB* PHi PPL

645　Philadelphia, Pa.
RELF'S PHILADELPHIA GAZETTE

The carriers of Relf's Philadelphia Gazette to their patrons, 1811.

First line: Another year has roll'd in haste away

50 x 34 cm. (43.5 x 32.0 cm.) Verse within architectural border in two columns divided by double rule. Cuts of two ships and two allegorical figures at head.

PPL*

Author: Joseph Hutton. Collected in *Leisure Hours,* 77–81.

646　Philadelphia, Pa.
TICKLER

Address of the carriers of the Tickler, to their patrons, on the commencement of the New Year, 1811.

First line: If father Hesiod's not a liar

53 x 43 cm. (43.8 x 35.0 cm.) Verse within architectural border in three columns.

PPL*

647　Philadelphia, Pa.
TRUE AMERICAN

Address of the carriers of the True American & Commercial Advertiser, to their patrons, on the commencement of the New Year . . . January 1, 1811.

First line: My noble patrons I again appear

46 x 28 cm. (37.5 x 24.3 cm.) Verse within ornamental border in two columns divided by line of type ornaments.

PPL*

648　Philadelphia, Pa.
UNITED STATES GAZETTE

For the patrons of the United States Gazette. Almanack for the year of our Lord 1811.

29 x 22 cm. (26.5 x 17.8 cm.) Calendar within ornamental border.

PHi*

649　Reading, Pa.
READINGER ADLER

Neu-Jahrs-Wunsch des Herumträgers des Readinger Adlers, an seine Kunden. Reading, 1 sten, Januar, 1811.

First line: Moge jeder Acker Land

27 x 23 cm. (20.5 x 18.0 cm.) Verse within ornamental border in two columns.

MWA* PRHi

650　Newport, R.I.
NEWPORT MERCURY

New-Year's address. Office of the Newport Mercury, January 1, 1811.

First line: Once more the wing of hoary time

35 x 25 cm. (34.1 x 24.2 cm.) Verse in three columns divided by single rules.

RPHi*

651   Providence, R.I.
      RHODE-ISLAND AMERICAN

Address of the carrier of the Rhode-Island American, to his patrons, wishing them a happy New Year. . . . January 1, 1811.

First line: Once more old time's untired career |
Signed: The carrier.

44 x 27 cm. (42.0 x 21.4 cm.) Verse within architectural border in three columns divided by curvilinear line.

RPHi*

652   Charleston, S.C.
      CITY GAZETTE

New-Year's address. To the generous patrons of the City Gazette. Charleston, January 1, 1811.

First line: The almanac has made it clear

50 x 22 cm. (40.3 x 14.7 cm.) Type ornaments and small cuts form side and bottom borders; the initials 'J.S.F.' appear near the head of each side border.

MWA*

653   WEEKLY VISITOR

New-Year's address, of the carrier of the Weekly Visitor. . . . January 1, 1811.

First line: Hail, hail, dear patrons, I appear

20 x 12 cm. (16.8 x 9.7 cm.) Verse in two columns divided by double rule.

NN*

1812

654   New Haven, Conn.
      CONNECTICUT JOURNAL

Address of the Journal carrier for 1812. . . . New-Haven, January 1, 1812.

First line: The news-man numbers one more year

46 x 20 cm. (38.0 x 12.5 cm.) Verse in two columns.

CtY*

655   Wilmington, Del.
      AMERICAN WATCHMAN

Address from the carrier to the patrons of the Watchman. . . . Watchman Office, 1st January, 1812.

First line: Time with a rapid flight and even

45 x 28 cm. (38.5 x 16.8 cm.) Verse within architectural border in two columns divided by curvilinear line, with six cuts at head.

DeHi*

656   Paris, Ky.
      WESTERN CITIZEN

Abram Ward's address to the patrons of the Western Citizen of both town and country. January 1st, 1812.

First line: Hail New-Year morning, with eventful seasons

32 x 18 cm. (30.2 x 17.4 cm.) Verse within ornamental border in two columns divided by single rule; last stanza centered.

NHi*

657   Portland, Me.
      EASTERN ARGUS

New-Year's address to the patrons of the Eastern Argus. . . . Argus-Office, January, 1812.

First line: Kind patrons, generous and good

30 x 25 cm. (28.0 x 17.2 cm.) Verse in two columns divided by curvilinear line.

MeHi*

658   Boston, Mass.
      BOSTON GAZETTE, 1800–1820

The printers boy's song; most humbly dedicated to the patrons of the Boston Gazette in sure and certain hope, 'that they will enable their humble servants to sing it this evening with grateful and cheerful hearts. . . . Boston, January 1st, 1812.

First line: Come on, brother 'Printers,' another new year

44 x 16 cm. (30.0 x 14.0 cm.) Verse within ornamental border.

NHi*

659   Boston, Mass.
COLUMBIAN CENTINEL

Address of the carriers of the Centinel, to its patrons, Boston, January 1st, 1812.

First line: I am the carrier—listen to my lay—

35 x 27 cm. (25.5 x 20.0 cm.) Verse within ornamental border in two columns divided by line of type ornaments.

MHi MWA NHi*

660   Boston, Mass.
INDEPENDENT CHRONICLE

The carriers of the Independent Chronicle, to their generous patrons, on the commencement of the year, 1812. . . . Chronicle Office, Jan. 1, 1812.

First line: Oft has the muse, in simple lay

35 x 21 cm. (31.4 x 16.3 cm.) Verse within ornamental border in two columns divided by line of type ornaments.

MWA WHi*

661   Newburyport, Mass.
NEWBURYPORT HERALD

The carrier's address to the patrons of the Newburyport Herald. . . . January 1, 1812.

First line: The newsboy comes, and brings th' expected lay | *Signed:* The carrier . . .

44 x 25 cm. (37.4 x 16.1 cm.) Verse within ornamental border in two columns divided by line of type ornaments.

MWA*

662   Salem, Mass.
SALEM GAZETTE

New-Year verses of the carriers of the Salem Gazette, to its patrons, 1812.

First line: Once more with our humble address

34 x 21 cm. (27.5 x 17.8 cm.) Verse in two columns divided by single rule.

MSaE RPB*

663   Concord, N.H.
NEW-HAMPSHIRE PATRIOT

News-boy's address to the patrons of the New-Hampshire Patriot. . . . January 1, 1812.

First line: While o'er his drear and desolate domain

50 x 32 cm. (44.5 x 28.3 cm.) Verse in three columns divided by single rules.

DLC MWA NhHD RPB*

664   Cooperstown, N.Y.
OTSEGO HERALD

The carrier of the Otsego Herald presents his kind customers the compliments of the season, with the following lines. . . . January 1, 1812.

First line: Seventeen times the earth's revolv'd

32 x 10 cm. (29.2 x 9.0 cm.)

NCooHi*

665   Geneva, N.Y.
GENEVA GAZETTE

The news-boy's address, to the patrons of the Geneva Gazette. . . . Geneva, January 1st, 1812.

First line: Excuse me, patrons, I can scarcely speak—

28 x 22 cm. (20.0 x 18.5 cm.) Verse in two columns divided by single rule with arched border of type ornaments at head.

N*

666   New York, N.Y.
NEW-YORK GAZETTE,
1795–1820+

New Year's bulletin. Or, address of the carriers of the New-York Gazette to their customers. January 1st, 1812.

First line: Our boat, which always keeps a look

37 x 18 cm. (26.5 x 11.2 cm.) Verse in two columns.

MWA*

667   New York, N.Y.
NEW-YORK MORNING POST

Address of the carrier of the New-York Morning Post, to his patrons. . . . January, 1812.

First line: The peaceful year with olive crown'd

34 x 14 cm. (32.4 x 10.0 cm.) Verse within ornamental border with thick-thin rules at head of text.

NHi*

668   New York, N.Y.
NEW-YORK PRICE-CURRENT,
1796–1817+

The carrier of the New-York-Price-Current, to his subscribers. . . . January 1, 1812.

First line: Hail, patrons all—the day returns

33 x 19 cm. (27.8 x 12.3 cm.) Verse within ornamental border.

NHi*

669   Chillicothe, Ohio
SCIOTO GAZETTE

My New Year's gift. Address of Thornley L. White, to the patrons of the Scioto Gazette. . . . January 1, 1812.

First line: Again behold the news-boy come [*sic*] |
Signed: Thornley L. White.

39 x 17 cm. (34.3 x 13.7 cm.) Verse in two columns divided by line of type ornaments, with double rule at head of text.

Sh 27538 / CSmH*

670   Lancaster, Pa.
LANCASTER JOURNAL

The carrier's address, to the patrons of the Lancaster Journal, on the commencement of the New Year, January 1, 1812.

First line: Tho' war's dark tempest frowning lowers

38 x 25 cm. (31.5 x 24.1 cm.) Verse within architectural border in two columns divided by line of type ornaments.

NHi*

671   Philadelphia, Pa.
DEMOCRATIC PRESS

The carriers of the Democratic Press, to their patrons on the commencement of the New Year, January 1, 1812.

First line: The air was bleak, the rude winds still

54 x 43 cm. (51.2 x 29.1 cm.) Verse within architectural border in two columns divided by chained line. Cut of trumpeting angel at head of border.

PPL*

672   Philadelphia, Pa.
FREEMAN'S JOURNAL
1804–1820+

Address of the carriers of the Freeman's Journal, and Philadelphia Mercantile Advertiser, to their patrons, on the commencement of the New Year. January 1, 1812.

First line: On fiery chariot and in smoking gear

45 x 27 cm. (35.5 x 19.5 cm.) Verse within ornamental border in two columns divided by line of type ornaments. Cut of eagle at head.

PPL*

Author: Joseph Hutton. Collected in *Leisure Hours*, 82–86.

673   Philadelphia, Pa.
HOPE'S PHILADELPHIA PRICE-
CURRENT

Address from the carrier of Hope's Philadelphia Price-Current, and Commercial Record, to its patrons on the commencement of the year 1812. January 1st, 1812.

First line: Just like the statesman whose prolific mind

45 x 37 cm. (42.5 x 27.0 cm.) Verse within architectural border in two columns divided by double rule. Cut of allegorical figure centered within border at head and end.

PHi*

674   Philadelphia, Pa.
RELF'S PHILADELPHIA
GAZETTE

Address of the carriers of Relf's Philadelphia Gazette, on the commencement of the year, 1812.

First line: Another sun has flung his blaze away

55 x 43 cm. (45.0 x 37.5 cm.) Verse within architectural border in two columns divided by curvilinear line, with cut of head centered at top.

PPL*

Author: Joseph Hutton. Collected in *Leisure Hours*, 87–91.

675   Philadelphia, Pa.
      TICKLER

Address of the carriers of the Tickler to their patrons, on the commencement of the New Year, 1812.

First line: Again around the station'd sun | *At end of text:* D. Heartt, Printer, Marshall's alley.

54 x 46 cm. (47.2 x 38.2 cm.) Verse within architectural border in three columns divided by curvilinear lines.

PPL RPB*

676   Philadelphia, Pa.
      TRUE AMERICAN

Address of the carriers of the True American & Commercial Advertiser, to its patrons, on the commencement of the New Year. . . . January 1, 1812.

First line: Not all the shifting scenes of life

48 x 32 cm. (43.5 x 21.3 cm.) Verse within ornamental border in two columns divided by line of type ornaments.

PPL*

677   Philadelphia, Pa.
      UNITED STATES GAZETTE

The address of the carriers of the United States' Gazette to their patrons, on the commencement of the year 1812; wishing them a happy New Year, long life, contentment, competency, and better times. January 1, 1812.

First line: Patrons accept on this New Year

54 x 34 cm. (41.1 x 28.1 cm.) Verse within architectural border in two columns divided by line of type ornaments.

PPL*

678   Reading, Pa.
      READINGER ADLER

Neujahrs-Wunsch des Herumträgers des Readinger Adlers, an seine Kunden, bey dem Eintritt des Jahrs, 1812.

First line: Es ist für jezt [*sic*] und immerdar

28 x 22 cm. (20.5 x 17.4 cm.) Verse within ornamental border in two columns divided by curvilinear line.

MWA*

679   Providence, R.I.
      PROVIDENCE GAZETTE

The Gazette carrier's New-Year address, to his patrons. . . . January 1, 1812.

First line: The constant news-boy once again

27 x 11 cm. (25.1 x 8.5 cm.) Verse within ornamental border.

RPB*

1813

680   Hartford, Conn.
      CONNECTICUT MIRROR

War, and proclamations. Addressed to the readers of the Connecticut Mirror. . . . Hartford, January 1, 1813.

First line: The day is past—th' election's o'er

44 x 28 cm. (38.8 x 20.7 cm.) Verse within ornamental border in three columns divided by curvilinear lines.

NHi RPB* / Reprinted in *Poulson's American Daily Advertiser* (Philadelphia), January 6, 1813.

681   New Haven, Conn.
      CONNECTICUT JOURNAL

Journal carrier's address. Out of the many great events of the past year, the carrier has selected a single one to transmit to immortality; and that is the first conquest of Canada. . . . Jan. 1, 1813.

First line: A warrior so bold, and an army so brave

52 x 21 cm. (43.0 x 16.8 cm.) Verse in two columns.

CtY*

682 Savannah, Ga.
REPUBLICAN

Republican and Evening Ledger. The News-boy to his patrons. Savannah, January 1, 1813.

First line: Another year, the child of time

46 x 29 cm. (37.5 x 22.4 cm.) Verse within architectural border in two columns divided by curvilinear line.

PPL*

683 Frankfort, Ky.
ARGUS OF WESTERN AMERICA

To the generous patrons of the Argus. . . . January 1st, 1813.

First line: Come on ye brave Kentuckians

29 x 22 cm. (21.1 x 14.1 cm.) Verse within ornamental border in two columns divided by single rule with double rule at head of text.

ICU*

684 Portland, Me.
EASTERN ARGUS

[New Year's address, to the patrons of the Eastern Argus.]

Verse in two columns.

Williamson 6838 / No copy located.

685 Portland, Me.
GAZETTE

[Address of the carriers of the Portland Gazette to its patrons.]

Sh 27659 / No copy located.

686 Baltimore, Md.
AMERICAN

Carrier's address to the patrons of the American & Commercial Daily Advertiser. Jan. 1, 1813.

First line: Oft times, on the wings of rapture borne

34 x 20 cm. (25.0 x 17.1 cm.) Verse within ornamental border in two columns divided by line of type ornaments.

MdHi*

687 Boston, Mass.
BOSTON GAZETTE, 1800–1820+

A New-Year medley, patriotic, personal and pathetic: presented by the carrier of the Boston Gazette, to his friends and patrons. January 1, 1813.

First line: The New Year's bard resumes the annual lyre

26 x 22 cm. (23.0 x 18.4 cm.) Verse within ornamental border in two columns divided by curvilinear line.

NHi*

688 Boston, Mass.
COLUMBIAN CENTINEL

The carrier's wish, respectfully dedicated to those he loves best—the generous patrons of the Columbian Centinel. January 1, 1813.

First line: Since one more stage, on life's long road, is run

48 x 21 cm. (47.9 x 20.3 cm.) Verse within ornamental border in two columns divided by single rule.

MB* MWA NHi NN

689 Boston, Mass.
INDEPENDENT CHRONICLE

Address of the carriers of the Independent Chronicle, to their patrons on the commencement of the year 1813. . . . Chronicle Office January 1, 1813.

First line: 'What does not fade?' the poet sung

41 x 25 cm. (37.0 x 17.9 cm.) Verse within ornamental border in two columns divided by line of type ornaments.

MWA*

690   Boston, Mass.
WEEKLY MESSENGER

Address of the carrier of the Boston Weekly Messenger to his highly respected friends and patrons. . . . January 1st, 1813.

First line: Patrons good day a novice carrier sues

32 x 19 cm. (31.4 x 17.7 cm.) Verse within ornamental border in two columns divided by curvilinear line.

MWA*

691   Newburyport, Mass.
NEWBURYPORT HERALD ◊

The news-carrier's annual address to the patrons of the Newburyport Herald. . . .

First line: On rapid wings last year has fled

33 x 16 cm. (28.3 x 12.9 cm.) Verse in two columns divided by line of type ornaments.

Sh 29366 / CSmH*

692   Salem, Mass.
ESSEX REGISTER

The news-boy's address to the patrons of the 'Essex Register.' . . . January 1, 1813.

First line: Fain would I greet my patrons kind

30 x 24 cm. (26.0 x 16.2 cm.) Verse on silk within ornamental border in two columns divided by curvilinear ornamental line. Paper copy: 36 x 21 cm. (26.0 x 16.4 cm.)

Tapley, 432 / MSaE*

693   Salem, Mass.
SALEM GAZETTE

New-Year address of the carriers of the Salem Gazette, to its patrons,—1813.

First line: Once more our little globe has run

32 x 26 cm. (24.6 x 18.5 cm.) Verse in three columns divided by single rules.

Sh 29713 / MSaE* MWA

694   St. Louis, Mo.
MISSOURI GAZETTE

The carrier of the Missouri Gazette, to the subscribers—Jan. 1, 1813.

First line: Again! so soon, must I the theme rehearse?

32 x 20 cm. (27.4 x 9.7 cm.)

MWA*

695   Portsmouth, N.H.
PORTSMOUTH ORACLE

New-Year's address to the patrons of the Portsmouth Oracle. . . . Portsmouth, January 1, 1813.

First line: I come, your News-boy, and a herald true

43 x 28 cm. (40.8 x 22.0 cm.) Verse within ornamental border in two columns divided by curvilinear line.

MWA RPB*

696   New Brunswick, N.J.
GUARDIAN

The news-carrier's address, to the patrons of the Guardian, &c. . . . New-Brunswick, January 1, 1813.

First line: When blissful numbers swell the song

46 x 41 cm. (40.9 x 32.2 cm.) Verse in four columns.

Sh 28681 / NjR*

697   Trenton, N.J.
TRENTON FEDERALIST

The New-Boy's address, to the patrons of the Trenton Federalist, January 1, 1813.

First line: Chain'd neck and heels to Bona's car

44 x 27 cm. (37.6 x 22.6 cm.) Verse within architectural border in two columns divided by curvilinear line.

PPL*

698   Albany, N.Y.
ALBANY GAZETTE

The carriers of the Albany Gazette, mosty humbly present to its patrons and friends, the compliments of the New Year; and respectfully lay before them the contrast: peace and war! . . . January 1, 1813.

First line: Handmaid of plenty! mildly smiling peace!

45 x 29 cm. (40.1 x 23.6 cm.) Verse within ornamental border in two columns divided by curvilinear line; cut at head followed by four lines of verse.

Albany Institute of History and Art*

699   New York, N.Y.
COLUMBIAN

Address of the carrier of the Columbian, to his patrons. . . . New-York, January 1, 1813.

First line: Hail, patrons hail! a happy year!

56 x 29 cm. (37.6 x 21.0 cm.) Verse within ornamental border in three columns divided by single rules.

PPL*

700   New York, N.Y.
MERCANTILE ADVERTISER

New-Year's address of the carrier of the Mercantile Advertiser. For January 1st, 1813.

First line: Another old year, broken hearted

32 x 20 cm. (30.0 x 14.0 cm.) Verse within ornamental border in two columns divided by curvilinear line.

NHi*

701   New York, N.Y.
NEW-YORK PRICE-CURRENT,
1796–1817+

On the New Year. Respectfully submitted by the carriers of Ming's New-York Price-Current. . . . January 1, 1813.

First line: Time, like the dove of rapid flight

27 x 15 cm. (23.8 x 13.8 cm.) Verse within curvilinear line border in two columns divided by double rule.

NHi*

702   Poughkeepsie, N.Y.
POUGHKEEPSIE JOURNAL

The carrier's address to the respectable supporters of the Poughkeepsie Journal and Constitutional Republican. January 1st, 1813.

First line: From types and balls, and ink and paper | *Signed:* John Doughty. Jan 1st, 1813.

40 x 22 cm. (35.8 x 17.0 cm.) Verse within ornamental border in two columns divided by curvilinear line.

DLC*

703   Philadelphia, Pa.
AURORA

The carriers of the Aurora to their patrons of the commencement of the New Year. January 1, 1813.

First line: Before you, dear patrons, once more we appear

50 x 34 cm. (47.1 x 34.0 cm.) Verse within architectural border in two columns divided by ornamental line.

PPL*

704   Philadelphia, Pa.
BUREAU

Address of the carrier of the Bureau to his patrons, on the commencement of the New Year, 1813.

First line: Round creation's red centre our planet has run

34 x 21 cm. (30.1 x 17.3 cm.) Verse within ornamental border in two columns divided by curvilinear line.

PPL*

705   Philadelphia, Pa.
FREEMAN'S JOURNAL,
1804–1820+

Address of the carriers of the Freeman's Journal and Philadelphia Mercantile Advertiser, to their patrons on the commencement to the New Year, one thousand eight hundred and thirteen. . . . January 1, 1813.

First line: Now, with the coming year, we strive again

46 x 30 cm. (36.7 x 21.5 cm.) Verse within orna-

mental border in two columns divided by curvilinear line.

PPL*

706 Philadelphia, Pa.
POLITICAL AND COMMERCIAL
REGISTER

Address of the carrier of the Political and Commercial Register, to their patrons, on the commencement of the year 1813.

First line: On this gay morn, when ev'ry care's at rest

56 x 29 cm. (38.3 x 20.3 cm.) Verse within double curvilinear line border in two columns.

PPL*

707 Philadelphia, Pa.
POULSON'S AMERICAN DAILY
ADVERTISER

The address of the carriers of Poulson's American Daily Advertiser, to its patrons, on the commencement of the year 1813.

First line: Year after year we still have hop'd to find

49 x 33 cm. (42.7 x 24.3 cm.) Verse within architectural border in two columns divided by line of type ornaments. Cuts of eagle and two ships above border. Cut of wharf at end.

DLC MWA PPL*

708 Philadelphia, Pa.
RELF'S PHILADELPHIA
GAZETTE

Address of the carriers of Relf's Philadelphia Gazette, to their patrons, on the commencement of the year, 1813.

First line: Around the sun again had roll'd our sphere

50 x 34 cm. (40.2 x 28.4 cm.) Verse within architectural border in two columns divided by double rule, with cut of head centered at top.

PPL*

709 Philadelphia, Pa.
TICKLER

Address of the carriers of the Tickler, to their patrons, on the commencement of the New-Year, 1813.

First line: Now on her broad and flying wheels

45 x 45 cm. (40.2 x 28.5 cm.) Verse within architectural border in three columns, with cuts at head and text.

PPL RPB*

710 Philadelphia, Pa.
TRUE AMERICAN

Address of the carriers of the True American & Commercial Advertiser, to its patrons on the commencement of the New Year. . . . January 1, 1813.

First line: Custom has long decreed that we should pay

41 x 36 cm. (26.0 x 20.0 cm.) Verse within ornamental border in two columns divided by line of type ornaments.

PPL*

711 Philadelphia, Pa.
UNITED STATES GAZETTE

Address of the carriers of the United States' Gazette, to their patrons, on the commencement of the New Year—1813.

First line: Once more, kind friends, we greet with hearty cheer

46 x 30 cm. (41.3 x 21.0 cm.) Verse within architectural border; title within oblong block of type ornaments.

NjR* PPL

712 Reading, Pa.
READINGER ADLER

Neujahrs-Wunsch des Herumträgers des Readinger Adlers, an seine Kunden, bey dem Eintritt Jahrs 1813.

First line: Mein Wunsch ist der—daß wir reichen Segen

28 x 23 cm. (23.9 x 19.5 cm.) Verse within ornamental border in two columns.

MWA* PRHi

713   Newport, R.I.
      NEWPORT MERCURY

To the patrons of the Newport Mercury, the carrier presents the compliments of the season, and the following address . . . January 1, 1813.

First line: Progressive time, whose rapid wings—

32 x 14 cm. (29.9 x 10.5 cm.) Verse within ornamental border.

MWA*

714   Newport, R.I.
      RHODE-ISLAND REPUBLICAN

The carrier of the Rhode-Island Republican, with the customary compliments on this occasion, wishes its patrons 'a happy New Year.' . . . Newport, Jan. 1, 1813.

First line: See! Patron's see! your faithful boy appear

33 x 20 cm. (26.6 x 15.7 cm.) Verse in two columns divided by single rule.

RPB*

715   Providence, R.I.
      PROVIDENCE GAZETTE

The Gazette carrier's New Year address, to his generous friends. . . . Providence, January 1, 1813.

First line: Time has revolv'd another year

27 x 9 cm. (25.3 x 8.5 cm.) Verse within ornamental border.

RPB*

1814

716   New Haven, Conn.
      CONNECTICUT JOURNAL

The Journal carrier's address to his patrons, for January 1, 1814.

First line: 'Twas said, by one who saw with piercing eyes

29 x 23 cm. (24.3 x 16.7 cm.) Verse in two columns divided by curvlinear line with short double rule at head of text.

CtY*

717   Louisville, Ky.
      WESTERN COURIER

The carriers address, to the patrons of the Western Courier. . . . January 1st, 1814.

First line: My muse now strain the vocal lay | *Signed:* John M Patton.

32 x 20 cm. (29.6 x 16.7 cm.) Verse within architectural border in two columns divided by curvilinear line.

PPL*

718   Baltimore, Md.
      AMERICAN

Address to the patrons of the American Commercial Daily Advertiser; by the carriers. . . . Baltimore, January 1, 1814.

First line: In silence and in haste, at twelve

34 x 21 cm. (20.5 x 17.0 cm.) Verse within ornamental border in two columns divided by double rule.

MdHi*

719   Baltimore, Md.
      BALTIMORE PATRIOT

Carrier's address to the patrons of the Baltimore Patriot & Evening Advertiser. . . . January 1st, 1814.

First line: The circle of the year complete

37 x 24 cm. (33.9 x 19.2 cm.) Verse within ornamental border in two columns divided by line of type ornaments.

PPL*

720   Baltimore, Md.
      NILES' NATIONAL REGISTER

The carrier's address to the patrons of the Weekly Register. January 1, 1814.

First line: Again we hail the rising New-Year's day | *At head of text:* The patrons of the Register are respectfully informed that the following lines were actually written by a 'Printer's boy,'. . . .

32 x 19 cm. (31.3 x 18.0 cm.) Verse within ornamental border in two columns divided by double rule. Date with short double rule at head of text.

MdHi*

721　Fredericktown, Md.
BARTGIS'S REPUBLICAN
GAZETTE

Address of the carrier of Bartgis's Republican Gazette, to his patrons, on the commencement of another year. . . . Fredericktown, January 1st, 1814.

First line: Hail, patrons, hail! a happy year!

40 x 30 cm. (32.2 x 24.3 cm.) Verse within architectural border in two columns divided by line of type ornaments.

PPL*

722　Fredericktown, Md.
FREDERICK-TOWN HERALD

New Year's address of the carrier of the Herald. January 1st 1814.

First line: The wide flood of time whose rapid career

29 x 20 cm. (23.8 x 18.0 cm.) Verse within ornamental border in two columns divided by curvilinear line. Cut of eagle at head.

PPL*

723　Boston, Mass.
BOSTON DAILY ADVERTISER,
1813–1820+

The carrier's address to his kind patrons. . . . January 1, 1814.

First line: At dawning of this newborn year

48 x 21 cm. (40.5 x 20.5 cm.) Verse within architectural border. Star emblem at head of text includes word 'The'.

MHi*

724　Boston, Mass.
BOSTON GAZETTE, 1800–1820+

The carriers of the Boston Gazette, respectfully present their annual congratulations to its numerous friends and patrons. . . . January 1st, 1814.

First line: Good people! I'm the printer's lad

32 x 25 cm. (29.6 x 22.6 cm.) Verse within ornamental border in two columns divided by curvilinear line.

NHi*

725　Boston, Mass.
CHRISTIAN DISCIPLE AND
THEOLOGICAL REVIEW ◊

The carrier of the Christian Disgiple [*sic*] to his patrons.

First line: Ye, who my monthly pages turn

22 x 13 cm. (18.9 x 8.2 cm.)

MWA*

The Christian Disciple was published in Boston between May 1813 and December 1823.

726　Boston, Mass.
COLUMBIAN CENTINEL

The carrier of the Columbian Centinel, begs leave to present his heartfelt wish to the generous patrons of that paper, and his best friends—and to offer them the compliments of the season. January 1, 1814.

First line: . . . I look around and view with drooping heart the gloom profound | *Preliminary verse with title:* Watchmen, what of the night?

41 x 21 cm. (40.7 x 19.8 cm.) Verse within ornamental border in single and double columns divided by line of type ornaments.

MWA NHi PHi*

727　Boston, Mass.
INDEPENDENT CHRONICLE

Address of the carriers of the Independent Chronicle to its patrons, on the commencement of the year 1814. . . . January 1, 1814.

First line: His youngest child while yet in manly bloom

47 x 26 cm. (33.0 x 19.2 cm.) Verse within ornamental border in two columns.

MWA* WHi

728　Salem, Mass.
ESSEX REGISTER

The carriers of the Essex Register with the compliments of the season, present its patrons with the following piece for their amusement, entitled 'Eighteen hundred and thirteen.' . . . January 1, 1814.

First line: . . . Go forth, fair maids and cull the early flowers

46 x 19 cm. (42.4 x 15.3 cm.) Playlet in two columns divided by decorative curvilinear line.

Tapley, 435 / MSaE*

729   Salem, Mass.
        SALEM GAZETTE

New Year address of the carriers of the Salem Gazette, to its patrons, 1814.

First line: Again the joyous season has come round

29 x 24 cm. (22.5 x 19.0 cm.)

Tapley, 437 / MSaE*

730   Washington, Mississippi Territory
        WASHINGTON REPUBLICAN

News-Boy's Budget. For the carrier of the Washington Republican. . . . Town of Washington (M.T.) January 1st, 1814.

First line: As happy New-Year, begins its career |
Within arch: I hold the maxim no less applicable to public than to private affairs, that honesty is the best policy.

43 x 28 cm. (22.4 x 18.7 cm.) Verse within architectural border in two columns divided by curvilinear line. Cut of eagle surrounded by eighteen stars at head.

InU*

731   Concord, N.H.
        CONCORD GAZETTE

The carrier of the Concord Gazette, to his patrons. . . . Concord, January 1st, 1814.

First line: Old time still rolls his ceaseless course along

47 x 29 cm. (40.3 x 17.7 cm.) Verse in two columns divided by curvilinear line.

MWA*

731A   Hudson, N.Y.
        NORTHERN WHIG

News-boy's address to the patrons of the Northern Whig.

First line: Again old time has brought the day along

23 x 20 cm. (20.3 x 16.2 cm.) Verse in two columns within ornamental border.

STE 4877 / MWA*

732   New York, N.Y.
        NEW-YORK GAZETTE,
        1795–1820+

Address of the carriers of the New-York Gazette, to their patrons. January 1st, 1814.

First line: Our news-boat now no longer trips

38 x 18 cm. (33.0 x 11.5 cm.) Verse in two columns.

PPL*

733   New York, N.Y.
        NEW-YORK PRICE-CURRENT,
        1796–1817+

Address of the carrier of the New-York Price-Current to his patrons. January 1, 1814.

First line: With sithe [sic] and glass, and phiz profound

30 x 16 cm. (25.7 x 11.7 cm.) Verse within ornamental border.

NHi*

734   New York, N.Y.
        WAR

The carrier of the War, to his generous friends and patrons. January 1, 1814.

First line: Fatigued with bustle, noise and strife

50 x 25 cm. (43.5 x 22.8 cm.) Verse in three columns with thick-thin rules at head of text.

RPB*

Author: Samuel Woodworth. See R. S. Guernsey, *New York City and Vicinity During the War of 1812 . . .*, 2 vols. (New York, 1889–95) 2: 8.

735   Newburgh, N.Y.
        POLITICAL INDEX

The carrier of the Political Index, to his patrons with the compliments of the season. Newburgh, 1814.

First line: Two years have passed, since news-boy's lays

14 p.   21 cm.

Sh 51373 / PU*

736   Poughkeepsie, N.Y.
POUGHKEEPSIE JOURNAL

The news-boy's address, to the patrons of the Poughkeepsie Journal, and Constitutional Republican. Poughkeepsie, January 1, 1814.

First line: The sun and moon and this fair world | *At end of text:* The patrons of the Poughkeepsie Journal will please to accept of this puny effort of their ever devoted and much obliged John Doughty, carrier of the Journal.

35 x 23 cm. (34.6 x 22.1 cm.) Verse in two columns divided by curvilinear line.

DLC*

737   Chillicothe, Ohio
SUPPORTER

The carriers' address, to the patrons of the Supporter.

First line: Faithful as time, I now appear | *At head of border:* 1814 | *Signed:* William Monroe.

40 x 33 cm. (36.1 x 23.5 cm.) Verse within architectural border in three columns divided by curvilinear lines.

PPL*

738   Philadelphia, Pa.
AURORA

The carriers of the Aurora, to their patrons, on the commencement of the New Year. January 1, 1814.

First line: Dear patrons and friends, since the old year is past

50 x 34 cm. (44.0 x 34.0 cm.) Verse within architectural border in two columns divided by line of type ornaments.

PPL*

739   Philadelphia, Pa.
DEMOCRATIC PRESS

The carriers of the Democratic Press to their patrons, on the commencement of the New-Year. . . . 1814.

First line: The faithful carrier would his patrons cheer

50 x 33 cm. (48.5 x 33.0 cm.) Verse within architectural border in two columns divided by curvilinear line. Cut of eagle at head of border.

PPL*

740   Philadelphia, Pa.
FREEMAN'S JOURNAL, 1804–1820+

Address of the carriers of the Freeman's Journal, and Philadelphia Mercantile Advertiser, to their patrons on the commencement of the New Year, one thousand eight hundred and fourteen. . . . January 1, 1814.

First line: The carrier now, with his accustom'd lay

46 x 29 cm.(38.5 x 20.2 cm.) Verse in two columns divided by curvilinear line.

PPL*

741   Philadephia, Pa.
LITERARY REGISTER

Address of the carrier of the Literary Register, to its patrons, on the commencement of the New Year. . . . January 1, 1814.

First line: Borne on the wings of time, revolving years

28 x 22 cm. (24.8 x 18.7 cm.) Verse within ornamental border in two columns divided by curvilinear line.

RPB*

742   Philadelphia, Pa.
POLITICAL AND COMMERCIAL REGISTER

Address of the carriers of the Political and Commercial Register to their patrons, on the commencement of the year 1814.

First line: To wish his patrons many happy years

42 x 28 cm. (37.0 x 22.0 cm.) Verse in two columns divided by curvilinear line. Cut of ship at head.

PPL*

743   Philadelphia, Pa.
RELF'S PHILADELPHIA
GAZETTE

Address of the carriers of Relf's Philadelphia Gazette, to their patrons, on the commencement of the year, 1814.

First line: Grateful for favors past, I now appear

55 x 45 cm. (45.0 x 37.9 cm.) Verse within architectural border in two columns divided by curvilinear line, with cut of head centered at top.

PPL*

744   Philadelphia, Pa.
TICKLER

Address of the carrier of the Tickler, to his patrons, on the commencement of the year, 1814.

First line: Round about the bursting sun

49 x 45 cm. (40.4 x 29.0 cm.) Verse within architectural border in three columns with cut at head of text.

PPL RPB*

745   Philadelphia, Pa.
TRUE AMERICAN

Address of the carriers of the True American and Commercial Advertiser, to their patrons, on the commencement of the New Year—January 1, 1814.

First line: Once more the earth has circled round the sun

46 x 29 cm. (34.8 x 20.6 cm.) Verse within ornamental border in two columns divided by curvilinear line.

PPL*

746   Philadelphia, Pa.
UNITED STATES GAZETTE

Address of the carriers of the United States' Gazette to their patrons, on the commencement of the New Year, January 1, 1814.

First line: Hail glorious days! so long foretold by Fate

47 x 29 cm. (41.5 x 27.0 cm.) Verse within architectural border.

NjR* PPL

747   Reading, Pa.
READINGER ADLER

Neujahrs-Wunsch des Herumträgers des Readinger Adlers, bey dem Eintritt des Jahrs 1814, an seine Kunden.

First line: Zum Neujahr wünsch' ich euch und mir

26 x 20 cm. Verse within ornamental border in two columns divided by line of type ornaments, with cut at head; last two lines centered on page.

MWA*

748   Wilkes-Barre, Pa.
VISITOR

Address, from the carrier of the Visitor, to his patrons. . . . Wilkes-Barre, January, 1814.

First line: How shall the news-boy strike a jocund lay

28 x 24 cm. (21.7 x 20.0 cm.) Verse within ornamental border in two columns.

PPL*

749   Newport, R.I.
NEWPORT MERCURY

To the patrons of the Newport Mercury, the carrier presents the compliments of the season, and the following address. . . . January 1, 1814.

First line: When rival nations, great in arms

45 x 14 cm. (41.6 x 11.7 cm.) Verse within ornamental border.

MWA*

750   Richmond, Va.
VIRGINIA ARGUS

The news carriers' address to the patrons of the Virginia Argus, December 25, 1813.

First line: Another year away has past!—

34 x 27 cm. (27.0 x 20.3 cm.) Verse within archi-

tectural border in two columns divided by line of type ornaments.

PPL*

1815

751   New Haven, Conn.
     CONNECTICUT JOURNAL

The carrier to his patrons. January 1, 1815.

First line: Again the carrier comes through frost and snow

35 x 21 cm. (30.6 x 15.4 cm.) Verse in two columns.

Sh 34429 / CtY*

752   Lexington, Ky.
     WESTERN MONITOR

. . . of the carrier of the Western Monitor, to his patrons, on the first day of January 1815. . . . Lexington, January 1st, 1815.

First line: My name is William Parrish, sir

25 x 17 cm. (21.3 x 15.9 cm.) Verse within ornamental border in two columns divided by curvilinear line.

WvU*

753   Hallowell, Me.
     HALLOWELL GAZETTE

The carrier's address to the patrons of Hallowell Gazette. . . . Hallowell, January 1st, 1815.

First line: Old Tempus now in mad career

46 x 28 cm. (33.7 x 18.8 cm.) Verse within ornamental border in two columns divided by line of type ornaments.

MeHa*

754   Baltimore, Md.
     FEDERAL GAZETTE

Address of the carriers of the Baltimore Federal Gazette; to their patrons. . . . January 1, 1815.

First line: Tho' custom would lead us to pass in review

31 x 20 cm. (27.0 x 15.1 cm.) Verse within ornamental double line border.

MdHi*

755   Boston, Mass.
     BOSTON GAZETTE, 1800–1820+

The carriers of the Boston Gazette, respectfully present their annual congratulations to its numerous friends and patrons. . . . January 1st, 1815.

First line: As some tall ship, with spreading sails

34 x 24 cm. (30.3 x 21.5 cm.) Verse within ornamental border in two columns divided by line of type ornaments.

NHi*

756   Boston, Mass.
     BOSTON SPECTATOR

Address. The carrier to the patrons of the Boston Spectator. . . . January 2, 1815.

First line: Whence come the ills of life? | *Signed:* The Carrier.

39 x 23 cm. (29.2 x 19.2 cm.) Verse in two columns.

MWA* NHi

757   Boston, Mass.
     CHRISTIAN DISCIPLE AND
     THEOLOGICAL REVIEW

The carrier of the Christian Disciple, begs leave to present his heart-felt wish to the generous patrons of that work, and his best friends, and to offer them the compliments of the season. . . . January, 1815.

First line: Patrons and friends, O! may you hail | *At end of text:* Written by Daniel Jones, carrier of the Christian Disciple. . . .

22 x 16 cm. (16.8 x 7.6 cm.)

MWA*

758   Boston, Mass.
     COLUMBIAN CENTINEL

An address for the New-Year 1815. Respectfully dedicated to the numerous patrons of the Colum-

bian Centinel and Massachusetts Federalist. . . .
January 1, 1815.—Third year of the War.

First line: With scarce a smile to greet the new-born year

45 x 27 cm. (36.7 x 19.0 cm.) Verse within ornamental border in two columns divided by line of type ornaments.

MH MWA*

759   Boston, Mass.
        EVENING GAZETTE

Address of the carrier of the Evening Gazette to its patrons. . . . Boston, January 1st, 1815.

First line: A simple acorn, dropping once, 'tis said | *Signed:* The carrier.

47 x 30 cm. (37.1 x 25.3 cm.) Verse within architectural border in two columns divided by single rule. Cut of Mercury with banner bearing words 'Latest News' within title.

MWA PPL*

760   Boston, Mass.
        INDEPENDENT CHRONICLE

Chronicle news-boy's address. . . . January 1st, 1815.

First line: O for the muse whose genius kind

33 x 20 cm. (26.9 x 16.8 cm.) Verse within ornamental border in two columns divided by curvilinear line.

MB MWA*

761   Boston, Mass.
        NEW-ENGLAND PALLADIUM

The carriers' of the New England Palladium, to its patrons. Palladium Office, January 1, 1815.

First line: It has been in the fashion, from time out of mind

53 x 25 cm. (49.5 x 20.5 cm.) Verse within ornamental border in two columns divided by double rule.

MH*

762   Boston, Mass.
        YANKEE

The carrier of the Yankee, to his patrons, with the compliments of the New Year. . . . January 1, 1815.

First line: Again the carrier comes, to show his rhymes

39 x 32 cm. (30.8 x 24.5 cm.) Verse within ornamental border in two columns.

MWA*

763   Newburyport, Mass.
        NEWBURYPORT HERALD

New year address of the carriers of the Newburyport Herald to its patrons. . . . January 1, 1815.

First line: Patrons accept the salutation

51 x 21 cm. (39.0 x 17.5 cm.) Verse within ornamental border in two columns divided by single rule.

PHi RPB*

764   Salem, Mass.
        ESSEX REGISTER

The carrier presents, to the patrons of the Essex Register, the compliments of the season, and the following address. . . . January 2, 1815.

First line: Fatigued with bustle, noise and strife

33 x 20 cm. (28.1 x 15.0 cm.) Verse within ornamental border in two columns divided by curvilinear line.

Tapley p. 438 / MSaE*

765   Salem, Mass.
        SALEM GAZETTE

New Year address of the carriers of the Salem Gazette to its patrons. 1815.

First line: Patrons, accept the salutation

50 x 30 cm. (41.5 x 17.9 cm.) Verse within ornamental border in two columns.

MSaE RPB*

766   Concord, N.H.
        CONCORD GAZETTE

The carrier of the Concord Gazette, to his patrons. . . . Jan. 1st, 1815.

First line: Awake! awake! my muse awake!

43 x 12 cm. (edges trimmed to text) Verse in two columns.

NHi*

767   Portsmouth, N.H.
NEW-HAMPSHIRE GAZETTE

The news-boy's address, to the patrons of the New-Hampshire Gazette. . . . Portsmouth, January 1, 1815.

First line: Welcome day of joy and gladness

45 x 29 cm. (36.3 x 19.3 cm.) Verse within ornamental border in two columns divided by line of type ornaments.

RPB*

768   Newark, N.J.
CENTINEL OF FREEDOM

. . . Centinel to its patrons. . . . January 1, 1815.

First line: Within a circle of a year

27 x 22 cm. (21.9 x 18.6 cm.) Verse in two columns divided by curvilinear line.

NjHi*

769   Albany, N.Y.
ALBANY ARGUS

The carrier's address to the patrons of the Albany Argus. January, 1815.

First line: Most generous patrons, may the coming year

46 x 31 cm. (39.8 x 27.0 cm.) Verse within architectural border in two columns divided by curvilinear line. Cut of eagle with banner bearing words 'E Pluribus Unum' at head; lower ornamental border includes words 'Where liberty dwells, there is my country.'—Franklin.

N*

770   New York, N.Y.
COLUMBIAN

Address of the carrier of the Columbian, to its patrons and friends. January 1, 1815.

First line: Patrons and friends! The tide of time

39 x 27 cm. (32.6 x 18.2 cm.) Verse in three columns divided by single rules.

NHi*

771   New York, N.Y.
NEW-YORK GAZETTE,
1795–1820+

Address of the carrier of the New-York Gazette to his patrons, on the commencement of the New Year. . . . January 1, 1815.

First line: I have to tell you dear patrons—but I suppose

35 x 22 cm. (30.3 x 16.8 cm.) Verse in three columns with thick-thin rules at head of text.

NHi*

772   New York, N.Y.
NEW-YORK WEEKLY MUSEUM

The carriers' New Year's address, to the patrons of the New York Weekly Museum. January 1, 1815.

First line: On time's swift wings, again, has flown

30 x 25 cm. (24.4 x 19.6 cm.) Verse within ornamental border in two columns divided by curvilinear line. Short double rule at head of text; ornament at end.

NHi*

773   Poughkeepsie, N.Y.
POUGHKEEPSIE JOURNAL

The news-boy's address to the respectable patrons of the Journal. . . . January 1st, 1815.

First line: Replete with much event—important—vast! | *At end of text:* Permit me gentlemen, to avail myself of this occasion to express the high consideration, &c. &c. &c. John Doughty. Poughk. Journal Office, Jan. 1, 1815.

35 x 19 cm. (34.0 x 16.4 cm.) Verse within ornamental border in two columns divided by curvilinear line.

DLC*

774   Downington, Pa.
AMERICAN REPUBLICAN

Address, of the carrier of the American Republican, Jan. 1, 1815.

First line: Once more

36 x 11 cm. (34.5 x 8.8 cm.)

PWcHi*

775   Harrisburg, Pa.
CHRONICLE

Address, by the carrier of the Chronicle, to his patrons, on the commencement of the year 1815. . . . Harrisburg, January 2, 1815.

First line: This morn I arose with thoughts on my mind

43 x 27 cm. (33.5 x 24.6 cm.) Verse within architectural border in two columns divided by line of type ornaments.

CSmH*

776   Philadelphia, Pa.
AMERICAN DEMOCRATIC
HERALD

The carriers of the American Democratic Herald, to their patrons on the commencement of the New Year: January 1, 1815.

First line: Twas a cold rainy night, when the carrier's mother

45 x 27 cm. (34.5 x 19.4 cm.) Verse within architectural border in two columns divided by curvilinear line.

PPL*

777   Philadelphia, Pa.
AURORA

The carriers of The Aurora, to their patrons on the commencement of the New Year: January 1, 1815.

First line: To custom's voice, the news-man still attends

45 x 30 cm. (35.9 x 23.8 cm.) Verse within architectural border in two columns divided by line of type ornaments

PPL*

778   Philadelphia, Pa.
CORRECTOR

Address of the carriers of the Corrector and American Weekly Review to their patrons on the commencement of the year 1815.

First line: In his old car, has Phoebus run

50 x 33 cm. (42.8 x 30.0 cm.) Verse within architectural border in three columns. Two lines of type ornaments at end of text.

PPL*

779   Philadelphia, Pa.
DEMOCRATIC PRESS

The carriers of the Democratic Press to their patrons, on the commencement of the New-Year. . . . 1815.

First line: As opens to-day, another welcome year

45 x 28 cm. (37.9 x 25.8 cm.) Verse within architectural border in two columns divided by curvilinear line. Cut of eagle at head of border.

PPL*

780   Philadelphia, Pa.
FREEMAN'S JOURNAL,
1804–1820+

Address of the carriers of the Freeman's Journal and Philadelphia Mercantile Advertiser, to their patrons on the commencement of the New Year, one thousand eight hundred and fifteen. . . . January 2, 1815.

First line: In times like these, when virtue's self is made

46 x 27 cm. (37.6 x 20.9 cm.) Verse in two columns divided by double line of type ornaments.

PPL*

781   Philadelphia, Pa.
POLITICAL AND COMMERCIAL
REGISTER

Address of the carriers of the Political and Commercial Register, to their patrons on the commencement of the New Year. . . . January 1, 1815.

First line: Custom demands and we present the lay

46 x 29 cm. (40.6 x 20.8 cm.) Verse within ornamental border in two columns divided by double line of type ornaments.

PPL*

782   Philadelphia, Pa.
       RELF'S PHILADELPHIA
             GAZETTE

Address of the carriers of Relf's Philadelphia Gazette, to their patrons on the commencement of the year 1815.

First line: In course eccentric, round the stedfast [*sic*] sun

50 x 34 cm. (46.2 x 31.5 cm.) Verse within architectural border in two columns, with cut of head at top within border.

PPL*

783   Philadelphia, Pa.
       TRUE AMERICAN

Address of the carriers of the True American and Commercial Advertiser to its patrons, on the commencement of the New Year, 1815.

First line: The New Year opens and the night is past

50 x 33 cm. (46.7 x 23.6 cm.) Verse within ornamental border in two columns divided by curvilinear line. Cut of wharf scene at head.

PPL*

784   Philadelphia, Pa.
       UNITED STATES GAZETTE

Address of the carriers of the United States Gazette to their patrons, on the commencement of the New Year, January 1, 1815.

First line: The web of life is a mingled yarn

46 x 30 cm. (41.8 x 25.0 cm.) Verse within architectural border in two columns divided by curvilinear line.

PPL*

785   Reading, Pa.
       READINGER ADLER

Neujahrs-Wunsch des Herumträgers des Rea-

dinger Adlers, an seine Kunden, bey dem Eintritt des Jahrs 1815.

First line: Zum jez'gen lieben neuen Jahr

28 x 23 cm. (21.5 x 17.5 cm.) Verse within ornamental border in two columns divided by curvilinear line, with cut at head.

MWA*

786   Newport, R.I.
       NEWPORT MERCURY

To the patrons of the Newport Mercury the carrier presents the compliments of the season and the following address. . . . Newport, January 1, 1815.

First line: Accept oh! my patrons, the efforts of youth

31 x 13 cm. (28.9 x 11.6 cm.) Verse within ornamental border.

MWA*

787   Nashville, Tenn.
       CLARION

The carriers of the Clarion to their patrons.

First line: On Christmas Day, I have heard say | *Calendar at end entitled:* Almanac, for the year 1815.

41 x 19 cm. (34.1 x 17.0 cm.) Verse within ornamental border in two columns divided by line of type ornaments.

MWA*

788   Richmond, Va.
       VIRGINIA ARGUS

The new's carriers' address to the patrons of the Virginia Argus. December 25th 1814.

First line: The time has been, your printer's boy could bring | *At head of text:* Carriers plea

29 x 23 cm. (27.5 x 18.6 cm.) Verse within architectural border.

PPL ViW*

789   EVENING POST ◊

New-Year's address of the carriers of the Evening Post, to their kind patrons.

First line: One year has gone—fled like a ghost!

29 x 23 cm. (24.4 x 16.1 cm.) Verse within ornamental border in two columns divided by line of type ornaments.

PPL*

790   EXAMINER

The carrier of the Examiner to his patrons. . . . January 1st, 1815.

First line: Hail, patrons kind! your carrier brings, this morn

49 x 21 cm. (43.1 x 14.0 cm.) Verse within ornamental border, with thick-thin rules at head of text.

NHi*

1816

791   Hartford, Conn.
CONNECTICUT COURANT

The news carrier's address, to the readers of the Connecticut Courant. . . . Hartford, January 1, 1816.

First line: Cold, hungry, destitute and poor

47 x 20 cm. (37.5 x 15.5 cm.) Verse within ornamental border in two columns divided by curvilinear line.

MWA*

792   New Haven, Conn.
CONNECTICUT JOURNAL

Dorman's address to the patrons of the Connecticut Journal, January 1, 1816.

First line: A carrier, I have been

30 x 24 cm. (23.4 x 16.4 cm.)

CtY*

793   Washington, D.C.
NATIONAL INTELLIGENCER

Address of the carrier of the National Intelligencer, to its patrons. . . . January 4, 1816.

First line: To wake the soul by transient gleams of reason

33 x 28 cm. (27.1 x 16.4 cm.) Verse within ornamental border in two columns divided by curvilinear line.

DLC* / Extract printed in the *New-York Spectator*, January 13, 1816.

794   Bangor, Me.
BANGOR WEEKLY REGISTER

Address of the carrier of the Bangor Weekly Register to its patrons, presenting them with the compliments of the season. . . . Register Office, Bangor, Jan. 1, 1816.

First line: This morn, my patrons, with a heart sincere

35 x 20 cm. (28.5 x 11.9 cm.) Verse within ornamental border.

MWA*

795   Hallowell, Me.
HALLOWELL GAZETTE

The carrier's address to the patrons of the Hallowell Gazette. . . . Hallowell, January 1st, 1816.

First line: Hail! morning, thrice welcome, rejoice in the sight!

48 x 29 cm. (47.2 x 23.0 cm.) Verse within ornamental border in two columns divided by curvilinear line.

MeHa*

796   Baltimore, Md.
BALTIMORE TELEGRAPH

The address of the carriers of the Baltimore Telegraph, to its patrons. . . . January, 1st. 1816.

First line: Another year, and lo our country

31 x 20 cm. (28.9 x 17.3 cm.) Verse within ornamental border in two columns divided by curvilinear line.

MdHi*

797   Baltimore, Md.
FEDERAL GAZETTE

A song, substituted as the address of the carriers to the patrons of the Federal Gazette. . . . January 1, 1816.

First line: The year eighteen hundred and fifteen is done | *At head of text:* Tune-Young Lochinvar

34 x 20 cm. (27.7 x 14.7 cm.) Verse within double line ornamental border.

MdHi*

798   Boston, Mass.
BOSTON GAZETTE, 1800–1820+

1815–1816. A song, addressed by the carriers of the Boston Gazette, to its patrons. . . . January, 1st, 1816.

First line: We, news-boys, so smart, have long time found it thus

46 x 16 cm. (33.0 x 13.8 cm.) Verse within ornamental border.

NHi*

799   Boston, Mass.
BOSTON PATRIOT

The carriers of the Boston Patriot beg leave respectfully to congratulate their patrons on the auspicious circumstances under which the New-Year commences, and to urge their acceptance of a few lines in imitation of rhyme. . . . January 1, 1816.

First line: An ancient people, taught on freedom's plan

38 x 12 cm. (31.8 x 7.8 cm.) Verse within curvilinear border.

DLC*

800   Boston, Mass.
CHRISTIAN DISCIPLE AND
THEOLOGICAL REVIEW

The carrier of the Christian Disciple begs leave to present to its patrons his heartfelt wish for their welfare, and to congratulate them on the return of peace and prosperity to our beloved country, as well as to most of the Christian world. He also solicits permission to present them the compliments of the season. January-1816.

First line: Patrons, another year is past | *At end of text:* Written by Daniel Jones, carrier of the Christian Disciple.

28 x 10 cm. (24.6 x 7.6 cm.)

NHi*

801   Boston, Mass.
COLUMBIAN CENTINEL

A year of jubilee. The carriers of the Columbian Centinel, with the kindest wishes of the day, congratulate their patrons—on the restoration of peace to the whole world:—on the revival of commerce, and the mechanic arts:—return of good times to industry and enterprize out of office; and the general enjoyment of health and prosperity:— and take leave, respectfully to dedicate to them the following hastily written lines:—. . . Centinel Office, January 1, 1816.

First line: Oh! listen!—Time heeds no man's praying

40 x 22 cm. (edges trimmed to border) Verse within architectural border in two columns divided by double curvilinear line. 'New Year 1816' centered in border in ornament.

MWA PHi*

802   Boston, Mass.
EVENING GAZETTE

The carrier of the Evening Gazette, &c. to its patrons, wishing them health and a happy New Year! . . . Evening Gazette Office, Jan. 1, 1816.

First line: Good folks, the carrier!—fill'd with fear

35 x 24 cm. (27.0 x 20.3 cm.) Verse within architectural border in two columns divided by single rule.

MHi* NHi

803   Boston, Mass.
INDEPENDENT CHRONICLE

The carrier of the Independent Chronicle congratulates his kind customers on the present elevated and honorable rank our beloved country sustains among the nations of the earth—the blessings of peace acquired by the firm and dignified conduct of our illustrious chief magistrate, and his brave compatriots,—and respectfully begs leave to offer the following lines on the commencement of the year 1816.

First line: As when on Andes' awful height

34 x 21 cm. (31.9 x 19.6 cm.) Verse within ornamental border in two columns divided by curvilinear line.

MB* MWA

804   Boston, Mass.
YANKEE

New Year's address, to the patrons of the Yankee. . . . January 1, 1816.

First line: Reader, when you and I met last

54 x 34 cm. (46.0 x 30.0 cm.) Verse within ornamental border in five columns.

MWA*

805   Salem, Mass.
SALEM GAZETTE

The carriers of the Salem Gazette wish health and happiness to its patrons, and beg leave to present them with the following New Year's minstrelsey [sic]. 1816.

First line: Again the year has gone its round

47 x 29 cm. (36.5 x 19.2 cm.) Verse in two columns divided by curvilinear line.

Tapley, 443 / MSaE*

806   Concord, N.H.
NEW-HAMPSHIRE PATRIOT

News-boy's address, to the patrons of the New-Hampshire Patriot. . . . January 1, 1816.

First line: Sol's fiery coursers to the south have sped

56 x 32 cm. (48.7 x 24.9 cm.) Verse in three columns divided by single rules, with ornamental line at head of text.

NhHi*

807   Portsmouth, N.H.
INTELLIGENCER

Address of the carrier of the Intelligencer, to his patrons—wishing them all a happy New-Year. . . . Portsmouth, January 1, 1816.

First line: Kind patrons pray attend the song

31 x 18 cm. (24.7 x 8.3 cm.)

MWA NhHi*

808   Albany, N.Y.
ALBANY ARGUS

The carrier's address to the patrons of the Albany Argus. January, 1816.

First line: A news-boy, never taught to ring

45 x 29 cm. (34.7 x 25.0 cm.) Verse within architectural border in two columns divided by curvilinear line. Cut of eagle at head.

N*

809   Albany, N.Y.
CHRISTIAN VISITANT

The carrier of the Christian Visitant, presents his patrons with the compliments of the season, and the following address. . . . Albany, January 1, 1816.

First line: See! another year is gone!

47 x 19 cm. (34.2 x 13.9 cm.) Verse in two columns divided by single rule.

MWA*

810   Binghamton, N.Y.
PHOENIX

New Year's address. The carrier of the Phoenix to his patrons. . . . January 1, 1816.

First line: The boy, who weekly brings the news

45 x 18 cm. (40.5 x 13.3 cm.) Verse in two columns divided by double rule.

NBu*

811   New York, N.Y.
COMMERCIAL ADVERTISER

Address of the carrier of the Commercial Advertiser, to his patrons. . . . New-York, January 1, 1816.

First line: Attendant in the New Year's train

46 x 24 cm. (40.6 x 20.0 cm.) Verse within ornamental border in three columns divided by line of type ornaments.

NHi*

812   New York, N.Y.
COURIER

The carrier's address to the patrons of the New-York Courier. January 1, 1816.

First line: A year has pass'd from human sight

30 x 20 cm. (26.4 x 13.4 cm.) Verse in two columns.

NHi*

813   New York, N.Y.
       NEW-YORK EVENING POST,
          1801–1820+

The carrier of the New-York Evening Post, to his patrons. . . . New-York, January 1, 1816.

First line: Silent, unseen, unweari'd, endless, slow

34 x 26 cm. (27.0 x 12.7 cm.) Verse in two columns with thick-thin rules at head.

NHi*

814   New York, N.Y.
       NEW-YORK GAZETTE,
          1795–1820+

Address of the carrier of the New-York Gazette, to his patrons. . . . New-York, January 1, 1816.

First line: The shining orbs that cheer our sight

39 x 17 cm. (31.0 x 11.5 cm.) Verse within ornamental border in two columns divided by curvilinear line.

NHi*

815   New York, N.Y.
       NEW-YORK PRICE-CURRENT,
          1796–1817+

New-Year's address of the carrier of the New-York Price-Current, for 1816.

First line: The festive season comes again

38 x 19 cm. (29.7 x 12.6 cm.) Verse within ornamental border, with thick-thin rules at head of text.

NHi*

816   New York, N.Y.
       NEW-YORK WEEKLY MUSEUM

The carriers' New-Year's address, to the patrons of the New-York Weekly Museum. January 1, 1816.

First line: Hail! patron hail! with livelier heart

29 x 23 cm. (23.5 x 19.0 cm.) Verse within ornamental border in two columns divided by curvilinear line, with double rule at head. Last verse centered.

NHi*

817   Poughkeepsie, N.Y.
       POUGHKEEPSIE JOURNAL

The carrier of the Poughkeepsie Journal to his patrons. . . . January 1st, 1816.

First line: Farewell, fifteen, farewell forever! | *Signed:* Frederick T. Parsons.

45 x 28 cm. (39.9 x 20.1 cm.) Verse within ornamental border in two columns divided by single rule. Cut of eagle with shield at head.

DLC*

818   Cincinnati, Ohio
       LIBERTY HALL

A New Year's lay dedicated to the patrons of Liberty Hall and Cincinnati Gazette. January 1, 1816.

First line: O thou! who oft within the rolling year

Sh 39042 / DLC OCHi / Copy not located.

Author: Peyton S. Symmes. See Coggeshall, William T., *The Poets and Poetry of the West* (Columbus, 1860), 31. Carriers were Wesley Smead and Stephen S. L'Hommedieu.

819   Philadelphia, Pa.
       DEMOCRATIC PRESS

The carriers of the Democratic Press, to their patrons, on the commencement of the New-Year. . . . 1816.

First line: At custom's call, the news-man comes to cheer

43 x 31 cm. (37.9 x 24.6 cm.) Verse within architectural border in two columns divided by curvilinear line. Cut of eagle at head.

PPL*

820   Philadelphia, Pa.
FREEMAN'S JOURNAL,
1804–1820+

Address of the carriers of the Freeman's Journal and Philadelphia Mercantile Advertiser, to their patrons, on the commencement of the New Year, one thousand eight hundred and sixteen. . . . January 1, 1816.

First line: Time, on his rapid wings, demands again

35 x 25 cm. (31.5 x 18.4 cm.) Verse in two columns divided by line of type ornaments.

PPL*

821   Philadelphia, Pa.
POLITICAL AND COMMERCIAL
REGISTER

Address of the carriers of the Political and Commercial Register, to their patrons, on the commencement of the New Year, January 1, 1816.

First line: Once more the muse attempts th' accustomed lay

44 x 25 cm. (39.0 x 21.3 cm.) Verse within ornamental border in two columns divided by curvilinear line.

PPL*

822   Philadelphia, Pa.
POULSON'S AMERICAN DAILY
ADVERTISER

The address of the carriers of Poulson's Daily American Advertiser, to its patrons, on the commencement of the year 1816.

First line: When last we pour'd the unassuming lay

50 x 33 cm. (33.4 x 27.6 cm.) Verse within architectural border in two columns divided by line of type ornaments. Three cuts at head; cut of wharf scene at end.

PHi PPL*

823   Philadelphia, Pa.
RELF'S PHILADELPHIA
GAZETTE

Address of the carriers of Relf's Philadelphia Gazette, to its patrons, on the commencement of the year 1816.

First line: Wrapt in his robes of frost, another year

50 x 34 cm. (37.8 x 31.6 cm.) Verse within architectural border in two columns divided by double rules. Cut of head centered at top.

PPL*

824   Philadelphia, Pa.
UNITED STATES GAZETTE

Address of the carriers of the United States' Gazette to their patrons, on the commencement of the New Year, January 1, 1816.

First line: Around the sun, once more, the earth has roll'd

45 x 23 cm. (40.4 x 29 cm.) Verse within architectural border in two columns divided by curvilinear line.

PPL*

825   Reading, Pa.
READINGER ADLER

Neujahrs-Wunsch des Herumträgers des Readinger Adlers, an seine Kunden, bey dem Eintritt des jahrs 1816.

First line: Dem Manne der mit Biederkeit

28 x 23 cm. (22.2 x 19.1 cm.) Verse within ornamental border in two columns divided by curvilinear line.

MWA*

826   Newport, R.I.
RHODE-ISLAND REPUBLICAN

Carrier's address to the patrons of the Rhode Island Republican. Wishing them a 'Happy New-Year' . . . Office of the R.I. Republican, Jan. 1, 1816.

First line: Precious time, how important 'tis to man

30 x 22 cm. (23.2 x 14.5 cm.)

Sh 37187 / RNHi*

827   Norfolk, Va.
NORFOLK HERALD

Ode, inscribed to the patrons of the Norfolk Herald, by the carriers. Norfolk, Monday, December 15, 1815.

First line: Long have we watch'd the rolling year

31 x 21 cm. (28.6 x 19.2 cm.) Verse within architectural border.

MdHi* / Ms. inscription on verso of Maryland Historical Society copy: Written by Wm. Simmons.

828 Gazette carrier's New Year address to his patrons. January 1, 1816.

First line: Hail, patrons all, my merry horn

28 x 23 cm. (25.7 x 17.3 cm.) Verse within ornamental border in two columns divided by curvilinear line.

PPL*

829 The news-boy's address, to his patrons. January 1, 1816.

First line: When now the circling year is past

45 x 15 cm. (37.7 x 12.0 cm.) Verse within ornamental border.

PPL*

1817

830 New Haven, Conn.
CONNECTICUT JOURNAL

Address of the carrier to the patrons of the Connecticut Journal, January 1, 1817.

First line: Hard times! hard times! old Gripus cries

31 x 25 cm. (27.0 x 22.0 cm.) Verse in three columns.

CtY*

831 Hallowell, Me.
HALLOWELL GAZETTE

The carrier's address to the patrons of the Hallowell Gazette.... Hallowell, January 1st, 1817.

First line: Our old and worn-out year 'tis said

38 x 28 cm. (29.6 x 20.0 cm.) Verse within ornamental border in two columns divided by curvilinear line.

MeHa*

832 Baltimore, Md.
AMERICAN

Address to the patrons of the American and Commercial Advertiser; by the carriers.... Baltimore, January 1, 1817.

First line: Behold! once more from out the stormy North

33 x 23 cm. (29.8 x 17.4 cm.) Verse within ornamental border in two columns divided by double rule.

Sh 36680 / MdHi*

833 Baltimore, Md.
BALTIMORE PATRIOT

The carriers' address to the patrons of the Baltimore Patriot & Evening Advertiser. . . . Baltimore, January 1, 1817.

First line: Since last the carrier greeted you, the sun

34 x 23 cm. (27.8 x 18.9 cm.) Verse within ornamental border in two columns divided by single rule.

MdHi*

834 Baltimore, Md.
FEDERAL GAZETTE

Address of the carriers of the Baltimore Federal Gazette; to their patrons.... January 1st, 1817.

First line: To rhyme without reason a fault would appear

35 x 21 cm. (22.6 x 15.9 cm.) Verse in two columns.

MdHi*

835 Boston, Mass.
BOSTON GAZETTE, 1800–1820+

The carrier's wish dedicated, by special permission, to his friends, the generous patrons, of the Boston Gazette.... January, 1st, 1817.

First line: Another year has rolled away

51 x 24 cm. (46.0 x 18.5 cm.) Verse within ornamental border in two columns divided by curvilinear line.

MWA NHi RPB*

Author: William Ray. Collected in his *Poems on various Subjects, Reilgious, Moral, Sentimental and Humorous* (Auburn, N.Y., 1812), 65–69.

836   Boston, Mass.
BOSTON INTELLIGENCER

Address of the carrier of the Boston Intelligencer, and Morning & Evening Advertiser, to its patrons, with the customary compliments for the year 1817. . . . January 1st, 1817.

First line: 'Tis roll'd away! another year

47 x 29 cm. (41.7 x 26.5 cm.) Verse within architectural border in two columns divided by single rule, with line of type ornaments at head of text.

DLC MWA NCooHi* NHi

837   Boston, Mass.
BOSTON WEEKLY MAGAZINE

A New Year's address, by the carriers of the Boston Weekly Magazine, dedicated to their patrons. . . . Boston Weekly Magazine Office, January 1st, 1817.

First line: Stern winter now crowns the chill brow of the mountain | *At head within arch:* Born to no master, of no sect are we.

43 x 29 cm. (41.9 x 22.1 cm.) Verse within architectural border in two columns divided by curvilinear line, with thick-thin rules at head and end.

MB* MWA

838   Boston, Mass.
CHRISTIAN DISCIPLE AND
THEOLOGICAL REVIEW

The carrier of the Christian Disciple, begs leave to present his compliments to its patrons, and to inform them, that on account of sickness in his family he was unable to present his address in season, but requests the permission to present it with this number of the work. . . . Boston January - 1817.

First line: Once more, with frank, well-wishing tones | *Signed:* The carrier.

24 x 16 cm. (19.6 x 12.7 cm.) Verse in two columns.

MWA* NHi

839   Boston, Mass.
COLUMBIAN CENTINEL

The following ode is respectfully dedicated—with the best wishes for their prosperity and happiness during this and every other year of their lives—to the patrons of the Centinel, by their grateful servant, the carrier. . . . Centinel Office, January 1, 1817.

First line: Hail to this year; but, memory will recall | *At head within arch:* Ode, to the New Year.

49 x 31 cm. (33.9 x 19.9 cm.) Verse within architectural border in two columns divided by line of type ornaments.

MWA NCooHi RPB*

840   Boston, Mass.
INDEPENDENT CHRONICLE

New Year's address of the carrier of the Chronicle. . . . January 1, 1817.

First line: From regions where with earliest ray | *At head of text:* [Voluntarily communicated by an old and much respected correspondent.] | *Preliminary elegiac verse to Abijah Adams with first line:* Unlike my song of former days

32 x 20 cm. (26.6 x 15.4 cm.) Verse within ornamental border in two columns divided by curvilinear line. Preliminary verse within ornamental border.

MWA RPB* WHi

841   Boston, Mass.
NEW-ENGLAND PALLADIUM

The carriers of the Palladium, to its patrons. . . . Palladium-Office, Jan. 1, 1817.

First line: Enlighten'd men, with pride confess

40 x 14 cm. (29.9 x 12.0 cm.) Verse within ornamental border.

MWA*

842   Salem, Mass.
ESSEX REGISTER

The carrier of the Essex Register, respectfully presents to his patrons, with the compliments of the season, the following address: . . . January 1, 1817.

First line: Time, like a river, rolls its varied stream

41 x 25 cm. (38.0 x 23.5 cm.) On silk.

MSaE*

843   Salem, Mass.
SALEM GAZETTE

To the patrons of the Salem Gazette. 1817.

First line: Whereas, when New Year's day doth first come

29 x 24 cm. (20.5 x 19.4 cm.) Verse within ornamental border in two columns divided by curvilinear line.

Tapley, 446 / MSaE*

844   Portsmouth, N.H.
INTELLIGENCER

New-Year's ode. 1817. The carrier of the Intelligencer to his patrons. . . . Portsmouth, January 1, 1817.

First line: Life is a vapour!—so the poet sings

48 x 29 cm. (40.8 x 19.2 cm.) Verse in two columns divided by line of type ornaments. Cut of eagle bearing words 'A little cash' at head.

NhHi RPB*

845   Portsmouth, N.H.
NEW-HAMPSHIRE GAZETTE

The news-boy's address to the patrons of the New-Hampshire Gazette. . . . New-Hampshire Gazette Office, January 1, 1817.

First line: Scarce has the new-fledg'd year its flight begun

49 x 28 cm. (43.1 x 22.0 cm.) Verse within ornamental border in two columns divided by line of type ornaments.

MWA NhHi*

846   New York, N.Y.
COMMERCIAL ADVERTISER

Address of the carrier of the New-York Commercial Advertiser to his patrons. . . . January 1st, 1817.

First line: As constant as old winter sheds | *At head of text:* Happy New Year!

38 x 23 cm. (36.4 x 20.6 cm.) Verse within ornamental border in three columns.

NHi*

847   New York, N.Y.
COURIER

Address of the carriers of the New-York Courier, to its patrons, on the commencement of the year 1817.

First line: Patrons—revolving time's career

35 x 26 cm. (31.8 x 20.1 cm.) Verse within architectural border in two columns divided by line of type ornaments. Cut of tombstone at head inscribed, 'Sacred to the memory of the illustrious Washington,' with trumpeting angel above and allegorical mourning figure of Liberty in foreground.

NHi*

848   New York, N.Y.
NEW-YORK GAZETTE,
          1795–1820+

Address of the carrier of the New-York Gazette, to his patrons, on the New Year 1817. January 1, 1817.

First line: Like sun-beam darted through a cloud

35 x 20 cm. (28.3 x 14.8 cm.) Verse within ornamental border in two columns divided by curvilinear line.

NHi*

849   New York, N.Y.
NEW-YORK PRICE-CURRENT,
          1796–1817+

New-Year's address of the carrier of Ming's New-York Price-Current for 1817.

First line: This day, when smiling friends, and (foes)

34 x 16 cm. (32.4 x 12.6 cm.) Verse within ornamental border. Receipt for carrier's tip with three line verse printed vertically before last verse.

NHi*

850   New York, N.Y.
       NEW-YORK WEEKLY MUSEUM

The carriers' New-Year's address to the patrons of the New-York Weekly Museum January 1, 1817.

First line: Season of song, hail! once again

29 x 23 cm. (21.0 x 18.5 cm.) Verse within ornamental border in two columns divided by curvilinear line.

NHi*

851   Cincinnati, Ohio
       LIBERTY HALL

A New-Year's-lay. Dedicated to the patrons of Liberty Hall and Cincinnati Gazette. January first, 1817. [Cincinnati, printed by Thomas Palmer, 1817.]

First line: Old winter, in his northern icy car

9 p.   19 cm.

Sh 42976 Wegelin 1221 / RPB* / Shaw 42976 is listed as 'A New-Year's-Day' [*sic*]; and 39042 is erroneously attributed to Peyton S. Symmes. Wegelin 1221 attributes to Gorham A. Worth. Last line of poem reads, 'Where nature opes her stores—and Worth presents her charms.'

852   Cincinnati, Ohio
       WESTERN SPY

A present from the carrier of the Western Spy, to its patrons, on the commencement of the New Year. January 1, 1817. [Cincinnati, 1817]

First line: Despotic time—whose power no spell can lay

12p.   18 cm.

Sh 39791 / OCHi* / Ms. note on Cincinnati Historical Society copy: By T. Peirce.

853   Philadelphia, Pa.
       AURORA

The carriers of the Aurora, to their patrons, on the commencement of the New Year, January 1, 1817.

First line: As usual on the New Year's day

42 x 17 cm. (41.5 x 16.3 cm.) Verse within architectural border in three columns divided by single rules.

PHi*

854   Philadelphia, Pa.
       FREEMAN'S JOURNAL,
       1804–1820+

Address of the carriers of the Freeman's Journal and Philadelphia Mercantile Advertiser, to their patrons of the commencement of the New Year, one thousand eight hundred and seventeen. . . . January 1, 1817.

First line: With yesterday another year's withdrawn | *At end of text:* The carrier.

Fragments

PHi*

855   Philadelphia, Pa.
       GROTJAN'S PHILADELPHIA
       PUBLIC-SALE REPORT

The carriers of Grotjan's Philadelphia Public-Sale Report, to their patrons, on the commencement of the New-Year—1817.

First line: On fiery chariot, and in smoaking [*sic*] gear

38 x 24 cm. (37.5 x 24.0 cm.) Verse within architectural border in two columns divided by curvilinear line. Cut of ship at head.

PHi*

856   Philadelphia, Pa.
       RELF'S PHILADELPHIA
       GAZETTE

Address of the carriers of Relf's Philadelphia Gazette, to its patrons, on the commencement of the year 1817.

First line: Hark! snow-crowned time has struck his solemn bell

44 x 29 cm. (41.3 x 29.0 cm.) Verse within architectural border in two columns divided by double rule.

PHi*

857   Philadelphia, Pa.
TRUE AMERICAN

Address of the carriers of the True American & Commercial Advertiser, on the commencement of the year 1817.

First line: And thou my country, cast retracting view

Fragments. Verse within architectural border in two columns.

PHi*

858   Reading, Pa.
READINGER ADLER

Neujahrs-Wunsch des Herumträgers des Readinger Adlers, an seine Kunden, bey dem Eintritt des jahrs 1817.

First line: Zum kunft'gen lieben neuen jahr

29 x 23 cm. (20.1 x 17.4 cm.) Verse within ornamental border in two columns divided by curvilinear line; last stanza centered on page.

MWA*

859   Newport, R.I.
[NEWPORT MERCURY]

Mercury carrier's New Year address to his patrons. January 1, 1817.

First line: Custom, long has mark'd the way

27 x 15 cm. (22.7 x 10.8 cm.)

RNHi*

860   Richmond, Va.
VIRGINIA PATRIOT

The carriers of the Virginia Patriot, with their warm wishes that the patrons of that paper may enjoy a cheerful Christmas and happy New Year, offer the usual tribute of a few rhymes. Christmas, 1816.

First line: 'Clip, clip time's wings,' the lover cries

52 x 31 cm. (51.0 x 25.4 cm.) Verse within architectural border in three columns, with cut of eagle at head.

NHi*

861   DEMOCRATIC PRESS ◊

The carriers of the Democratic Press to their patrons.

First line: Tho winter with his surly blast

46 x 28 cm. (36.0 x 21.5 cm.) Verse within ornamental border in two columns divided by line of type ornaments. Cut of printing press within title.

PPL*

1818

862   New Haven, Conn.
CONNECTICUT JOURNAL

Address of the carrier to the patrons of the Connecticut Journal, Jan. 1, 1818.

First line: Harken, my friends; while I indite ye

34 x 27 cm. (25.1 x 21.7 cm.) Verse in three columns.

CtY*

863   Hallowell, Me.
HALLOWELL GAZETTE

The carrier's address to the patrons of the Hallowell Gazette. Hallowell, January 1, 1818.

First line: Marked with events of varied hue

48 x 28 cm. (35.5 x 20.4 cm.) Verse within ornamental border in two columns divided by line of type ornaments.

MeHa*

864   Boston, Mass
BOSTON GAZETTE, 1800–1820+

The carrier's New Year's address, to his friends, the patrons of the Boston Commercial Gazette. . . . January 1, 1818.

First line: Kind patrons, with the new-born year

45 x 24 cm. (40.6 x 21.5 cm.) Verse within orna-

mental border in two columns divided by curvilinear line. Short thick-thin rules at head of text.

NHi*

865   Boston, Mass.
BOSTON INTELLIGENCER

Address of the carrier of the Boston Intelligencer and Morning and Evening Advertiser, to its patrons, for the year 1818.

First line: Time runs his ceaseless race,—another year

35 x 25 cm. (30.0 x 17.7 cm.) Verse in two columns divided by double rule.

NHi*

866   Boston, Mass.
BOSTON PATRIOT

News boy's address to the patrons of the Chronicle & Patriot, on the commencement of the year 1818. . . . January 1, 1818.

First line: Old time, the grand monarch who rules o'er us all

42 x 14 cm. (38.2 x 12.1 cm.) Verse within ornamental border.

MWA NHi*

867   Boston, Mass.
BOSTON WEEKLY MAGAZINE

The carriers of the Boston Weekly Magazine present their annual congratulations to its patrons . . . January 1, 1818.

First line: Custom, the tyrant of the present age

33 x 19 cm. (31.6 x 18.8 cm.) Verse within ornamental border in two columns divided by curvilinear line.

NHi*

868   Boston, Mass.
COLUMBIAN CENTINEL

Boston, January 1, 1818. The carrier's address, devoted to the friends and patrons of the Columbian Centinel.

First line: With joyful heart and gratitude sincere

31 x 19 cm. (25.3 x 18.8 cm.) Verse within ornamental border with thick-thin rules at head of text. Cut of eagle in title.

Sh 43542 / MWA*

869   Boston, Mass.
NEW-ENGLAND GALAXY

The carrier of the New England Galaxy and Masonic Magazine, to his patrons. Boston, Jan. 1, 1818.

First line: With my bundle and cane, at your doors I appear

20 x 13 cm. (15.2 x 8.7 cm.)

NHi*

870   Salem, Mass.
ESSEX REGISTER

The carrier of the Essex Register, respectfully presents to its patrons, with the compliments of the season, the following address: . . . January 1, 1818.

First line: Hag of the sunken eye and wrinkled brow

37 x 23 cm. (34.2 x 18.5 cm.) Verse on silk within ornamental border in two columns divided by curvilinear line.

MSaE*

871   Salem, Mass.
SALEM GAZETTE

Address of the carriers of the Salem Gazette, to its patrons, to whom they wish a happy New Year. 1818. . . . January 1st, 1818.

First line: Janus once more his temple closes

47 x 29 cm. (35.1 x 19.1 cm.) Verse within ornamental border in two columns divided by line of type ornaments.

Sh 45621 / MSaE* MWA

872   Portsmouth, N.H.
PORTSMOUTH ORACLE

Address of the carrier of the Portsmouth Oracle, to its customers—to wish them a happy New-Year. 1818.

First line: Janus once more his temple closes

33 x 25 cm. (27.2 x 17.1 cm.) Verse within ornamental border in two columns divided by single rule.

NhHi*

873   New York, N.Y.
NEW-YORK GAZETTE, 1795–1820+

Address of the carrier, of the New-York Gazette and General Advertiser, to his patrons, for the year 1818. . . . January 1st, 1818.

First line: Once more, dear friends, you see me here

29 x 13 cm. (25.8 x 11.8 cm.) Verse within ornamental border in two columns divided by single rule.

RPB*

874   New York, N.Y.
REPUBLICAN CHRONICLE

The carrier of the Republican Chronicle to his generous friends and patrons, wishing them a happy New Year—January 1818.

First line: Dear patrons, a happy, thrice happy New Year

51 x 32 cm. (46.4 x 25.3 cm.) Verse within ornamental border in three columns divided by curvilinear lines. Cut centered within title, beneath double rules enclosing words, 'The tale of times that are.'

NjR*

875   Cincinnati, Ohio
LIBERTY HALL

A New Year's lay, dedicated to the patrons of the Liberty Hall and Cincinnati Gazette, on the commencement of the year 1818. By the news boy. Cincinnati, 1818.

First line: Old time, who marks decay on all that pass

10 p.   18 cm.

RPB* / Ms. note on Brown University copy: By Mr. Wright.

876   Cincinnati, Ohio
WESTERN SPY

A poetical gift, to the patrons of 'The Western Spy,' on the commencement of the year 1818. By the carrier. Accompanied with notes, critical and explanatory. By the printer's devil. Cincinnati: January first, 1818.

First line: In gay, good humor with his friends and foes

23 p.   18 cm.

Sh 41821 / OCHi RPB* / Ms. note on Brown University copy: by Tom Peirce.

877   Easton, Pa.
SPIRIT OF PENNSYLVANIA

A New Year's verse, for the year 1818; by the carrier of the 'Spirit of Pennsylvania.' Easton, January 1st, 1818.

First line: Time, ever varying, ever changing

29 x 17 cm. (28.7 x 12.2 cm.) Verse within architectural border with line of large type ornaments outside border at end. Cut of subscriber receiving carrier's address from carrier at head.

PHi*

878   Harrisburg, Pa.
HARRISBURGH CHRONICLE

Address of the carrier of the Harrisburg Chronicle; to his patrons at the commencement of the year 1818.

First line: Good morning to you patrons dear

33 x 20 cm. (26.1 x 14.7 cm.) Verse within ornamental border.

MWA*

879   Philadelphia, Pa.
AURORA

The carriers of the Aurora, on the commencement of the New Year, January 1, 1818.

First line: His very best respects to pay

Fragments. Verse within architectural border in two columns divided by single line.

PHi*

880   Philadelphia, Pa.
DEMOCRATIC PRESS

The carriers of the Democratic Press, to their patrons, on the commencement of the New-Year—1818.

First line: At this glad season, when the joyous heart

Fragments. Verse in two columns.

PHi*

881   Philadelphia, Pa.
POULSON'S AMERICAN DAILY ADVERTISER

The address of the carriers of Poulson's American Daily Advertiser to its patrons, on the commencement of the year 1818.

First line: 'Tis New Year's day, and all expect to find

50 x 33 cm. (44.0 x 28.6 cm.) Sailing ship in oval medallion at left and right of title outside border. Scene of ships at anchor in harbor at end of text. Trumpeting angel bearing words. 'To the American people,—...' at head.

MB* NHi

882   Reading, Pa.
READINGER ALDER

Neujahrs-Wunsch des Herümtragers des Readinger Adlers an seine Kunden bey dem Eintritt des Jahrs 1818.

First line: Zwar wünsch ich zu jeder Zeit

30 x 24 cm. (20.0 x 18.8 cm.) Verse within ornamental border in two columns divided by curvilinear line; last stanza centered on page.

MWA* PRHi

883   Newport, R.I.
NEWPORT MERCURY

New-Year's address. . . . Office of the Newport Mercury, Jan. 1, 1818.

First line: The pensive muse, who long has ceas'd to sing

35 x 19 cm. (31.7 x 10.7 cm.)

CSmH*

884   Providence, R.I.
RHODE-ISLAND AMERICAN

New-Year address of the carriers of the Rhode-Island American to its patrons. Providence, January 1, 1818.

First line: Hark! from yon distant spire the midnight peal

32 x 18 cm. (30.8 x 14.7 cm.) Verse within ornamental border in two columns divided by single rule.

RPB*

885   TRUE AMERICAN

The carriers of the True American, to their patrons, on the commencement of the New Year 1818.

First line: The New Year's day, from olden time

53 x 35 cm. (49.0 x 33.0 cm.) Verse within architectural border in two columns divided by curvilinear line. Curvilinear line at head of text.

RPB*

1819

886   Hartford, Conn.
CONNECTICUT MIRROR

The carrier of the Connecticut Mirror to his patrons, January 1, 1819.

First line: Arrah! my honeys, and a pleasant good morning to you

55 x 40 cm. (51.5 x 30.9 cm.) Prose and verse within ornamental border in three columns divided by curvilinear lines. Two woodcuts at head of text.

CtY*

887   Vincennes, Ind.
WESTERN SUN

The carrier to the patrons of the Western Sun, on the first day of January 1819.

First line: Good morning patrons of the Western sun

29 x 23 cm. (20.8 x 16.0 cm.) Verse within architectural border in two columns divided by curvilinear line, with date at head.

Byrd 70 / In*

888   Hallowell, Me.
HALLOWELL GAZETTE

The carrier's address to the patrons of the Hallowell Gazette. . . . January 1, 1819.

First line: The tempest tolls the knell of parting year

33 x 14 cm. (27.3 x 10.2 cm.) Verse within ornamental border.

MeHa*

889   Baltimore, Md.
BALTIMORE PATRIOT

Carriers' address to the patrons of the Baltimore Patriot & Mercantile Advertiser.

First line: Kind patrons! again is the carrier sincere | *At head of text within short double rule:* January 1, 1819.

34 x 24 cm. (32.0 x 20.3 cm.) Verse within ornamental border in two columns divided by curvilinear line.

Sh 43543 / MdHi*

890   Boston, Mass.
BOSTON GAZETTE, 1800–1820+

Address of the carrier of the Boston Commercial Gazette, to his friends and patrons. . . . January 1, 1819.

First line: Old time, revolvent, in his steady race

37 x 27 cm. (33.1 x 20.8 cm.) Verse within ornamental border in two columns.

MWA*

891   Boston, Mass.
BOSTON PATRIOT

Address of the carrier of the Patriot & Chronicle, to his numerous and respectable patrons, on the commencement of the year 1819. . . . January 1, 1819.

First line: There is a strain belov'd by all

42 x 29 cm. (35.7 x 20.7 cm.) Verse within ornamental border in two columns.

MWA*

892   Boston, Mass.
BOSTON WEEKLY MAGAZINE

Address of the carrier of the Boston Weekly Magazine, to his patrons on the commencement of the year 1819. . . . January 1, 1819.

First line: Time's annual circuit has again come round | *Woodcut at head signed:* Bowen.

34 x 14 cm. (30.6 x 9.6 cm.) Verse within ornamental border.

MWA* NHi

893   Boston, Mass.
COLUMBIAN CENTINEL

The carrier of the Columbian Centinel presents to its numerous patrons the compliments of the season, with his most earnest desires for their individual health and happiness.—On this occasion while he humbly asks for something, he has something to give, and as a quid pro quo, he has tried his hand in the following Hudibras-tick, Pindar-ick, Walter Scott-ick, Byron-ick, Pope-ish, Swift-ish, Printer's Devil-ish ode: . . . Centinel Office, January 1, 1819.

First line: Oh for a muse, to help me dip my quill | *Signed:* The carrier.

41 x 24 cm. (35.2 x 20.9 cm.) Verse within ornamental border in two columns divided by curvilinear line.

MWA NHi RPB*

894   Boston, Mass.
IDIOT

Uncle Sam's address to the patrons of the Idiot. On the commencement of the New Year. . . . January 1st, 1819.

First line: Kind patronizers—Ha! Ha! Ha!

40 x 17 cm. (34.3 x 13.1 cm.) Verse in two columns divided by line of type ornaments. Partially hand-colored cut of caricatured scribe at head.

MWA*

Uncle Sam's Address

TO THE

PATRONS OF THE IDIOT.

On the Commencement of the New Year.

KIND PATRONIZERS—Ha! Ha! Ha!
I wish you a *Happy New Year's Day;*
Time, ever in his swift career,
Has brought about another year:
And if my Parents told me true,
'Tis Uncle SAMMY's birth day too;
Yes, thrice four months ago this morn,
The RAMBLING IDIOT was born!
Hence the gay suit I now display,
My coat of red, and breeches grey:
And hence this annual Address,
Issued from the 'SQUIRE's own Press:
Hence, Watchmen, Barbers, Undertakers,
Lamplighters, Printer's Boys and Waiters,
At every door this morn appear,
To bid ye all a ' Happy Year!'
To whom ye grant some trifling fee,
To manifest [Ha! ha! ha!] your regard for
    ME!
  Well may Columbia's Sons rejoice,
In extacy raise every voice,
For should old Time but stop *my* breath,
Where is *my equal* left on earth!
Fools much abound, no doubt, but then
['Lord] DEXTER' and *I*, were born *wise men!*
By Nature taught, in Nature's school,
Born to enlighten and to rule!
To rule! aye, place *me* at the head
Of *Town Affairs*, grant me the lead,
See what *improvements* then ensue,
What SAMMY SIMPLETON could do!
Could do! aye, to improve the town,
I'd every crazy but pull down,
Adorn the Mall—blow up the Hill,
And send the Prostitutes to H—!
Level the Grog-shops with the ground,
And turn their rum-jugs upside down:
Of night Parowlers clear the coast,
The Watchmen rally at their post:
Serve the Prophane with something greeting,
Send Sabbath-Breakers all to meeting;
Send Jugglers, Quacks, and Fencing Masters,
To toil for bread in fields and pastures:
REED-hook rogues, nocturnal Bawlers.
Cheats, Knaves, Sharpers, and Forestallers,
Vile Blackguards who insult the FAIR,
Who much abound in M——t Square!

The poor protect, by labour fed,
And regulate the weight of Bread:
Grant to the widow'd poor relief,
Reduce the price of Pork and Beef:
And what would prove for public good,
'Tend to the measurement of Wood.

Nor ought you think it monstrous strange,
Should SAMMY take a peep on *'Change*—
Tell who is who, that thereon walk,
And who of *Crowns* and *Kingdoms* talk.
Where Idlers rest their worthless bones,
Conjointly with their fellow drones:
Where Mushrooms prate of " Naval Right,"
But rather run away than fight:
Who curse the " vile Administration,"

Which won't encourage Navigation—
(For were it in a prosperous state,
One might go *Cook*, another *Mate!*)
Where brainless " Dandies" still presume
To figure with the borrow'd plume,
With corslets, bracelets, parasols,
And paints, and artificial curls,
(Apeing the fashions of the Belles,)
With pretty Indispensables.
Where epauletted Sons of Mars
Boast of their unreceived scars!
Of *Battles* which they never fought,
And *dangers* which they never sought!
Where empty sconc'd dull Politicians
And would-be wise and learn'd Physicians,
Where sly designing Speculators
Contrive to bite their fellow-creatures;
And self-assuming Pettifoggers
Foment law-suits between Plough joggers.

And still his honest course pursue,
Next Uncle SAM might take a view
Of that Connubial state of life,
Where little else prevails but strife—
By whom the *breeches* shall be worn,
Until from both the garment's torn!
And some advice might SAM impart,
To those who have more *tongue* than heart:
Old Maids he means, who snarl and rage,
And amply fill the gossip's page,
With tales of slander and detraction,
And envy fraught with truth's refraction.
While cynic Bachelors are stupid,
And bomb-proof to the shafts of Cupid;
Frigid, like the northern pole,
Without the warmth of heart or soul—
Who set at nought dame Nature's plan.
And lose the *essence* of the Man!

But, first your Town Incorporate,
'Ere we of REFORMATION prate;
For 'less ye dub ME ' Sir, the MAYOR!'
SAM's ' Building Castles in the Air!'

THE NEWS BOY.

And now permit the Printer's lad to rhyme,
Who for a year has serv'd you, in due time.
With *fun*, as well as knowledge, without fail,
Tho' rough the weather, & tho' hard the gale,
I've spar'd no pains my customers to serve,
And from my duty never meant to swerve.
Some new delight may each revolving day,
To your kind bosoms constantly display.
Blest in your friends, and to your conttry dear,
Long may you live, and ev'ry pleasure share;
Till Time shall in Eternity be lost,
And worlds and systems moulder into dust.
Now while I wish my friends a happy year
Something I need *my* sinking heart to cheer,
I 've toil'd for you thro' storms of hail & rain;
Hard was my lot, though very small my gain.
Now if you'll but unfold your purse and heart
And grant a FEE—I'll thankfully depart.
   January, 1st. 1819.

Fig. 12. McDonald 894. *Idiot*, Boston, Mass., January 1, 1819. American Antiquarian Society.

895 Boston, Mass.
NEW-ENGLAND GALAXY

Address to the patrons of the New-England Galaxy & Masonic Magazine. January 1, 1819.

First line: There's nothing new beneath the sun

38 x 23 cm. (26.9 x 15.4 cm.) Verse within ornamental border in two columns.

MHi MWA*

896 Boston, Mass.
NEW-ENGLAND PALLADIUM

New-Year's address of the carriers of the New-England Palladium, to its patrons. . . . Palladium Office, Jan. 1, 1819.

First line: Omnipotent is habit—from the child

25 x 19 cm. (22.1 x 15.5 cm.) Verse in two columns divided by curvilinear line.

MWA*

897 Salem, Mass.
ESSEX REGISTER

To the patrons of the Essex Register, the carrier presents the compliments of the season, and the following address: . . . Salem, January 1, 1819.

First line: Oh! you who often on my unfledg'd lines

29 x 17 cm. (28.2 x 14.6 cm.) Verse on silk within ornamental border in two columns divided by curvilinear line.

Sh 47914 / MHi MSaE MWA RPB*

898 Salem, Mass.
SALEM GAZETTE

Address of the carriers of the Salem Gazette, to its patrons, New Year's Day, 1819. . . . January 1st, 1819.

First line: Last year's last sands, last night, ran out

37 x 24 cm. (33.2 x 20.7 cm.) Verse within architectural border in two columns divided by curvilinear line. Cut of eagle at head. The words 'Fugit irreparabile tempus' centered in head of border.

Tapley, 456–57 / MSaE* MWA

899 New York, N.Y.
MERCANTILE ADVERTISER

New-Year's address, of the carrier of the Mercantile Advertiser, January 1, 1819.

First line: While at the genial board you pay

31 x 22 cm. (27.7 x 14.0 cm.) Verse within ornamental border in two columns divided by curvilinear line.

RPB*

900 New York, N.Y.
NEW-YORK EVENING POST,
1801–1820+

The carrier of the New-York Evening Post to his patrons. New York, January 1, 1819.

First line: Dear patrons! by order of time

38 x 27 cm. (32.7 c 23.3 cm.) Verse within ornamental border in three columns divided by curvilinear lines.

RPB*

901 New York, N.Y.
NEW-YORK GAZETTE,
1795–1820+

Address of the carrier, of the New-York Gazette and General Advertiser, to his patrons, for the year 1819. . . . January 1, 1819.

First line: Patrons! expecting and sincere

31 x 22 cm. (26.9 x 18.1 cm.) Verse within ornamental border in three columns.

RPB*

902 Poughkeepsie, N.Y.
POUGHKEEPSIE JOURNAL

The carrier of the Poughkeepsie Journal, to his patrons. . . . Jan. 1, 1819.

First line: Time, with his pinions broad and strong

46 x 28 cm. (33.7 x 20.5 cm.) Verse within architectural border in two columns divided by curvilinear line. Cut of eagle at head of text.

Sh 25819 / NPou*

Attributed to Henry Livingston, Jr. See A. P Ver Nooy, 'The Carrier's Address—A New Year's Greeting,' *Dutchess County Historical Society Yearbook* 29 (1944): 46–47.

903   Columbus, Ohio
OHIO MONITOR ◊

[The carrier of the Monitor, to his patrons. . . .]

Sh 47678 / No copy located.

904   Philadelphia, Pa.
INDEPENDENT BALANCE

Address of the carriers of the Independent Balance, to its patrons, on the commencement of the year, 1819.

First line: Hail! New Year! season when the festive board

50 x 37 cm. (47.2 x 28.6 cm.) Verse within architectural border in two columns divided by double rule, with double rule at head of text. Figure of Justice centered at head within border.

ICHi MB*

905   Philadelphia, Pa.
POULSON'S AMERICAN DAILY ADVERTISER

The address of the carriers of Poulson's American Daily Advertiser to its patrons, on the commencement of the year 1819.

First line: How vain are all the views and hopes of man

50 x 33 cm. (44.1 x 28.6 cm.) Sailing ship in oval medallion at left and right of title outside border. Trumpeting angel bearing words. 'To the American people,—. . .' at head. Scene of ships at anchor in harbor at end.

MB*

906   Reading, Pa.
READINGER ADLER

Etliche Fragen, Antworten und Wünsche des Herumträgers des Readinger Adlers, an seine Kunden, bey dem Eintritt des Jahrs 1819.

First line: Wo ist der Weg zum Glück der Liebe?

31 x 25 cm. (23.1 x 21.5 cm.) Verse within orna-mental border in two columns divided by curvi-linear line.

MWA*

907   Providence, R.I.
PROVIDENCE GAZETTE

The Gazette carriers' New Year address, to their friends. January 1, 1819.

First line: Just eighteen hundred years have rolled away

29 x 15 cm. (27.8 x 11.9 cm.) Verse within orna-mental border.

RPB*

1820

908   Washington, D.C.
CITY OF WASHINGTON GAZETTE

Verses, by the carrier of the City of Washington Gazette, on New-Year's-Day, 1820. Respectfully dedicated to the patrons of that print. . . . Washington, January 1, 1820.

First line: Some poets mount upon Pegasus

26 x 19 cm. (21.8 x 12.8 cm.) Verse in two columns divided by double rule.

NN*

909   Portland, Me.
EASTERN ARGUS

The carrier's address, to be said or sung. Argus Office, Portland, January 1, 1820.

First line: Father Time, in whose rapid career | *At head of text:* Tune—Yorkshireman.

47 x 26 cm. (38.1 x 21.1 cm.) Verse within orna-mental border in two columns divided by curvi-linear line.

MWA* RPB

910   Baltimore, Md.
FEDERAL GAZETTE

Address of the carriers of the Baltimore Federal Gazette to their patrons. . . . January 1st, 1820.

First line: Not often, Pegasus, thy back I straddle

34 x 21 cm. (24.9 x 15.9 cm.) Verse within ornamental border in two columns divided by double rule.

MdHi*

911 Baltimore, Md.
MORNING CHRONICLE

The carrier's address to the patrons of the Morning Chronicle, and Baltimore Advertiser. . . . January 1st, 1820.

First line: Where are the Caesars, Alexanders now

46 x 29 cm. (42.5 x 24.6 cm.) Verse within architectural border in two columns.

MdHi*

912 Boston, Mass.
BOSTON DAILY ADVERTISER

Carrier's song. . . . Boston, January 1, 1820.

First line: Will you think of the news, I have carried for you | *At head of text:* Air—Will you come to the bower . . .

33 x 17 cm. (30.8 x 11.9 cm.) Verse within ornamental border.

MB*

913 Boston, Mass.
BOSTON GAZETTE, 1800–1820+

The carrier of the Boston Commercial Gazette, presents to its patrons, the compliments of the season. . . . Boston, January 1, 1820.

First line: Kind patrons, hail! hail to the new-born year

41 x 26 cm. (37.4 x 20.4 cm.) Verse within ornamental border in two columns divided by curvilinear line. Floral headband at head of verse and thick-thin rule at head of text.

MB MWA NHi RPB*

914 Boston, Mass.
BOSTON INTELLIGENCER

The carrier of the Boston Intelligencer, to his patrons, with the best wishes of the season. . . . Boston, January 1, 1820.

First line: Hail gen'rous patrons of old Faustus, hail!

29 x 15 cm. (25.3 x 10.7 cm.) Verse within ornamental border.

MB* MWA NN

915 Boston, Mass.
BOSTON PATRIOT

Address of the carrier of the Patriot and Chronicle, on the commencement of the year 1820. . . . Boston, January 1, 1820.

First line: Here, printer, stop, and let me learn the news

29 x 23 cm. (26.4 x 17.0 cm.) Verse within ornamental border in two columns divided by line of type ornaments.

MWA NHi*

916 Boston, Mass.
BOSTON RECORDER

New Year's address of the carrier of the Boston Recorder, to his patrons. . . . Jan. 1, 1820.

First line: Once more, my kind patrons, with pleasure I meet you

29 x 24 cm. (21.0 x 16.8 cm.) Verse within architectural border in two columns divided by curvilinear line.

DLC*

917 Boston, Mass.
CHRISTIAN DISCIPLE AND THEOLOGICAL REVIEW

The carrier of the Christian Disciple, to its patrons. . . . Boston, Jan. 1, 1820.

First line: With dawning of the New Year's Day

25 x 15 cm. (18.5 x 8.5 cm.)

MWA*

918 Boston, Mass.
COLUMBIAN CENTINEL

The New-Year's lay. The carrier of the Columbia [*sic*] Centinel tenders to its patrons the thirty-fourth annual tribute of his respect, in the following humble address. . . . January 1, 1820.

First line: Patrons and friends! With welcome meet

35 x 21 cm. (32.6 x 17.0 cm.) Verse within ornamental border in two columns divided by line of type ornaments.

Sh 824 / MB*

919 Boston, Mass.
NEW-ENGLAND GALAXY

Address of the carriers of the New-England Galaxy, January 1, 1820.

First line: Time hurries on with rapid bound

31 x 22 cm. (26.0 x 16.2 cm.) Verse within ornamental border in two columns divided by curvilinear line, with thick-thin rules at head of text.

Sh 2410 / MB*

920 Boston, Mass.
NEW-ENGLAND PALLADIUM

The carriers of the Palladium, to its patrons. . . . Boston January 1, 1820.

First line: The news-boy comes with a New-Year's lay! | *At end of text:* '*Rolla,' the writer of several very patriotic New Year's addresses for the Chronicle carriers, during the 'Reign of Terror,' when we were burdened with a standing army in time of peace, direct taxes, stamp duties, a public debt, loan, a Navy, a national bank, exorbitant salaries, &c., &c.

35 x 18 cm. (33.3 x 16.5 cm.) Verse within heavy black line border in two columns divided by single rule.

Sh 2412 / MB*

921 Boston, Mass.
UNIVERSALIST MAGAZINE

The carrier's address, to the patrons of the Universalist Magazine. January 1, 1820.

First line: Kind patrons, while others present their address

26 x 21 cm. (23.2 x 16.7 cm.) Verse within ornamental border in two columns divided by curvilinear line. Cut at head by Samuel H. Dearborn; engraved by Abel Bowen with caption, 'Universalist magazine office . . . Congress Street, Boston.'

MWA*126

922 Boston, Mass.
YANKEE

News-boy's address to the patrons of the Boston Yankee. . . . Yankee Office, Jan. 1, 1820.

First line: A Yankee boy once more essays

27 x 19 cm. (22.6 x 14.1 cm.) Verse within ornamental border in two columns divided by curvilinear line.

Sh 549 / MB*

923 Salem, Mass.
ESSEX REGISTER

Carrier's address, to the patrons of the Essex Register, with the compliments of the season, Jan. 1, 1820.

First line: Old Time revolvent, with accustom'd pace

36 x 19 cm. (32.6 x 13.2 cm.) Verse on silk within ornamental border with short broken line at head of text. Paper copy: 36 x 19 cm. (32.3 x 13.1 cm.)

Tapley, 458 / MSaE*

924 Salem, Mass.
SALEM GAZETTE

To the patrons of the Salem Gazette, the carriers wish a happy New Year. . . . Jan. 1st, 1820.

First line: Compare ours with any foreign nation

34 x 21 cm. (32.5 x 19.4 cm.) On coral, coated paper. Verse within ornamental border in two columns divided by curvilinear line.

Sh 3093 / MeHi MSaE*

925 Albany, N.Y.
ALBANY REGISTER

The news-boy's address, to the patrons of the Albany Register. January 1, 1820.

First line: Time flaps his snowy pinions at the goal

44 x 22 cm. (35.0 x 13.4 cm.) Verse in two columns divided by curvilinear line.

NHi* NhHD

926 Hudson, N.Y.
NORTHERN WHIG

Address of the carrier of the Northern Whig. . . . Hudson, January 1, 1820.

First line: Still pressing on thy rude and powerful path

46 x 26 cm. (40.4 x 16.0 cm.) Verse in two columns divided by double rule.

NHi*

927   New York, N.Y.
        COMMERCIAL ADVERTISER

Address of the carrier of the Commercial Advertiser, to his patrons. . . . New-York, January 1st, 1820.

First line: The rhyming season's come again

46 x 28 cm. (38.0 x 20.0 cm.) Verse within ornamental border in three columns divided by curvilinear lines.

MWA*

928   New York, N.Y.
        NEW-YORK EVENING POST,
            1801–1820+

The carrier's address to the patrons of the New-York Evening Post, for the year 1820.

First line: At twelve last night, this spacious world

47 x 25 cm. (38.3 x 20.5 cm.) Verse within ornamental border in three columns divided by line of type ornaments.

MWA*

929   New York, N.Y.
        WEEKLY VISITOR, 1817–1820+

New-Year's address of the carrier of the Weekly Visitor, and Ladies' Museum. To his patrons, January the 1st, 1820.

First line: The day, which happy proves to many

31 x 14 cm. (29.4 x 12.6 cm.) Verse within ornamental border.

NN*

930   Poughkeepsie, N.Y.
        POUGHKEEPSIE JOURNAL

The carrier of the Poughkeepsie Journal, to his patrons. . . . January 1st, 1820.

First line: Time when advancing spreads his plumes | Signed: Frederick T. Parsons.

45 x 29 cm. (37.0 x 22.0 cm.) Verse within ornamental border in two columns divided by curvilinear line. Cut of eagle with shield at head. Inset poem 'To the memory of Com. Perry' in first column set off by ornamental border.

DLC*

931   Schoharie, N.Y.
        SCHOHARIE OBSERVER

The carrier of the Schoharie Observer presents his patrons with the compliments of the season and the following address: . . . January 1, 1820.

First line: Old Time with a visage, which most men of his age

46 x 28 cm. (30.1 x 20.0 cm.) Verse in two columns.

NHi*

932   Cincinnati, Ohio
        INQUISITOR

A New-Year's lay for 1820; dedicated to the patrons of the Inquisitor and Cincinnati Advertiser, by the carrier. Cincinnati, 1820.

First line: Through every age—o'er every clime | *Preliminary verse with first line:* The news-boy tenders to his patrons kind

11p.   18 cm.

Sh 47618 / RPB*

Author: Peyton S. Symmes. Ms. note on Brown University copy: by P.S.S.

933   Cincinnati, Ohio
        LIBERTY HALL

Address to the patrons of the Liberty Hall and Cincinnati Gazette, by the carrier; on the commencement of the year 1820.

First line: Patrons, that carrier of all truth and lies

43 x 27 cm. (38.4 x 20.9 cm.) Verse within ornamental border in two columns divided by curvilinear line.

MWA*

934   Downington, Pa.
AMERICAN REPUBLICAN

News boy's address, to the patrons of the American Republican, January 1, 1820,—Almanac included.

First line: A New-Year's gift! my friends—a New-Year's gift!

32 x 18 cm. (27.1 x 14.2 cm.) Verse in left column and almanac in right column, divided by single rule.

MWA PWcHi RPB*

935   Erie, Pa.
ERIE REFLECTOR

News-boy's address, to the patrons of the Erie Reflector. . . . January 1st, 1820.

First line: Another year, with silent tread | *At head of text within double rules:* We take no note of time, but by its loss.

33 x 21 cm. (23.3 x 14.4 cm.) Verse within ornamental border in two columns divided by curvilinear line.

Sh 51924 / PU*

936   Philadelphia, Pa.
POULSON'S AMERICAN DAILY
ADVERTISER

The address of the carriers of Poulson's American Daily Advertiser to its patrons, on the commencement of the year 1820.

First line: Again the New Year comes; but comes in clouds

49 x 31 cm. (44.5 x 28.5 cm.) Verse on silk within architectural border in two columns divided by line of type ornaments. Cut of trumpeting angel with banner bearing words, 'To the American people,—union, health and happiness,' at head. Cut of ship at head of each column and cut of harbor scene at end.

MB (paper) PHi* RPB (paper)

937   Reading, Pa.
READINGER ADLER

Neujahrs-Wunsch des Herumträgers des Readinger Adlers, an seine Kunden, bey dem Eintritt des Jahrs 1820.

First line: Auf dem Pfad der Hoffnung wallt

31 x 24 cm. (27.0 x 18.3 cm.) Verse within ornamental border in two columns divided by curvilinear line. Cut of eagle at head of text.

MWA*

938   Providence, R.I.
RHODE-ISLAND AMERICAN

A happy New Year. Reflections, on the New Year; respectfully inscribed to the patrons of the Rhode-Island American by the carriers. January 1, 1820.

First line: Again hath time, with swift career

47 x 33 cm. (41.5 x 29.1 cm.) Verse within architectural border in two columns divided by single rule.

MWA*

939   Petersburg, Va.
REPUBLICAN

The carrier's address to the patrons of the Petersburg Republican. Christmas, 1819.

First line: Kind sirs I've come again, with humble song

35 x 21 cm. (34.0 x 19.6 cm.) Text within architectural border. Verse in left column and calendar for 1820 in right column, divided by decorative line.

Hummel 3342 / NcD*

[n.d.]

940   Boston, Mass.
INDEPENDENT CHRONICLE

The carrier of the Independent Chronicle, wishes all his kind customers a happy New-Year, and presents them the following: . . .

First line: Once more indulgent heav'n rolls round the year

19 x 15 cm. (16.0 x 10.3 cm.) Double line of type ornaments at head and end.

PHi*

Canadian Carriers' Addresses

1767

941   Quebec, Que.
QUEBEC GAZETTE

The New-Year verses of the printers lad, who carries about the Quebec Gazette to the customers. January 1, 1767.

First line: The old year now is past and gone

34 x 20 cm. (28.0 x 17.2 cm.) Verse within ornamental border in two columns divided by decorative line, with decorated initial.

Vlach 0806 / CaQQS*

942   Quebec, Que.
[QUEBEC GAZETTE] ◊

Etrennes du garçon imprimeur à ses pratiques. Chanson.

First line: Qu'on ne me parle plus de vers

29 x 14 cm. (22.1 x 10.9 cm.) Verse within ornamental border, with decorated initial.

Vlach 0585 / CaQQS*

1778

943   Quebec, Que.
QUEBEC GAZETTE

Etrennes du garçon qui porte la Gazette de Quebec aux pratiques. Le 1 Janvier, 1778.

First line: En finissant

25 x 13 cm. (21.0 x 10.5 cm.) Verse within ornamental border.

Tremaine 269 / CaOOP*

1779

944   Quebec, Que.
QUEBEC GAZETTE

Etrennes du garçon qui porte la Gazette de Quebec aux pratiques. Le 1 Janvier, 1779.

First line: Dans ce jour d'allegresse

27 x 13 cm. (19.5 x 10.5 cm.) Verse within ornamental border.

Tremaine 299 / CaOOP*

1780

945   Quebec, Que.
QUEBEC GAZETTE

Etrennes du garçon qui porte la Gazette de Quebec aux pratiques. Le 1 Janvier, 1780.

First line: S'il faut que dans les premiers jours

23 x 15 cm. (18.8 x 11.7 cm.) Verse within ornamental border.

Tremaine 329 / CaOOP*

1781

946   Quebec, Que.
QUEBEC GAZETTE

New-Year's verses of the printer's boy, who carries about the Quebec Gazette to the customers. January 1, 1781.

First line: Serious and solemn be the song

26 x 18 cm. (21.5 x 13.0 cm.) Verse within ornamental border.

Tremaine 345 / CaOOP

1782

947   Quebec, Que.
QUEBEC GAZETTE

New-Year's verses of the printer's lad, who carries about the Quebec Gazette to the customers. January 1, 1782.

First line: Once more my days their circling race

26 x 19 cm. (22.0 x 13.0 cm.) Verse within ornamental line border.

Tremaine 362 / CaOOP*

1785

948   Quebec, Que.
QUEBEC GAZETTE

New-Year's verses of the printer's lad who carries about the Quebec Gazette to the customers. January 1, 1785.

First line: My worthy good masters, whether warriors or civil

36 x 24 cm. (32.0 x 19.0 cm.) Verse within ornamental border, with initial block.

Tremaine 440 / CaOOP*

1786

949   Quebec, Que.
QUEBEC GAZETTE

New-Year's verses of the printer's boy who carries about the Quebec Gazette to the customers. January 1, 1786.

First line: Since time, the old bald-pate, leads in a New-Year

36 x 24 cm. (32.5 x 21.0 cm.) Verse within ornamental line border.

Tremaine 465 / CaOOP

1787

950   Quebec, Que.
QUEBEC GAZETTE

Etrennes du garçon qui porte la Gazette de Québec aux pratiques. Le 1er. Janvier, 1787.

First line: Plus on vit, glose qui glose

28 x 22 cm. (24.5 x 17.0 cm.) Verse within ornamental border.

Tremaine 498 / CaOOP

1788

951   Quebec, Que.
QUEBEC GAZETTE

Etrennes du garçon, qui porte la Gazette de Quebec aux pratiques. Le 1 Janvier, 1788.

First line: Comme c'est l'utilite

27 x 19 cm. (23.5 x 15.5 cm.) Verse within ornamental line border.

Tremaine 539 / CaOOP

1789

952   Quebec, Que.
QUEBEC GAZETTE

Etrennes du garçon qui porte la Gazette de Quebec aux pratiques. Le 1er Janvier, 1789.

First line: Bonjour, bon an, me voici

31 x 18 cm. (27.0 x 15.0 cm.) Verse within ornamental triple line border.

Tremaine 565 / CaOOP

1790

953   Quebec, Que.
QUEBEC GAZETTE

Etrennes du garçon qui porte la Gazette de Quebec aux pratiques. Le 1er Janvier, 1790.

First line: Je viens ici gaillardement

31 x 19 cm. (27.0 x 12.5 cm.) Verse within ornamental border.

Tremaine 617 / CaOOP

1791

954   Quebec, Que.
QUEBEC GAZETTE

Verses of the printer's boy who carries the Quebec Gazette to the customers. January 1, 1791. / Etrennes du garçon qui porte la Gazette de Quebec aux pratiques. Le 1er Janvier, 1791.

First line: Since its freedom the press triumphant maintains / *First line:* Pour me conformer a l'usage

36 x 31 cm. (32.0 x 26.0 cm.) Verses in English and French. French verse in two columns.

Tremaine 671 / CaOOP

1792

955   Quebec, Que.
QUEBEC GAZETTE

Verses of the printer's boy who carries the Quebec Gazette to the customers. January 1, 1792. / Etrennes du garçon qui porte la Gazette aux pratiques. Le 1er Janvier, 1792.

First line: Help, help ye nine, a trembling devil aid / *First line:* Aujourd'hui par une chanson

41 x 33 cm. (34.5 x 27.0 cm.) Verses in English and French within double line border divided by decorative line.

Tremaine 736 / CaOOP*

1793

956   Quebec, Que.
QUEBEC GAZETTE

Verses of the printer's boy who carries the Quebec Gazette to the customers. January 1st, 1793. / Etrennes du garçon qui porte la Gazette de Quebec aux pratiques. Le 1er Janvier, 1793.

First line: Imprimis—news foreign, eventful, I've brought ye / *First line:* Un pais autrefois soumis au despotisme

35 x 31 cm. (33.5 x 26.5 cm.) Verses in English and French within ornamental line border.

Tremaine 798 / CaOOP

1794

957   Quebec, Que.
QUEBEC GAZETTE

Verses of the printer's boy who carries the Quebec Gazette to the customers. January 1, 1794. / Les souhaits sinceres du garçon qui porte la Gazette de Quebec aux pratiques. Le 1er Janvier, 1794.

First line: Again my good sirs the year has revolv'd / *First line:* Aujourd'hui par une chanson

39 x 31 cm. (35.5 x 29.0 cm.) Verses in English and French within ornamental border divided by decorative line. French verse in two columns.

Tremaine 854 / CaQMBN*

1795

958   Quebec, Que.
QUEBEC GAZETTE

Verses of the printer's boy who carries the Quebec Gazette to the customers. January 1st, 1795. / Chanson du garçon qui porte la Gazette aux pratiques. Le 1er Janvier, 1795.

First line: Oblig'd my annual verse to pay / *First line:* Du nouvel an

39 x 31 cm. (33.0 x 28.0 cm.) Verses in English and French within ornamental border divided by decorative line. French verse in two columns. Cuts of three crowns at head of text of English verse. Ornament at head of each stanza of French verse except first.

Tremaine 907 / CaOOP*

959   Quebec, Que.
TIMES

The printer's boy of the Times. To the subscribers. . . . Quebec, 1st January, 1795.

First line: Citizens, male and female all

(25 x 19 cm.) Verse within ornamental border.

Tremaine 914 / CaOOP

1796

960   Halifax, N.S.
        Royal Gazette ◊

The news-carrier's address to the customers of the Royal Gazette.

First line: Twelve months my weekly course I've run

(32 x 18 cm.) Verse within ornamental border.

Tremaine 963 / CaNsHa

961   Quebec, Que.
        Quebec Gazette

The printer's boy wishes his customers a happy New-Year. Cum re modoque. / Etrennes du garçon qui porte la Gazette de Quebec aux pratiques. Le 1er Janvier, 1796.

First line: Happiness where art thou found? / *First line:* Aristote n'a pas trouvé notre vrai nom

39 x 34 cm. (28.0 x 28.0 cm.) Verses in English and French within ornamental line border

Tremaine 962 / CaOOP

1797

962   Quebec, Que.
        Quebec Gazette

Verses of the printer's boy who carries the Quebec Gazette to the customers. January 1st, 1797. / Etrennes du garçon qui porte la Gazette de Quebec aux pratiques. Le 1er Janvier, 1797.

First line: Lo! a new Year! and, strange to tell / *First line:* Toujours de mes devoirs fidele observateur

36 x 31 cm. (33.5 x 29.5 cm.) Verses in English and French within ornamental line border.

Tremaine 1014 / CaOOP

1798

963   Quebec, Que.
        Quebec Gazette

Quebec, 1st January, 1798. Verses of the boy who carries the Quebec Gazette to the subscribers. / Quebee [*sic*] 1er Janvier, 1798. Etrennes du garçon qui porte la Gazette de Quebec, aux pratiques.

First line: Again his annual glass old time / *First line:* Que dans Paris on s'applique

36 x 31 cm. (26.5 x 24.0 cm.) Verses in English and French.

Tremaine 1065 / CaOOP

1799

964   Quebec, Que.
        Quebec Gazette

Verses of the boy who carries the Quebec Gazette to the subscribers. 1st January, 1799. / Etrennes du garçon qui porte la Gazette de Quebec aux pratiques. 1er Janvier, 1799.

First line: At this returning season of the year / *First line:* Aujourd'hui sans rancune

33 x 24 cm. (30.0 x 23.0 cm.) Verses in English and French within ornamental double line border divided by decorative line.

Tremaine 1101 / CaOOP*

1800

965   Quebec, Que.
        Quebec Gazette

Verses from the news-boy to his customers. 1st. January, 1800.

First line: Care enough—enough of sorrow

(18.0 x 7.0 cm.)

Tremaine 1141 / CaOA

1801

966   Montreal, Que.
MONTREAL GAZETTE

Etrennes du garçon qui porte la Gazette de Montreal aux pratiques. 1er Janvier, 1801 . . .

First line: Voici l'aimable saison

(25.0 x 17.0 cm.) Verse within ornamental border.

Tremaine 1187 / CaQQS

967   Quebec, Que.
QUEBEC GAZETTE

Address of the boy who carries the Quebec Gazette. January 1st. 1801. / Etrennes du garçon qui porte la Gazette de Quebec aux pratiques. 1er Janvier, 1801.

First line: Now in this season of the year / *First line:* Je ne viens point en Satyrique

32 x 30 cm. (29.5 x 33.0 cm.) Verses in English and French within ornamental border divided by decorative line. French verse in two columns divided by rule.

Tremaine 1195 / CaOOP*

1802

968   Quebec, Que.
QUEBEC GAZETTE

The news boy's New Year's gift to his customers. 1st. January 1802. / Etrennes du garçon qui porte la Gazette de Quebec.

Verses in English and French in two columns.

Hare 38 No copy located.

1803

969   Montreal, Que.
MONTREAL GAZETTE

Etrennes du garçon qui porte la Gazette de Montreal, à ses pratiques. Premier Janvier, 1803.

First line: Vous favez qu'a tout nouvel an

33 x 21 cm. (27.0 x 14.0 cm.) Verse within ornamental border.

Vlach 0586 / CaQMBN*

970   Quebec, Que.
QUEBEC GAZETTE ◊

The news boy's New Year's gift to his customers. / Etrennes du garçon qui porte la Gazette de Quebec.

Verses in English and French in two columns.

Hare 56 No copy located.

1804

971   Quebec, Que.
QUEBEC GAZETTE

Etrennes du garçon qui porte la Gazette de Quebec aux pratiques; 1er. Janvier, 1804. / The news-boy's New Year's gift to his customers; 1st January, 1804.

First line: Oh! le bon siècle mes frères / *First line:* The humble news boy at your door

4 p.   19 cm. French text on page one in two columns divided by single rule, with single rule at head of verse. English text on page three.

Vlach 0591 / CaQMBN*

1805

972   Halifax, N.S.
WEEKLY CHRONICLE

Lines for the New Year; respectfully addressed to the patrons of the Weekly Chronicle, by the lad who delivers it. . . . Dec. 27, 1804.

First line: Bless me! how swift time rolls away

26 x 20 cm. (21.0 x 15.1 cm.) Verse within ornamental border in two columns divided by single rule.

RPB*

973   Quebec, Que.
QUEBEC GAZETTE

Etrennes du garçon qui porte la Gazette de Quebec aux pratiques; 1er. Janvier, 1805. / The New

Year's address of the boy who carries the Quebec Gazette to the subscribers.

First line: Couvrons de fleurs la faulx du tems / *First line:* A happy year and length of days

4 p.   19 cm. French text on page one with short single rule at head of verse. English text on page three with short single rule at head of verse.

Vlach 0592 / CaQMBN*

1806

974   Quebec, Que.
QUEBEC GAZETTE

Etrennes du garçon qui porte la Gazette de Quebec à ses pratiques. Premier Janvier, 1806.

First line: En vain je fais diligence

27 x 20 cm. (24.8 x 9.2 cm.) Verse on silk within ornamental border.

Vlach 0588 / CaQMM*

974A   Quebec, Que.
QUEBEC GAZETTE

The newsboy's address, to the subscribers of the Quebec Gazette; on the New-Year 1806./ Etrennes du garçon qui porte la Gazette de Quebec à ses pratiques. Premier Janvier 1806.

First line: On this day when the world and his wife all appear / *First line*: En vain je fais diligence

35 x 36 cm. [24.4 x 31.1 cm.] Verses in English and French within ornamental border divided by decorative line. English verse in two columns divided by decorative line.

Vlach 0820 / CaQQS*

975   Quebec, Que.
QUEBEC MERCURY

New Year's verses of the printer's boy that carries the Quebec Mercury, most respectfully addressed to the subscribers. Quebec, 1st. January, 1806.

First line: Custom commands, and I obey

32 x 20 cm. (27.5 x 16.4 cm.) Verse within ornamental border in two columns. Thick-thin rules set off place and date.

Vlach 0807 / CaQQS*

1807

976   Montreal, Que.
MONTREAL GAZETTE

Etrennes du garçon qui porte la Gazette de Montreal respectueusement adressées à ses pratiques. Le 1er Janvier, 1807.

First line: D'ou vient qu'au premier jour de l'an

19 x 15 cm. (15.2 x 10.4 cm.) Verse within ornamental border.

Vlach 0587 / CaQQS*

977   Quebec, Que.
LE CANADIEN

Etrennes du Canadien, 1er. Janvier, 1807.

First line: Je veux vous complimenter

23 x 14 cm. (18.0 x 10.3 cm.) Verse in two columns.

Vlach 0581 / CaQQS*

978   Quebec, Que.
QUEBEC GAZETTE

The news boy's address, to the subscribers of the Quebec Gazette, on the New Year. 1807. . . . / Etrennes du garçon qui porte la Gazette de Quebec a ses pratiques. Premier Janvier, 1807.

40 x 19 cm. Verses in English and French within ornamental border in two columns divided by line of type ornaments.

Vlach 0821 / CaQQS

979   Quebec, Que.
QUEBEC MERCURY

New Year's verses of the printer's boy that carries the Quebec Mercury. Most respectfully addressed to the subscribers. Quebec, 1st. January, 1807.

First line: Once more the annual glass of time

31 x 20 cm. (27.5 x 16.9 cm.) Verse within ornamental border in two columns. Thick-thin rules set off place and date.

Vlach 0808 / CaQQS*

1808

980   Montreal, Que.
CANADIAN COURANT

The news boy's address, to the patrons of the Canadian Courant. . . . Canadian Courant Office, Montreal, January 1, 1808.

32 x 20 cm.

Vlach 0818 / CaQMBN

981   Quebec, Que.
LE CANADIEN

Etrennes du Canadien, 1er. Janvier, 1808.

First line: Au milieu du sombre orage

25 x 17 cm. (21.0 x 12.5 cm.) Verse in two columns; last stanza centered.

Vlach 0582 / CaQQS*

982   Quebec, Que.
QUEBEC GAZETTE

The newsboy's address, to the subscribers of the Quebec Gazette, on the New-Year 1808. / Etrennes du garçon qui porte la Gazette de Quebec à ses pratiques. Premier Janvier 1808.

First line: Some people think Life like the ocean / *First line:* La douzieme maison

44 x 27 cm. (42.5 x 24.7 cm.) Verses in English and French within ornamental border in two columns divided by decorative line. French verse set off by decorative line.

Vlach 0822 / CaQQS*

983   Quebec, Que.
QUEBEC MERCURY

New Year's verses of the printer's boy that carries the Quebec Mercury, most respectfully addressed to the subscribers. Quebec, 1st. January, 1808. . . . New Printing Office.

First line: Again, the god, with locks of gold

32 x 20 cm. (28.0 x 19.0 cm.) Verse within oval ornamental border in two columns. Thick-thin rules set off place and date. Triangular design of type ornaments at end of text.

Vlach 0809 / CaQQS*

1809

984   Quebec, Que.
[LE CANADIEN]

Etrennes du garçon gazetier. 1er. Janvier, 1809.

First line: Si souvent on me critique

23 x 18 cm. (22.5 x 17.6 cm.) Verse in two columns.

Vlach 0583 / CaQQS*

985   Quebec, Que.
QUEBEC GAZETTE

1809. The boy's New Year's gift.—Etrennes du garçon qui porte la Gazette de Quebec.

First line: Attend fellow Britons, we tune the bold lyre / *First line:* Il est passe, le tems [*sic*] l'entraine

39 x 36 cm. (37.0 x 34.9 cm.) Verses in English and French within architectural border in two columns divided by decorative line. French verse in two columns. Cut at head.

Vlach 0253 / CaQQS*

986   Quebec, Que.
QUEBEC MERCURY

New Year's verses of the printer's boy that carries the Quebec Mercury, most respectfully addressed to the subscribers. Quebec, January 1, 1809.

First line: Hard is the case of that poor man

35 x 20 cm. (31.2 x 20.0 cm.) Verse within architectural border in two columns divided by decorative line, with cut of Royal coat of arms at head. Thick-thin rules set off place and date.

Vlach 0810 / CaQQS*

1810

987   Quebec, Que.
[LE CANADIEN]

Etrennes du garçon gazetier, 1er. Janvier, 1810.

First line: Je ne suis point de ville

28 x 21 cm. (25.0 x 17.9 cm.) Verse within ornamental border in two columns divided by decorative line.

Vlach 0584 / CaQQS*

988   Quebec, Que.
QUEBEC GAZETTE

1810. The boy's New Year's gift.—Etrennes du garçon qui porte la Gazette de Quebec.

Verses in English and French.

Hare 245 / No copy located.

1811

989   Montreal, Que.
CANADIAN COURANT

The news boy's address, to the patrons of the Canadian Courant. January 1st. 1811. . . . Canadian Courant Office, Montreal, January 1, 1811.

30 x 19 cm. Verse within ornamental border in two columns divided by line of type ornaments.

Vlach 0819 / CaQMBN

990   Quebec, Que.
QUEBEC GAZETTE

1811. The boy's New Year's gift.—Etrennes du garçon de la Gazette de Quebec.

First line: Some travel East, some travel West / *First line:* Si je viens vous importuner

42 x 27 cm. (38.2 x 24.0 cm.) Verses in English and French within architectural border in two columns divided by single rule. Cut at head.

Vlach 0249 / CaQQS*

991   Quebec, Que.
QUEBEC MERCURY

New Year's verses of the printer's boy that carries the Quebec Mercury, most respectfully addressed to the subscribers. Quebec, 1st January, 1811.

First line: Hail, Janus, with the double face

25 x 19 cm. (21.5 x 15.0 cm.) Verse within ornamental border in two columns.

Vlach 0811 / CaQQS*

1813

992   Quebec, Que.
QUEBEC GAZETTE

1813. The boy's New Year's gift.—Etrennes du garçon de la Gazette de Quebec.

First line: Permit a bashful, inexperienc'd boy / *First line:* Douze laisse a minuit

48 x 31 cm. (38.0 x 25.8 cm.) Verses in English and French within architectural border. French verse in two columns. Cut at head.

Vlach 0250 / CaQQS*

993   Quebec, Que.
QUEBEC MERCURY

New Year's verses of the printer's boy that carries the Quebec Mercury, most respectfully addressed to the subscribers. Quebec, 1st January, 1813.

First line: Old Janus, with thy backward face

30 x 24 cm. (27.2 x 19.8 cm.) Verse within ornamental border in two columns.

Vlach 0812 / CaQQS*

1814

994   Halifax, N.S.
WEEKLY CHRONICLE

Lines for the approaching New Year, respectfully addressed to the subscribers for the Weekly Chronicle. By the lads who deliver it. . . . Friday, December, 1813.

First line: High seated on a rock sublime

33 x 20 cm. (26.0 x 15.5 cm.) Verse within curvilinear line border in two columns divided by decorative line.

RPB*

995   Quebec, Que.
QUEBEC GAZETTE ◊

The boy's New Year's gift.—Etrennes du garçon de la Gazette de Quebec.

First line: Hard times, and sad, our patrons say /
First line: Pendant toute la guerre

45 x 29 cm. (37.8 x 24.2 cm.) Verses in English and French within architectural border in two columns divided by single rule.

NN*

996   Quebec, Que.
Quebec Mercury

New Year's verses of the printer's boy that carries the Quebec Mercury, most respectfully addressed to the subscribers. Quebec, January 1st, 1814.

First line: Again old Time another year

30 x 24 cm. (27.7 x 19.0 cm.) Verse within ornamental border in two columns divided by decorative line. Thick-thin rules set off place and date.

Vlach 0813 / CaQQS*

1815

997   Quebec, Que.
Quebec Gazette

1815. The boy's New Year's gift.—Etrennes du garçon de la Gazette de Quebec.

First line: Permit me, sirs, upon this day / *First line:* Jour de l'an tu es venu

51 x 30 cm. (39.0 x 24.8 cm.) Verses in English and French within architectural border divided by decorative line. Cut at head.

Vlach 0252 / CaQQS*

998   Quebec, Que.
Quebec Mercury

New Year's verses of the printer's boy that carries the Quebec Mercury, most respectfully addressed to the subscribers. Quebec, January 1st, 1815.

First line: The annual muse her wings once more

34 x 24 cm. (27.9 x 18.5 cm.) Verse within ornamental border in two columns divided by decorative line. Thick-thin rules set off place and date.

Vlach 0815 / CaQQS*

1817

999   Halifax, N.S.
Weekly Chronicle

Stanzas for the New-Year; respectfully addressed to the subscribers for the Weekly Chronicle. By the lads who deliver it. . . . Halifax, N.S. 27th December, 1816.

First line: Know ye the land, sirs, of fish and potatoes

33 x 20 cm. (27.7 x 14.7 cm.) Verse within curvilinear line border.

RPB*

1820

1000   Quebec, Que.
Quebec Gazette

1820. Quebec Gazette.

First line: Struggling with modesty and pride / *First line:* L'an se montre, l'an s'ecoule

44 x 29 cm. (38.2 x 25.8 cm.) Verses in English and French within architectural border divided by decorative line. Cut at head.

RPB*

1001   Quebec, Que.
Quebec Mercury

New Year's verses of the printer's boy that carries the Quebec Mercury, most respectfully addressed to the subscribers. Quebec, January 1st. 1820.

First line: Again old Time has run his race

33 x 22 cm. (31.9 x 20.9 cm.) Verse within ornamental border in two columns divided by double rule. Ornaments set off place and date.

Vlach 0816 / CaQQS*

[n.d.]

1002   Halifax, N.S.
Nova-Scotia Gazette and the Weekly Chronicle or Nova-Scotia Gazette and the Weekly Advertiser

New-Year's verses. Addressed to the customers of the Nova-Scotia Gazette, by the printer's lad that carries them.

First line: Again my good friends, behold Boreas approaching

44 x 26 cm. (34.5 x 16.2 cm.) Verse within ornamental border.

MWA* / American Antiquarian Society copy bears ms. note signed: Warburton. A printing date between 1770 and 1805 is suggested by American Antiquarian Society based on typographical evidence.

Bibliography

[Alsop, Richard.] *The Echo, with Other Poems*. [New York]: Printed at the Porcupine Press by Pasquin Petronius, 1807.

Alden, John Eliot. *Rhode Island Imprints, 1727–1800*. New York: Published for the Bibliographical Society of America [by] R. R. Bowker Company, 1949.

Blanck, Jacob. *Bibliography of American Literature, compiled by Jacob Blanck for the Bibliographical Society of America*. 9 vols. New Haven: Yale University Press, 1955–1983.

Brigham, Clarence S. *History and Bibliography of American Newspapers. 1690–1820*. 2 vols. Worcester: American Antiquarian Society, 1947.

——. *Journals and Journeymen: A Contribution to the History of Early American Newspapers*. Philadelphia: University of Pennsylvania Press, 1950.

Bristol, Roger P. *Supplement to Charles Evans' American Bibliography*. Charlottesville: Published for the Bibliographical Society of the University of Virginia by the University Press of Virginia, 1970.

Buckingham, Joseph T. *Personal Memoirs and Recollections of Editorial Life*. 2 vols. Boston: Ticknor, Reed and Fields, 1852.

——. *Specimens of Newspaper Literature: with Personal Memoirs, Anecdotes, and Reminiscences*. 2 vols. Boston: C. C. Little and J. Brown, 1850.

Byrd, Cecil K. , and Howard H. Peckham. *A Bibliography of Indiana Imprints, 1804–1853*. Indianapolis: Indiana Historical Bureau, 1955.

Coggeshall, William T. *The Poets and Poetry of the West*. Columbus: Follett, Foster and Company, 1860.

Evans, Charles. *American Bibliography*. 13 vols. Chicago: Privately printed for the author by the Blakely Press, 1903–1959.

Evans, Nathaniel. *Poems on Several Occasions, with Some Other Compositions*. Philadelphia: John Dunlap, 1772.

Ford, Worthington Chauncey. *Broadsides, Ballads, &c. Printed in Massachusetts, 1639–1800*. Boston: Massachusetts Historical Society, 1922.

Freneau, Philip. *The Miscellaneous Works of Mr. Philip Freneau Containing his Essays, and Additional Poems*. Philadelphia: Printed by Francis Bailey, 1788.

——. *The Poems of Philip Freneau. Written Chiefly during the Late War*. Philadelphia: Printed by Francis Bailey, 1786.

——. *Poems Written Between the Years 1768 and 1794 by Philip Freneau of New Jersey. A new ed., rev. and corrected by the author; including a considerable number of pieces never before published*. . . . Monmouth, N.J.: Printed at the Press of the author, 1795.

Gaines, Pierce W. *William Cobbett and the United States, 1792–1835*. Worcester: American Antiquarian Society, 1971.

Guernsey, Rocellers Sheridan. *New York City and Vicinity During the War of 1812. . . . With an Account of the Citizens' Movements, and of the Military and Naval Officers, Regiments, Companies, etc., in Service There*. 2 vols. New York: C. L. Woodward, 1889–95.

Hare, John and Jean-Pierre Wallot. *Les Imprimes dans le Bas-Canada. 1801–1810.* Montreal: Les Presses de L'Universite de Montreal, 1967.

Harrington, K. P. *Richard Alsop 'A Hartford Wit.'* Middletown, Conn: Mattabesett Press, 1939.

Hildeburn, Charles R. *A Century of Printing. The Issues of the Press in Philadelphia 1685–1784.* 2 vols. Philadelphia: Press of Matlack & Harvey, 1885–86.

Hummel, Ray O. *Southeastern Broadsides before 1877: A Bibliography.* Richmond, Va: Virginia State Library, 1971.

Hutton, Joseph. *Leisure Hours; or Poetic Effusions.* Philadelphia: Hellings and Aitken, 1812.

McCorison, Marcus A. *Vermont Imprints: 1778–1820: A Check List of Books, Pamphlets, and Broadsides.* Worcester: American Antiquarian Society, 1963.

McDonald, Gerald D. 'New Year's Addresses of American Newsboys.' *In Bookman's Holiday. Notes and Studies Written and Gathered in Tribute to Harry Miller Lydenberg,* edited by Deoch Fulton. New York: The New York Public Library, 1943.

Ray, William. *Poems on Various Subjects, Religious, Moral, Sentimental and Humorous.* Auburn, N.Y.: Printed by U. F. Doubleday, 1821.

Reilly, Elizabeth C. *A Dictionary of Colonial American Printers' Ornaments and Illustrations.* Worcester: American Antiquarian Society, 1975.

Rink, Evald. *Printing in Delaware, 1761–1800: A Checklist.* Wilmington: Eleutherian Mills Historical Society Library, 1969.

Rose, Aquila. *Poems on several Occasions. To which are prefixed some other Pieces writ to him, and to his Memory after his Decease. Collected and published by his Son Joseph Rose, of Philadelphia.* Philadelphia: Printed at the New Printing-Office, near the Market, 1740.

Shaw, Ralph R., and Richard H. Shoemaker, *American Bibliography.* New York: Scarecrow Press, 1958–.

Shipton, Clifford K. *Sibley's Harvard Graduates. Biographical Sketches of Those Who Attended Harvard College . . . with Bibliographical and Other Notes.* 17 vols. Boston: Massachusetts Historical Society, 1937–75. Vol. 11, 1741–45.

Shipton, Clifford K., and James E. Mooney. *National Index of American Imprints through 1800: The Short-Title Evans.* 2 vols. Worcester: American Antiquarian Society and Barre Publishers, 1969.

Shoemaker, Richard H. *A Checklist of American Imprints for 1820.* New York & London: The Scarecrow Press, Inc., 1964.

Skeel, Emily E. F., comp., *A Bibliography of the Writings of Noah Webster.* Edited by Edwin H. Carpenter, Jr. New York: New York Public Library, 1958.

Stoddard, Roger E. *A Catalogue of Books and Pamphlets Unrecorded in Oscar Wegelin's 'Early American Poetry, 1650–1820.'* Providence: Friends of the Library of Brown University, 1969.

Tapley, Harriet S. *Salem Imprints, 1768–1825.* Salem: The Essex Institute, 1927.

Tremaine, Marie. *A Bibliography of Canadian Imprints. 1751–1800.* Toronto: University of Toronto Press, 1952.

Trumbull, James H. *List of Books Printed in Connecticut, 1709–1800.* Acorn Club Publications, no. 9. Hartford: Case, Lockwood, and Brainard Co. , 1904.

Ver Nooy, A. P. 'The Carrier's Address—A New Year's Greeting.' *Dutchess County Historical Society Yearbook* 29 (1944): 46.

Vlach, Milada, and Yolande Buono. *Catalogue collectif des Impressions Quebeçoises, 1764–1820*. Quebec: Bibliothèque nationale du Québec, Bibliothèque nationale du Canada, 1984.

Wegelin, Oscar. *Early American Poetry; a Compilation of the Titles and Volumes of Verse and Broadsides by Writers Born or Residing in North America, North of the Mexican Border [1650–1820]*. 1930. 2d ed., rev. and enl. Gloucester, Mass.: Peter Smith, 1965.

Williamson, Joseph. *A Bibliography of the State of Maine from the Earliest Period to 1891*. 2 vols. Portland: The Thurston Print, 1896.

Winslow, Ola E., ed. *American Broadside Verse*. New Haven: Yale University Press, 1930.

Woodworth, Samuel. Letter. January 3, 1802. Brown University Library.

Zunder, Theodore A. *The Early Days of Joel Barlow, a Connecticut Wit*. New Haven: Yale University Press, 1934.

Location Index

CONNECTICUT

Hartford

American Mercury 208, 217, 221, 233, 241, 249, 262, 270, 283, 298, 316, 347, 366, 382, 410, 548

Connecticut Courant 190, 199, 209, 222, 242, 250, 263, 271, 284, 288, 299, 317, 330, 348, 367, 383, 396, 411, 443, 612, 791

Connecticut Mirror 573, 613, 680, 886

Freeman's Chronicle 199A

[n.p.n.] 234

Litchfield

Litchfield Monitor 349, 368

Middletown

Middlesex Gazette 300, 318, 526

New Haven

Connecticut Gazette 87, 350, 550

Connecticut Journal 301, 384, 549, 654, 681, 716, 751, 792, 830, 862

Federal Gazetteer 321

New-Haven Gazette, and Connecticut Magazine 210

[n.p.n.] 223

New London

Weekly Oracle 332

Newfield

American Telegraphe 369

Norwich

Courier 351

Norwich Packet 264, 370

DELAWARE

Wilmington

American Watchman 655

Delaware Gazette 332A

Mirror of the Times 486

DISTRICT OF COLUMBIA

Georgetown

Georgetown Weekly Ledger 272

Washington Federalist 464

Washington

City of Washington Gazette 908

National Intelligencer 793

GEORGIA

Augusta

Augusta Herald 551

Savannah

Republican 614, 682

INDIANA

Vincennes

Western Sun 887

KENTUCKY

Frankfort

Argus of Western America 683

Lexington

Western Monitor 752

Lousiville

Western Courier 717

Paris

Western Citizen 656

MAINE

Augusta

Kennebec Gazette 397

Bangor

Bangor Weekly Register 794

Hallowell

Hallowell Gazette 753, 795, 831, 863, 888

Portland

    Eastern Argus 465, 504, 527, 552, 574, 657, 684, 909

    Eastern Herald 319

    Freeman's Friend 553, 575

    Gazette 685

    Herald of Gospel Liberty 615

MARYLAND

  Baltimore

    American 444, 616, 686, 718, 832

    Baltimore Daily Intelligencer 289

    Baltimore Daily Repository 273

    Baltimore Evening Post, 1805–1811 617

    Baltimore Patriot 719, 833, 889

    Baltimore Telegraphe 333

    Baltimore Telegraph 796

    Federal Gazette 352, 398, 423, 445, 618, 754, 797, 834, 910

    Federal Republican 576

    Maryland Gazette 218, 235, 251, 265

    Maryland Journal 173, 211, 212, 224, 290

    Niles' National Register 720

    North American 554

  Fredericktown

    Bartgis's Republican Gazette 721

    Frederick-Town Herald 722

    Hornet 487, 619

MASSACHUSETTS

  Boston

    American Apollo 291

    American Herald 213

    Boston Chronicle 116

    Boston Daily Advertiser, 1813–1820+ 723, 912

    Boston Eveing-Post, 1735–1775 69, 78, 88, 96, 106, 117, 126

    Boston Evening-Post, 1781–1784 200

    Boston Gazette, 1719–1798 70, 79, 97, 107, 118, 252

    Boston Gazette, 1800–1820+ 385, 424, 466, 577, 620, 658, 687, 724, 755, 798, 835, 864, 890, 913

    Boston Intelligencer 836, 865, 914

    Boston Magazine 488

    Boston Mirror 578

    Boston News-Letter 54, 71, 98, 108, 119, 139, 146, 153

    Boston Patriot 579, 799, 866, 891, 915

    Boston Post-Boy 51, 58, 80, 89, 99, 120

    Boston Recorder 916

    Boston Spectator 756

    Boston Weekly Magazine 446, 467, 837, 867, 892

    Censor 131

    Christian Disciple and Theological Review 725, 757, 800, 838, 917

    Columbian Centinel 274, 292, 303, 320, 353, 371, 386, 412, 425, 468, 580, 659, 688, 726, 758, 801, 839, 868, 893, 918

    Constitutional Telegraph 413

    Courier 321

    Emerald 528

    Evening Gazette 759, 802

    Federal Orrery 304, 322

    Herald of Freedom 243

    Idiot 894

    Independent Chronicle 323, 334, 354, 372, 387, 399, 414, 426, 447, 469, 489, 529, 555, 581, 621, 660, 689, 727, 760, 803, 840, 940

    Independent Ledger 214

    Massachusetts Centinel 218A, 225, 236

    Massachusetts Magazine 275, 293

    Massachusetts Mercury 294, 324, 388, 400

    Massachusetts Spy 127, 132

    New-England Galaxy 869, 895, 919

New-England Palladium 427, 470, 490, 505, 556, 761, 841, 896, 920

Repertory 471, 491, 506, 530, 557, 622

Universalist Magazine 921

Weekly Messenger 690

Yankee 762, 804, 922

[n.p.n.] 66, 325

Dedham

Minerva 355

Greenfield

Greenfield Gazette 335

Haverhill

Guardian of Freedom 305

Newburyport

Newburyport Herald 356, 373, 428, 448, 472, 492, 558, 623, 661, 691, 763

Political Gazette 336

Northampton

Hampshire Gazette 582

Hive 473

Republican Spy 493

Salem

Essex Gazette 109, 133, 140, 147

Essex Register 531, 559, 583, 624, 692, 728, 764, 842, 870, 897, 923

Salem Gazette 337, 357, 401, 415, 429, 474, 494, 532, 560, 584, 625, 662, 693, 729, 765, 805, 843, 871, 898, 924

Salem Register 416, 430, 475, 495, 507

Stockbridge

Western Star 266

MISSISSIPPI TERRITORY

Washington

Washington Republican 730

MISSOURI

St. Louis

Missouri Gazette 694

NEW HAMPSHIRE

Amherst

Farmer's Cabinet 476

Concord

Concord Gazette 561, 731, 766

Courier of New-Hampshire 338, 417

Mirrour 306, 374

New-Hampshire Patriot 626, 663, 806

Exeter

Freeman's Oracle 226

Hanover

Dartmouth Gazette 449

Eagle 307

Portsmouth

New-Hampshire Gazette 90, 100, 141, 174, 585, 627, 767, 845

Portsmouth Oracle 695, 872

NEW JERSEY

New Brunswick

Guardian 696

Newark

Centinel of Freedom 339, 358, 375, 389, 508, 628, 768

Wood's Newark Gazette 295

Trenton

New-Jersey State Gazette 376

Trenton Federalist 697

True American 431, 496

NEW YORK

Albany

Albany Argus 769, 808

Albany Centinel 377

Albany Gazette 698

Albany Register 253, 326, 533, 562, 925

Christian Visitant 809

Guardian 534

Republican Crisis 509

Brooklyn
Long Island Star 586, 629
Binghamton
Phoenix 810
Cooperstown
Otsego Herald 664
Geneva
Geneva Gazette 665
Hudson
Bee 477, 510
Northern Whig 731A, 926
Kingston
Ulster Gazette 535
Lansingburgh
Farmer's Register 450, 497
Lansingburgh Gazette 511, 536, 587
Lansingburgh Recorder 308
New York
American Citizen 432, 498, 563, 588
Argus 340, 378
Columbian 589, 699, 770
Commercial Advertiser 390, 564, 590, 630, 811, 846, 927
Courier 812, 847
Daily Advertiser, 1785–1806 244, 254, 276, 285, 309, 341, 379
Daily Advertiser, 1808–1809 565
Diary 310
Gazette of The United States 255
Independent Republican 512
Lady's Monitor 418
Mercantile Advertiser 402, 433, 591, 700, 899
Minerva 327
Morning Chronicle 451, 513, 911
New-York Daily Gazette 277
New-York Evening Post, 1801–1820+ 434, 452, 592, 813, 900, 928
New-York Gazette, 1795–1820+ 514, 537, 566, 593, 631, 666, 732, 771, 814, 848, 873, 901
New-York Gazette [Weyman's] 81
New-York Gazette, and Weekly Mercury 110
New-York Gazette, or Weekly Post Boy 30, 55, 61, 72, 91
New-York Journal, 1784–1793 245, 256, 311
New-York Mercury, 1752–1768 45, 73
New-York Morning Post 257, 278, 632, 667
New-York Packet, 1783–1792 219, 237, 258
New-York Price-Current, 1796–1817+ 594, 668, 701, 733, 815, 849
New York Spy 515
New-York Weekly Museum 259, 267, 279, 286, 296, 312, 328, 342, 359, 380, 391, 404, 419, 435, 453, 516, 538, 567, 772, 816, 850
New-York Weekly Post-Boy 11, 15
Observer 633
People's Friend 517
Public Advertiser 595, 634
Republican Chronicle 874
Rivington's New-York Gazetteer 148, 154
Temple of Reason 403
Time Piece 360
War 734
Weekly Visitor, 1802–1807(?) 539
Weekly Visitor, 1817–1820+ 929
Newburgh
Political Index 518, 540, 735
Recorder of the Times 454, 499
Poughkeepsie
Country Journal 227
Political Barometer 436
Poughkeepsie Journal 343, 420, 635, 702, 736, 773, 817, 902, 930
Schoharie
Schoharie Observer 931

Troy
  Farmer's Oracle 361
  Northern Budget 405
  Troy Gazette 596
Wardsbridge
  Orange County Republican 519

NOVA SCOTIA, CANADA
Halifax
  *Nova-Scotia Gazette and the Weekly Chronicle
    or Nova-Scotia Gazette and the Weekly
    Advertiser* 1002
  Royal Gazette 960
  Weekly Chronicle 972, 994, 999

OHIO
Chillicothe
  Scioto Gazette 669
  Supporter 737
Cincinnati
  Inquisitor 932
  Liberty Hall 818, 851, 875, 933
  Western Spy 636, 852, 876
Columbus
  Ohio Monitor 903

PENNSYLVANIA
Carlisle
  Carlisle Gazette 637
  Carlisle Herald 638
  Cumberland Register 597, 639
Downington
  American Republican 774, 934
Easton
  Spirit of Pennsylvania 877
Erie
  Erie Reflector 935
Harrisburg
  Chronicle 775, 878

Lancaster
  Intelligencer 392, 406, 455, 598, 807, 844
  Lancaster Journal 437, 456, 478, 599, 670
  Neue Unpartheyische Lancaster Zeitung 280
Philadelphia
  American Democratic Herald 776
  American Weekly Mercury 4, 7, 8A, 9, 12, 16,
    19
  Aurora 407, 479, 520, 600, 640, 703, 738,
    777, 853, 879
  Bureau 704
  Corrector 778
  Democratic Press 601, 671, 739, 779, 819, 880
  Dunlap's American Daily Advertiser 313
  Evening Star 641
  Federal Gazette 246, 260
  Freeman's Journal, 1781–1792 183, 191, 201,
    215, 228, 238
  Freeman's Journal, 1804–1820+ 602, 672,
    705, 740, 780, 820, 854
  Gazette of the United States 314, 329, 344
  Gemeinnützige Philadelphische Correspondenz
    184, 192, 202
  Grotjan's Philadelphia Public-Sale Report 855
  Hope's Philadelphia Price-Current 568, 673
  Independent Balance 904
  Independent Gazetteer 193, 203, 229
  Literary Register 741
  Merchants Daily Advertiser 362
  Pennsylvania Chronicle 101, 111, 121, 128,
    134, 142, 149
  Pennsylvania Evening Post 158, 163, 165, 169,
    175, 179, 185, 194
  Pennsylvania Gazette 5, 6, 8, 10, 13, 17, 20,
    22, 24, 26, 28, 31, 33, 35, 37, 39, 41, 43,
    46, 49, 52, 56, 59, 62, 67, 74, 82, 92, 102,
    112, 122, 129, 135, 143, 150, 155, 159,
    170, 176, 180, 186, 195, 204, 216, 261,
    297
  Pennsylvania Journal 14, 18, 21, 23, 25, 27,

29, 32, 34, 36, 38, 40, 42, 44, 47, 50, 53, 57, 60, 63, 68, 75, 83, 93, 103, 113, 123, 130, 136, 144, 151, 156, 160, 171, 177, 181, 187, 196, 205

Pennsylvania Ledger 161, 166

Pennsylvania Mercury 281

Pennsylvania Packet 137, 145, 152, 157, 162, 164, 167, 172, 178, 182, 188, 197, 206, 230, 239

Philadelphia Repertory 643

Philadelphia Repository 421, 438, 457

Political and Commerical Register 480, 642, 706, 742, 781, 821

Porcupine's Gazette 363

Poulson's American Daily Advertiser 408, 439, 458, 481, 500, 521, 541, 569, 603, 644, 707, 822, 881, 905, 936

Relf's Philadelphia Gazette 501, 522, 542, 604, 645, 674, 708, 743, 782, 823, 856

Tickler 570, 605, 646, 675, 709, 744

True American 381, 393, 459, 482, 543, 606, 647, 676, 710, 745, 783, 857

United States Gazette 544, 607, 648, 677, 711, 746, 784, 824

Wöchentliche Philadelphische Staatsbote 76, 84

[n.p.n.] 1, 2, 3, 198

Reading

Readinger Adler 483, 523, 545, 608, 649, 678, 712, 747, 785, 825, 858, 882, 906, 937

Wilkes-Barre

Visitor 748

QUEBEC, CANADA

Montreal

Canadian Courant 980, 989

Montreal Gazette 966, 969, 976

Quebec

Le Canadien 977, 981, 984, 987

Quebec Gazette 941, 943, 944, 945, 946, 947, 948, 949, 950, 951, 952, 953, 954, 955, 956, 957, 958, 961, 962, 963, 964, 965, 967, 968, 970, 971, 973, 974, 974A, 978, 982, 985, 988, 990, 992, 995, 997, 1000

Quebec Mercury 975, 979, 983, 986, 991, 993, 996, 998, 1001

Times 959

RHODE ISLAND

Newport

Newport Herald 240, 247

Newport Mercury 114, 115, 124, 231, 268, 440, 524, 546, 609, 650, 713, 749, 786, 859, 883

Rhode-Island Republican 460, 502, 714, 826

Providence

Columbian Phenix 610

Providence Gazette 287, 364, 394, 441, 525, 571, 679, 715, 907

Rhode-Island American 572, 651, 884, 938

United States Chronicle 315, 365, 461

SOUTH CAROLINA

Charleston

City Gazette 248, 409, 652

Columbian Herald 220, 232

South-Carolina and American General Gazette 104

South-Carolina Gazette 125

South-Carolina Gazette; and Country Journal 94

TENNESSEE

Nashville

Clarion 787

VERMONT

Bennington

Vermont Gazette 462

Burlington

Burlington Advertiser 269

Middlebury

Middlebury Mercury 484, 547

Virginia

Alexandria

Alexandria Advertiser 442, 503

Alexandria Expositor 485

Norfolk

Norfolk Herald 827

Petersburg

Republican 939

Richmond

Enquirer 463, 611

Virginia Argus 750, 788

Virginia Patriot 860

Winchester

Virginia Centinel 282

Unidentified Newspapers

Democratic Press 861

Evening Post 789

Examiner 790

True American 885

Weekly Register 302

Weekly Visitor 653

[n.p.n.] 48, 64, 65, 77, 85, 86, 95, 105, 138, 168, 189, 207, 345, 346, 395, 422, 828, 829

Newspaper Name Index

Albany Argus 769, 808
Albany Centinel 377
Albany Gazette 698
Albany Register 253, 326, 533, 562, 925
Alexandria Advertiser 442, 503
Alexandria Daily Advertiser
 see *Alexandria Advertiser*
Alexandria Expositor 485
American (Baltimore, Md.) 444, 616, 686, 718, 832
American (Providence, R.I.)
 see *Rhode Island American*
American and Commercial Advertiser
 see *American* (Baltimore, Md.)
American and Commercial Daily Advertiser
 see *American* (Baltimore, Md.)
American Apollo 291
American Citizen 432, 498, 563, 588
American Commercial Daily Advertiser
 see *American* (Baltimore, Md.)
American Daily Advertiser
 see *Dunlap's American Daily Advertiser*
American Democratic Herald 776
American Herald 213
American Mercury 208, 217, 221, 233, 241, 249,
 262, 270, 283, 298, 316, 347, 366, 382, 410,
 548
American Republican 774, 934
American Telegraphe 369
American Watchman 655
American Weekly Mercury 4, 7, 8A, 9, 12, 16, 19
Argus 340, 378
 see also *Argus of Western America*
Argus of Western America 683
Augusta Herald 551
Aurora 407, 479, 520, 600, 640, 703, 738, 777,
 853, 879
Baltimore Daily Intelligencer 289
Baltimore Daily Repository 273
Baltimore Evening Post, 1805–1811 617
Baltimore Federal Gazette
 see *Federal Gazette* (Baltimore, Md.)
Baltimore Patriot 719, 833, 889
Baltimore Patriot & Evening Advertiser
 see *Baltimore Patriot*

Baltimore Patriot & Mercantile Advertiser
 see *Baltimore Patriot*
Baltimore Telegraphe 333
Baltimore Telegraph 796
Bangor Weekly Register 794
Bartgis's Republican Gazette 721
Bee 477, 510
Boston Chronicle 116
Boston Daily Advertiser, 1813–1820+ 723, 912
Boston Evening Courier
 see *Courier* (Boston, Mass.)
Boston Evening-Post, 1735–1775 69, 78, 88, 96,
 106, 117, 126
Boston Evening-Post, 1781–1784 200
Boston Gazette, 1719–1798 70, 79, 97, 107, 118,
 252
Boston Gazette, 1800–1820+ 385, 424, 466, 577,
 620, 658, 687, 724, 755, 798, 835, 864, 890,
 913
Boston Intelligencer 836, 865, 914
*Boston Intelligencer, and Morning & Evening
 Advertiser*
 see *Boston Intelligencer*
Boston Magazine 488
Boston Mirror 578
Boston News-Letter 54, 71, 98, 108, 119, 139, 146,
 153
Boston Patriot 579, 799, 866, 891, 915
Boston Post-Boy 51, 58, 80, 89, 99, 120
Boston Recorder 916
Boston Spectator 756
Boston Weekly Magazine 446, 467, 837, 867, 892
Boston Weekly Messenger
 see *Weekly Messenger*
Boston Yankee
 see *Yankee*
Bureau 704
Burlington Advertiser 269
Canadian Courant 980, 989
Le Canadien 977, 981, 984, 987
Carlisle Gazette 637
Carlisle Herald 638
Censor 131
Centinel

see *Centinel of Freedom*
   Massachusetts Centinel
Centinel of Freedom 339, 358, 375, 389, 508, 628,
   768
Chelsea Courier
   see *Courier* (Norwich, Conn.)
Christian Disciple
   see *Christian Disciple and Theological Review*
Christian Disciple and Theological Review 725, 757,
   800, 838, 917
Christian Visitant 809
Chronicle (Boston, Mass.)
   see *Independent Chronicle*
Chronicle (Harrisburg, Pa.) 775, 878
Chronicle and Patriot
   see *Boston Patriot*
City Gazette 248, 409, 652
City of Washington Gazette 908
Clarion 787
Columbian 589, 699, 770
Columbian Centinel 274, 292, 303, 320, 353, 371,
   386, 412, 425, 468, 580, 659, 688, 726, 758,
   801, 839, 868, 893, 918
Columbian Centinel and Massachusetts Federalist
   see *Columbian Centinel*
Columbian Herald 220, 232
Columbian Phenix 610
Columbian USA Centinel
   see *Columbian Centinel*
Commercial Advertiser 390, 564, 590, 630, 811,
   846, 927
Concord Gazette 561, 731, 766
Connecticut Courant 190, 199, 209, 222, 242, 250,
   263, 271, 284, 288, 299, 317, 330, 348, 367,
   383, 396, 411, 443, 612, 791
Connecticut Gazette 87, 350, 550
Connecticut Journal 301, 384, 549, 654, 681, 716,
   751, 792, 830, 862
Connecticut Mirror 573, 613, 680, 886
Constitutional Telegraph 413
Corrector 778
Corrector and American Weekly Review
   see *Corrector*
Country Journal 227
Courier (Boston, Mass.) 321
Courier (Norwich, Conn.) 351
Courier (New York, N.Y.) 812, 847
Courier of New-Hampshire 338, 417
Cumberland Register 597, 639
Daily Advertiser, 1785–1806 244, 254, 276, 285,
   309, 341, 379

Daily Advertiser, 1808–1809 565
Daily Advertiser
   see *City Gazette*
Dartmouth Gazette 449
Delaware Gazette 332A
Democratic Press 601, 671, 739, 779, 819, 861, 880
Dessert to the True American
   see *True American*
Diary 310
Dunlap's American Daily Advertiser 313
Eagle 307
Eastern Argus 465, 504, 527, 552, 574, 657, 684,
   909
Eastern Herald 319
Emerald 528
Enquier 463, 611
Erie Reflector 935
Essex Gazette 109, 133, 140, 147
Essex Register 531, 559, 583, 624, 692, 728, 764,
   842, 870, 897, 923
Evening Gazette 759, 802
Evening Post (n.p) 789
Evening Post
   see *New-York Evening Post*, 1801–1820+
   Pennsylvania Evening Post
Evening-Post
   see *Boston Evening-Post*, 1735–1775
Evening Star 641
Examiner 790
Farmer's Cabinet 476
Farmer's Oracle 361
Farmer's Register 450, 497
Federal Gazette (Baltimore, Md.) 352, 398, 423,
   445, 618, 754, 797, 834, 910
Federal Gazette (Philadelphia, Pa.) 246, 260
Federal Gazette, & Baltimore Daily Advertiser
   see *Federal Gazette*
Federal Gazetteer 321
Federal Orrery 304, 322
Federal Republican 576
Frederick-Town Herald 722
Freeman's Chronicle 199A
Freeman's Friend 553, 575
Freeman's Journal, 1781–1792 183, 191, 201, 215,
   228, 238
Freeman's Journal, 1804–1820+ 602, 672, 705,
   740, 780, 820, 854
*Freeman's Journal, and Philadelphia Mercantile
   Advertiser*
   see *Freeman's Journal*, 1804–1820+
Freeman's Oracle 226

Gazette (Portland, Me.) 685
Gazette (Providence, R.I.)
  see *Providence Gazette*
Gazette and Hornet
  see *Hornet*
Gazette of the United States 255, 314, 329, 344
Gemeinnützige Philadelphische Correspondenz 184,
  192, 202
Geneva Gazette 665
Georgetown Weekly Ledger 272
Greenfield Gazette 335
Grotjan's Philadelphia Public-Sale Report 855
Guardian 534, 696
Guardian of Freedom 305
Halloween Gazette 753, 795, 831, 863, 888
Hampshire Gazette 582
The Herald
  see *Frederick-Town Herald*
Herald of Freedom 243
Herald of Gospel Liberty 615
Hive 473
Hope's Philadelphia Price-Current 568, 673
Hope's Philadelphia Price-Current, and Commercial
  Record
  see *Hope's Philadelphia Price-Current*
Hornet 487, 619
Idiot 894
Independent Balance 904
Independent Chronicle 323, 334, 354, 372, 387,
  399, 414, 426, 447, 469, 489, 529, 555, 581,
  621, 660, 689, 727, 760, 803, 840, 940
Independent Gazetteer 193, 203, 229
Independent Ledger 214
Independent Republican 512
Inquisitor 932
Inquisitor and Cincinnati Advertiser
  see *Inquisitor*
Intelligencer 392, 406, 455, 598, 807, 844
Intelligencer, and Weekly Advertiser
  see *Intellingencer*
Journal
  see *Connecticut Journal* or
    Poughkeepsie Journal
Kennebec Gazette 397
Lady's Monitor 418
Lady's Weekly Miscellany
  see *Weekly Visitor, 1802–1807(?)*
Lancaster Journal 437, 456, 478, 599, 670
Lansingburgh Gazette 511, 536, 587
Lansingburgh Recorder 308
Liberty Hall 818, 851, 875, 933

Liberty Hall and Cincinnati Gazette
  see *Liberty Hall*
Litchfield Monitor 349, 368
Literary Register 741
Long Island Star 586, 629
Mail or Daily Advertiser
  see *Daily Advertiser, 1785–1806*
Maryland Gazette 218, 235, 251, 265
Maryland Gazette, or the Baltimore General
  Advertiser
  see *Maryland Gazette*
Maryland Journal 173, 211, 212, 224, 290
Maryland Journal, and Baltimore Advertiser
  see *Maryland Journal*
Massachusetts and Boston News-Letter
  see *Boston News-Letter*
Massachusetts Centinel 218A, 225, 236
Massachusetts Gazette
  see *Boston News-Letter*
Massachusetts Gazette & Boston News-Letter
  see *Boston News-Letter*
Massachusetts Gazette & Boston Post-Boy
  see *Boston Post-Boy*
Massachusetts Magazine 275, 293
Massachusetts Mercury 294, 324, 388, 400
Massachusetts Spy 127, 132
Mercantile Advertiser 402, 433, 591, 700, 899
Merchants Daily Advertiser 362
Mercury
  see *Massachusetts Mercury*
Middlebury Mercury 484, 547
Middlesex Gazette 300, 318, 526
Minerva 327, 355
Ming's New-York Price-Current
  see *New-York Price-Current, 1796–1817+*
Mirror
  see *Mirror of the Times*
Mirror of the Times 486
Mirrour 306, 374
Missouri Gazette 694
Monitor
  see *Litchfield Monitor*
Montreal Gazette 966, 969, 976
Morning Chronicle 451, 513, 911
Morning Chronicle, and Baltimore Advertiser
  see *Morning Chronicle*
Morning Post
  see *New-York Morning Post, 1783–1792*
National Intelligencer 793
Neue Unpartheyische Lancaster Zeitung 280
New York Spy 515

Newburyport Herald 356, 373, 428, 448, 472, 492, 558, 623, 661, 691, 763
New-England Galaxy 869, 895, 919
New-England Galaxy and Masonic Magazine
    see *New-England Galaxy*
New-England Palladium 427, 470, 490, 505, 556, 761, 841, 896, 920
New-Hampshire Gazette 90, 100, 141, 174, 585, 627, 767, 845
New-Hampshire Patriot 626, 663, 806
New-Haven Gazette, and Connecticut Magazine 210
New-Jersey State Gazette 376
Newport Herald 240, 247
Newport Mercury 114, 115, 124, 231, 268, 440, 524, 546, 609, 650, 713, 749, 786, 859, 883
New-York Commercial Advertiser
    see *Commercial Advertiser*
New-York Courier
    see *Courier* (New York, N.Y.)
New-York Daily Gazette 277
New-York Evening Post, 1801–1820+ 434, 452, 592, 813, 900, 928
New-York Gazette, 1795–1820+ 514, 537, 566, 593, 631, 666, 732, 771, 814, 848, 873, 901
New-York Gazette [Weyman's] 81
New-York Gazette and General Advertiser
    see *New-York Gazette, 1795–1820+*
New-York Gazette, and Weekly Mercury 110
New-York Gazette or Weekly Mercury
    see *New-York Gazette, and Weekly Mercury*
New-York Gazette, or Weekly Post Boy 30, 55, 61, 72, 91
New-York Journal, 1784–1793 245, 256, 311
New-York Journal & Weekly Register
    see *New-York Journal, 1784–1793*
New-York Mercury, 1752–1768 45, 73
New-York Morning Post 257, 278, 632, 667
New-York Morning Post, and Daily Advertiser
    see *New-York Morning Post, 1783–1792*
New-York Packet, 1783–1792 219, 237, 258
New-York Price-Current, 1796–1817+ 594, 668, 701, 733, 815, 849
New-York Weekly Museum 259, 267, 279, 286, 296, 312, 328, 342, 359, 380, 391, 404, 419, 435, 453, 516, 538, 567, 772, 816, 850
Weekly Post-Boy 30, 55, 61, 72
New-York Weekly Post-Boy 11, 15
Niles' National Register 720
Norfolk Herald 827
North American 554

Northern Budget 405
Northern Whig 731A, 926
Norwich Packet 264, 370
Nova-Scotia Gazette and the Weekly Chronicle or Nova-Scotia Gazette and the Weekly Advertiser 1002
Observer 633
Ohio Monitor 903
Orange County Republican 519
Otsego Herald 664
Palladium
    see *New England Palladium*
Patriot and Chronicle
    see *Boston Patriot*
Pennsylvania Chronicle 101, 111, 121, 128, 134, 142, 149
Pennsylvania Evening Post 158, 163, 165, 169, 175, 179, 185, 194
Pennsylvania Gazette 5, 6, 8, 10, 13, 17, 20, 22, 24, 26, 28, 31, 33, 35, 37, 39, 41, 43, 46, 49, 52, 56, 59, 62, 67, 74, 82, 92, 102, 112, 122, 129, 135, 143, 150, 155, 159, 170, 176, 180, 186, 195, 204, 216, 261, 297
Pennsylvania Journal 14, 18, 21, 23, 25, 27, 29, 32, 34, 36, 38, 40, 42, 44, 47, 50, 53, 57, 60, 63, 68, 75, 83, 93, 103, 113, 123, 130, 136, 144, 151, 156, 160, 171, 177, 181, 187, 196, 205
Pennsylvania Ledger 161, 166
Pennsylvania Mercury 281
Pennsylvania Packet 137, 145, 152, 157, 162, 164, 167, 172, 178, 182, 188, 197, 206, 230, 239
Pennsylvania Packet, and Daily Advertiser
    see *Pennsylvania Packet*
People's Friend 517
People's Friend and Daily Advertiser
    see *People's Friend*
Petersburg Republican
    see *Republican*
Philadelphia Federal Gazette
    see *Federal Gazette*
Philadelphia Repertory 643
Philadelphia Repository 421, 438, 457
Philadelphische Correspondenz
    see *Gemeinnutzige Philadelphische Correspondenz*
Phoenix 810
Political and Commerical Register 480, 642, 706, 742, 781, 821
Political Barometer 436
Political Gazette 336
Political Index 518, 540, 735

Porcupine's Gazette 363
Portsmouth Oracle 695, 872
Post-Boy and Advertiser
   see *Boston Evening-Post*, 1781–1784
Post-Boy & Advertiser
   see *Boston Post-Boy*
Poughkeepsie Advertiser
   see *Country Journal*
Poughkeepsie Journal 343, 420, 635, 702, 736, 773, 817, 902, 930
Poughkeepsie Journal and Constitutional Republican
   see *Poughkeepsie Journal*
Poulson's American Daily Advertiser 408, 439, 458, 481, 500, 521, 541, 569, 603, 644, 707, 822, 881, 905, 936
Providence Gazette 287, 364, 394, 441, 525, 571, 679, 715, 907
Public Advertiser 595, 634
Quebec Gazette 941, 943, 944, 945, 946, 947, 948, 949, 950, 951, 952, 953, 954, 955, 956, 957, 958, 961, 962, 963, 964, 965, 967, 968, 970, 971, 973, 974, 974A, 978, 982, 985, 988, 990, 992, 995, 997, 1000
Quebec Mercury 975, 979, 983, 986, 991, 993, 996, 998, 1001
Readinger Adler 483, 523, 545, 608, 649, 678, 712, 747, 785, 825, 858, 882, 906, 937
Recorder of the Times 454, 499
Relf's Philadelphia Gazette 501, 522, 542, 604, 645, 674, 708, 743, 782, 823, 856
Repertory 471, 491, 506, 530, 557, 622
Republican 614, 682, 939
Republican and Evening Ledger
   see *Republican*
Republican Chronicle 874
Republican Crisis 509
Republican Spy 493
Rhode-Island American 572, 651, 884, 938
Rhode-Island Republican 460, 502, 714, 826
Rivington's New-York Gazetteer 148, 154
Royal Gazette 960
Russell's Columbian Centinel
   see *Columbian Centinel*
Salem Gazette 337, 357, 401, 415, 429, 474, 494, 532, 560, 584, 625, 662, 693, 729, 765, 805, 843, 871, 898, 924
Salem Register 416, 430, 475, 495, 507
Schoharie Observer 931
Scioto Gazette 669
South-Carolina and American General Gazette 104
South-Carolina Gazette 125
South-Carolina Gazette; and Country Journal 94
Spirit of Pennsylvania 877
Supporter 737
Temple of Reason 403
Tickler 570, 605, 646, 675, 709, 744
Times 959
Time Piece 360
Trenton Federalist 697
Troy Gazette 596
True American 381, 393, 431, 459, 482, 496, 543, 606, 647, 676, 710, 745, 783, 857, 885
True American and Commercial Advertiser
   see *True American*
U.S. Chronicle
   see *United States Chronicle*
Ulster Gazette 535
United States Chronicle 315, 365, 461
United States Gazette 544, 607, 648, 677, 711, 746, 784, 824
Universalist Magazine 921
Vermont Gazette 462
Virginia Argus 750, 788
Virginia Centinel 282
Virginia Centinal, or, the Winchester Repository
   see *Virginia Centinel*
Virginia Patriot 860
Visitor 748
War 734
Washington Federalist 464
Washington Republican 730
Watchman
   see *American Watchman*
Weekly Chronicle 972, 994, 999
Weekly Messenger 690
Weekly Museum
   see *New-York Weekly Museum*
Weekly Oracle 332
Weekly Post-Boy
   see *New-York Weekly Post-Boy*
Weekly Register 302
   see *Niles' National Register*
Weekly Visitor 653
Weekly Visitor, 1802–1807(?) 539
Weekly Visitor, 1817–1820+ 929
Weekly Visitor, and Ladies' Museum
   see *Weekly Visitor*, 1817–1820+
Western Citizen 656
Western Courier 717
Western Monitor 752

Western Spy 636, 852, 876
Western Star 266
Western Sun 887
Wöchentliche Philadelphische Staatsbote 76, 84

Wood's Newark Gazette 295
Wood's Newark Gazette and Paterson Advertiser
    see *Wood's Newark Gazette*
Yankee 762, 804, 922

First Line Index

Accept oh! my patrons, the efforts of youth 786
According to custom, behold I appear 223
According to custom, once more I appear 198
Adieu to ninety-six—eventful year! 344
Again around the station'd sun 675
Again behold the news-boy come [*sic*] 669
Again bleak winter's frosty hand 290
Again hath time, with swift career 938
Again his annual glass old time 963
Again, kind patrons as we meet you 625
Again my good friends, behold Boreas
    approaching 1002
Again my good sirs the year has revolv'd 957
Again, my patrons dear, behold 511
Again old Time another year 996
Again old time has brought the day along 731A
Again old Time has run his race 1001
Again, revolving in his swift career 524
Again! so soon, must I the theme rehearse? 694
Again the carrier comes through frost and snow
    751
Again the carrier comes, to show his rhymes 762
Again the earth, in rapid flight, has run 562
Again, the god, with locks of gold 983
Again the joyous season has come round 729
Again the New Year comes; but comes in clouds
    936
Again the year has gone its round 805
Again we hail the rising New-Year's day 720
Again, with steady pace, our rolling sphere 376
Ah me! the sad minute is come 157
Air was bleak, the rude winds still 671
All hail! cry we heralds, who weekly diffuse 219
All hail the glorious New-Year's day 622
All hail to the season so jovial and gay 436
All have their hobbies;—this I'm bold t'assert
    442
Almanac has made it clear 652
Among th' attendant of this festive time 311
Among the fine New-Year's addresses 538
Ancient people, taught on freedom's plan 579, 799
And Jemmy is a silly dog, and Jemmy is a tool 81
And now the car of bright Phoebus once more
    605

And thou my country, cast retracting view 857
Annual muse her wings once more 998
Another memorable year is past 66
Another old year, broken hearted 700
Another sun has flung his blaze away 674
Another year, and lo our country 796
Another year away has past!—750
Another year from door to door 216
Another year has pass'd away—613
Another year has passed before our view 600
Another year has roll'd around 570
Another year has roll'd in haste away 645
Another year has roll'd its round 315
Another year has rolled away 835
Another year is gone! and past—that bourn 412
Another year is gone—and yet frail man 453
Another year is past and gone 460
Another year, the child of time 682
Another year, with silent tread 935
Another year's past—'tis gone! 519
Anxious to gain you smiles and praise 251
Approach ye happy years! when time shall bring
    281
Aristote n'a pas trouvé notre vrai nom 961
Around successive years have pass'd 373
Around the circling year has whirl'd 174
Around the sun again had roll'd our sphere 708
Around the sun, once more, the earth has roll'd
    824
Arrah! my honeys, and a pleasant good morning
    to you. 886
Arrived from ancient Chaos' den 593
Arrived, from climes beyond the line 566
Arrived this morning, full of freight 537
As another New-Year begins its career 585
As bridegroom joys on wedding morn 517
As constant as old winter sheds 846
As custom directs me, once more I appear 346
As glides our flying hours so swift away 261
As happy New-Year, begins its career 730
As late soft slumber clos'd my eyes 241
As life is said a stage to be 211
As long as customers we find 180
As on the broad Atlantic's beaten shore 110

As opens to-day, another welcome year 779
As rolling time, with swift career 351
As Rome high triumph'd in the sacred bays 112
As sol diffuseth his enliv'ning ray 463
As some tall ship, with spreading sails 755
As the bold merchant watches every gale 644
As 'tis the custom now a days 493
As usual on the New Year's day 853
As when on Andes' awful height 803
At custom's call, the news-man comes to cheer 819
At dawning of this newborn year 723
At Hartford, every New-Year's day 350
At school I've heard my master say 591
At this glad season, when the joyous heart 880
At this returning season of the year 964
At this revolving sun my masters hear 278
At this season of mirth, when the full tide of pleasure 451
At twelve last night, this spacious world 928
Attend fellow Britons, we tune the bold lyre 985
Attend, my dear readers, attend to my lore 52
Attend ye patrons of the printing art 512
Attendant in the New Year's train 811
Attir'd in storms and drifting snows 378
Au milieu du sombre orage 981
Auf dem Pfad der Hoffnung wallt 937
Aujourd'hui par une chanson 955, 957
Aujourd'hui sans rancune 964
Aurora ushers in the year 520
Awake! awake! my muse awake! 766
Awake, O! drooping muse and make a shift 45

Be it known to all the folks 535
Before the morning ray shines bright 563
Before you, dear patrons, once more we appear 703
Begin, mercurial muse, with quickest ears 5
Begin, thou bright celestial orb 334
Behold another year comes on! 291
Behold, another year is past 250
Behold, my friends! as roll the circling spheres 308
Behold! once more from out the stormy North 832
Behold! poor Boston sore distrest 153
Bey diesem und bey jedem Scheiden 545
Bless me! how swift time rolls away 972
Blest be th' indulgent hand of Heav'n 526
Blest be the man, the world has said 503

Blest be the man who early prov'd 201, 361
Blest be this morn! Hail, patrons, dear! 404
Blyth Christmas, joyous season, past 135
Bonjour, bon an, me voici 952
Borne on the rapid wings of time 498
Borne on the wings of time another year 641
Borne on the wings of time, revolving years 741
Boy, who weekly brings the news 810
Boy who weekly pads the streets 69
Bright issuing from th' ocean stream 74
Bright sol has run his annual course sublime 269
Bright sun! great source of light, of life and joy 148
By annual services estates are held 6
By old earth's journey round the heav'n 634
By the law of good nature 'tis always agreed 168
By your leave, gents and ladies all 554

Can nature, in her brumal [*sic*] hue 33
Care enough—enough of sorrow 965
Carrier, I have been 792
Carrier now, with his accustom'd lay 740
Chain'd neck and heels to Bona's car 697
Circle of the year complete 719
Citizens, male and female all 959
Clad in her icy robes the New-Year comes 637
Claim prescriptive, who will dare deny? 620
'Clip, clip time's wings;' the lover cries 860
Cold blows the blast: The snow and hail descend 522
Cold, hungry, destitute and poor 791
Come, generous patron, lend an ear 71
Come Guillotina, muse divine! 317
Come muse, I invoke thee, light up thy fire- 548
Come on, brother 'Printers,' another new year 658
Come on ye brave Kentuckians 683
Come, sisters of the tuneful nine 444, 606
Comme c'est l'utilite 951
Compare ours with any foreign nation 924
Constant lapse of rolling years 215, 407
Constant news-boy once again 679
Courier's lad, gent. folks, you see 321
Course of time again devolves 99
Couvrons de fleurs la faulx du tems 973
Custom commands, and I obey 975
Custom demands and we present the lay 781
Custom has long decreed that we should pay 710
Custom has, long since, made it customary 306
Custom, long has mark'd the way 859

Custom, the tyrant of mankind 275
Custom, the tyrant of the present age 867
Custom, whom all mankind obey 459

Dans ce jour d'allegresse 944
Day is past—th' election's o'er 680
Day, which happy proves to many 929
Dear patrons, a happy, thrice happy New Year 874
Dear patrons and friends, since the old year is past 738
Dear patrons! by order of time 900
Dem Manne der mit Biederkeit 825
Der Tag Deckt viler Herzen auf 184
Descend, ye powers of rhyme and reason 415
Despotic time—whose power no spell can lay 852
D'ou vient qu'au premier jour de l'an 976
Douze laisse a minuit 992
Du nouvel an 958

Eighty-nine is now past, and ninety's begun 253
Embargo! What a new year's theme! 560
En finissant 943
En vain je fais diligence 974, 974A
Encircled round with blessings far and near 98
Enlighten'd men, with pride confess 841
Es ist für jezt [*sic*] und immerdar 678
Europa still partakes the joys of peace 77
Events of all evolving time 299
Excuse me, patrons, I can scarcely speak— 665

Fain would I greet my patrons kind 692
Fair ladies, your servants, in hot, cold or dry 446
Faithful as time, I now appear 737
Faithful carrier would his patrons cheer 739
Far, far from hence be satire's aspect rude 383
Farewell, fifteen, farewell forever! 817
Fashion, that little flat'tring jade 558
Father Time, in whose rapid career 909
Fatigued with bustle, noise and strife 734, 764
Festive season comes again 815
Few short months have quickly roll'd away 533
For breaking faith, and eating frogs 91
For many years, the carrier's muse 490
From custom since 'tis wrong to vary 464
From last year's mark we now aspire 233
From reason's sacred altar fir'd 403
From regions where with earliest ray 840
From the regions of day, when fair science first came 419

From Thetis' lap, thou amber sun 67
From types and balls, and ink and paper 702
Full fifty times have roul'd their changes on 1
Full thirteen moons are gone and wasted 434, 461

Gay from the east the bright'ning hours appear 380
Geehrte Leser, was für Wechsel sind gewesen 84
Generous customers, I run 80
Gentlemen and ladies, permit a youth his compliments to pay 100
Glass has run—see ninety seven has fled 360
Glorious day by prophets long foretold 615
. . . Go forth, fair maids and cull the early flowers 728
Good bye t'ye, eighteen hundred nine 592
Good customers, since 'tis the fashion 417
Good folks, the carrier!—fill'd with fear 802
Good generous friends! as I am here 347
Good gentlemen, and ladies all 612
Good masters, gentle and genteel 544
Good mercy! how I tore my shoes 392
Good morning patrons of the Western sun 887
Good morning to you patrons dear 878
Good news, another year is past 438
Good parson, such a one (quoth I) 316
Good patrons, gentlemen, and ladies 543
Good people! I'm the printer's lad 724
Gorgeous palaces, and towers 468
Grateful and joyous once more I appear 115
Grateful for favors past, I now appear 743

Had we the powers of G. + D. 494
Hag of the sunken eye and wrinkled brow 870
Hail, aged time! thou mother of all years! 536
Hail! all hail! th' auspicious day 540
Hail brave Bostonians! still we live 119
Hail, festive morn! hail, dear auspicious day 375
Hail first-born offspring of the year! 623
Hail gen'rous patrons of old Faustus, hail! 914
Hail! gen'rous patrons! we, once more, do greet you 289
Hail glorious days! so long foretold by Fate 746
Hail, hail, dear patrons, I appear 653
Hail happy day, important year! 132
Hail, happy day, propitious be the year! 140
Hail, Janus, with the double face 991
Hail! morning, thrice welcome, rejoice in the sight! 795
Hail natal day! you usher from the skies 624

Hail New-Year morning, with eventful seasons 656

Hail! New Year! season when the festive board 904

Hail! O America! 163

Hail! patron hail! with livelier heart 816

Hail patrons all, my merry horn 828

Hail, patrons all—the day returns 668

Hail, patrons hail! a happy year! 699, 721

Hail patrons hail!!—behold your boy appears 372

Hail, patrons kind! your carrier brings, this morn 790

Hail sacred muse! Thou harbinger of fame 62

Hail to my happy friends—th' accustom'd lay 234

Hail to the New-born Year!—hail, festive day! 391

Hail to this year; but, memory will recall 839

Handmaid of plenty! mildly smiling peace! 698

Happiness where art thou found? 961

Happy the man, who cheers the paths of life 426

Happy year and length of days 973

Hard a lee, see the breakers! ahoi! all hands ahoi! 631

Hard is his lot who's strictly bound 617

Hard is the case of that poor man 986

Hard times, and sad, our patrons say 995

Hard times! hard times! old Gripus cries 830

Hark! from yon distant spire the midnight peal 884

Hark! snow-crowned time has struck his solemn bell 856

Harken, my friends; while I indite ye 862

Having labour'd to please you, by bringing you news 72

Heaven bless the heart that loves to give 288

Help, help ye nine, a trembling devil aid 955

Here, printer, stop, and let me learn the news 915

Here's Charley a good lad, and true to his word 370

High seated on a rock sublime 994

His very best respects to pay 879

His worth! His death, whose heaven-directed hand 393

His youngest child while yet in manly bloom 727

Holloa! friend time, said New-Year's day 318

Horror of the frozen north 147

How hard the hapless news-boy's fate? 43

How shall the news-boy strike a jocund lay 748

How short is time! and canst thou well complain 561

How swift the weeks in various changes run 2

How things have changed since last New-Year 204

How vain are all the views and hopes of man 905

How war rides forth on wheels of thunder 395

Howe'er the car of state may go— 425

Humble carriers of the Federal Print 352

Humble news boy at your door 971

Humbly a youth begs leave to pay 109

Huzza my good patrons! once more I am here 420

I am against the Stamp Act 85

I am the carrier—listen to my lay— 659

I come generous patrons (how can I neglect) 332

I come, your annual visitant once more 332A

I come, your News-boy, and a herald true 695

I have to tell you dear patrons—but I suppose 771

I look around and view with drooping heart the gloom profound 726

[I] think you would laugh—you would smile, I am certain 228

I'm come, my friends, as Post-Boys use 217

I'm come (you'll all expect) to express 199

Ich wünsch' Euch Frieden, auf daß weit 523

If ever printer's boy deserv'd regard 274

If father Hesiod's not a liar 646

If heroes seek for fame in fight 298

Il est passe, le tems [*sic*] l'entraine 985

Imprimis—news foreign, eventful, I've brought ye 956

In ages past, when not the typic art 402

In ancient days, in England's court 283

In course eccentric, round the stedfast [sic] sun 782

In days of yore, when Greece the sceptre sway'd 125

In England, where the poets scribble 190

In gay, good humor with his friends and foes 876

In heat and in cold, through rain and thro' snow 599

In his old car, has Phoebus run 778

In mammoth times, when wit is bought and sold 428

In scenes confus'd the busy year we've past 7

In silence and in haste, at twelve 718

In the days when old Jupiter held the prime station 208

In this wild, romantic age 213
In those insipid barren times 502
In times like these, when virtue's self is made 780
In vernal pride no more the woodlands bloom 362
Independent, dependent, depending 354
Induc'd by respect and benevolent view 210
Insatiate time, who nothing spares 531
Inspir'd with respect, and a prospect of meeting 485
Inspiring nine, ye virgins fair! 423
It has been in the fashion, from time out of mind 761
It hath been a fashion (I can't tell how long) 358
It is a custom to appear 356
It is a point will be agreed 87
It's an old saying, and perhaps 'tis wise 397
It's hard, confounded hard, this freezing weather 510

Ja, wieder, wieder schwand ein Jahr- 483
Janus once more his temple closes 871, 872
Janus, who, with sliding pace 102
Je ne suis point de ville 987
Je ne viens point en Satyrique 967
Je veux vous complimenter 977
Je viens ici gaillardement 953
Jour de l'an tu es venu 997
Joy! generous patrons!—see the day arrive 303
Joy! joy! enlighten'd patrons! cheer! 294
Joy to my friends; another year 441
Joy to my friends—The new-born year 365
Joy to my patron—may his face 521
Joy to the morn, and gladness to the day 549
Joyful day returns! th' illustrious time! 114
Joyful I see Aurora's blushing ray 214
Just eighteen hundred years have rolled away 907
Just like the statesman whose prolific mind 673

Kind friends and patrons of our daily page 409
Kind friends, once more on New-Year's Day 462
Kind gentlemen, I come once more 297
Kind patron—patron! aye the noun is common 530
Kind patronizers—Ha! Ha! Ha! 894
Kind patrons! again is the carrier sincere 889
Kind patrons and friends, of every clime 614
Kind patrons, generous and good 657
Kind patrons, hail! hail to the new-born year 913
Kind patrons pray attend the song 807

Kind patrons, while others present their address 921
Kind patrons will you hear your news boy's song? 458
Kind patrons, with a New-Year's face 565
Kind patrons, with the new-born year 864
Kind patrons your news-boy with heart most sincere 272
Kind sirs, a young and bashful boy 154
Kind sirs I've come again, with humble song 939
Kind sirs, you've lived another year 400
Kind to my wishes till this happy day 54
Know ye the land, sirs, of fish and potatoes 999

La douzieme maison 982
L'an se montre, l'an s'ecoule 1000
Ladies and gentlemen, here comes the news-boy, faithful, true, sincere 394
Ladies and gentlemen! Old father time, with scythe upheld 488
Ladies and gents, with vast humility 470
Last night December bow'd her aged head 323
Last year's last sands, last night, ran out 898
Led thro' a scene of blood, a dreadful year 51
Let faction's little-minded boys rehearse 382
Let festive mirth once more appear 173
Let gay festivity appear 224
Let others sing in am'rous strains 176
Let pleasure crown this smiling morn 92
Let those who will, in hackney'd rhyme 191
Life is a vapour!—so the poet sings 844
Like sun-beam darted through a cloud 848
Little infant (scarcely two months old) 534
Lo! a new Year! and, strange to tell 962
Lo! on the wings of time, sugacious [sic] borne 374
Lo! the fleet steps of feathery-footed time 342
Lo! winter's come, with all his hoary train 381
Long has it been, you know, our way 429
Long have we watch'd the rolling year 827
Loud let our songs of praise ascend 482

Mankind have been too apt to cherish 575
Mankind, in every clime and age 589
Marked with events of varied hue 863
Martin, the printer, with his humble lay 212
Master, my modesty's so great 70
Masters, I wish a happy year 21
May grateful omens now appear 127
May my infantine muse your attention arrest 633

May Providence, propitious, grant my pray'r 65
May't please your Honour's pow'r and glory- 471
Mein Wunsch ist der—daß wir reichen Segen
   712
Mercury, who was post of Jove 262
Midst all the gloom of winter's woe 371
Modest man, it hath been said 243
Moge jeder Acker Land 649
Money's the centre of attraction 474
'More honor'd,' as [we newsboys preach] 322
More than fill'd the poet's eye 329
Most generous patrons, may the coming year
   769
Most worthy citizens, accept these lays 295
Muse, to whom the talk belongs 581
Muse, who notes all changes here 466
My friends I appear to give you a cheer 284
My honour'd patrons, and my friends 94
My labour's done for one unreckon'd year 8
My muse now strain the vocal lay 717
My name is William Parrish, sir 752
My noble friends, this welcome day 271
My noble patrons I again appear 647
My worthy good masters, whether warriors or
   civil 948

Ned Modish, when once 'mongst his friends in
   debate 143
Neither Whig, nor Tory am I 116
Never-erring book of fate 529
New-born year now usher's in 95
New-born year, with rising lustre crown'd 546
New joys arise! new joys to cheer 305
New-Year once more, comes hast'ning o'er 454
New Year opens and the night is past 783
New Year's bard resumes the annual lyre 687
New Year's day, from olden time 885
New Year's gay morn appears 277
New-Year's gift! my friends—a New-Year's gift!
   934
New-Year's ode, the newsboy sighs- 495
New Year's wish is grown so common 139
News-boy comes with a New-Year's lay! 920
News-boy humbly greets you all 235
News-boy, never taught to ring 808
News-boy on this festal day 265
News-boy's friends, who ne'er can bear to leave
   292
New's-Man comes with hat in hand 389
News-man numbers one more year 654

News! news my generous friends, and sure 302
Newsboy comes, and brings th' expected lay 661
Newsboy comes—prepare the way— 598
Night was dark, loud roar'd the storm 457
Night's gloom departs, the shadows disappear 568
No more the stream meanders through the vale
   472
No more—to meditate on scenes of war 414
Not all the shifting scenes of life 676
Not often, Pegasus, thy back I straddle 910
Now eighteen hundred ten is gone 629
Now from the dreary north bleak blows the wind
   567
Now happily dawns the year—seventy two— 133
Now hoary winter's crowned the var'ing year 257
Now in this season of the year 967
Now like a ghost has eighty-six 229
Now on her broad and flying wheels 709
Now our grandame, earth has run 287
Now summer with her wanton court is gone 443
Now the fair volume of unfolding time 231
Now the Great Spirit of revolving time 232
Now, with the coming year, we strive again 705

O for the muse whose genius kind 760
O, nature! 'inexhaustive' pow'r 497
O thou, in airy garret perch'd 357
O thou! who oft within the rolling year 818
'O time!' exclaims the happy lover 398
O would the present year commence 572
O Yes! O yes! O yes!—On you, good friends 501
Oblig'd my annual verse to pay 958
Of all employments in this world of strife 542
Of all things ends abound the freest 366
Oft, gen'rous patron, to regale your taste 88
Oft gen'rous patrons, to regale your taste 146
Oft has the muse, in simple lay 660
Oft has the period been foretold 411
Oft times, on the wings of rapture borne 686
Oh for a muse, to help me dip my quill 893
Oh, gen'rous patrons of the news 390
Oh! le bon siècle mes frères 971
Oh! listen!—Time heeds no man's praying 801
Oh! you who often on my unfledg'd lines 897
Old customs teach ('tis said my [*sic*] many 209
Old earth, my dear patrons, once more has
   whirl'd round 492
Old eighty-five is past and gone 220
Old Father Time, once more has gone his round
   595

Old Janus, with thy backward face 993
Old surly winter frowns again 514
Old Tempus now in mad career 753
Old time again has run the circling year 126
Old time, commander of the sun 564
Old time his constant motion keeps 638
Old time (if fancy told the story right 331
Old time, revolvent, in his steady race 890
Old Time revolvent, with accustom'd pace 923
Old time, since when this crazy earth 547
Old time, sir, by his process queer 388
Old time still rolls his ceaseless course along 731
Old time, the grand monarch who rules o'er us all 866
Old time the meagre elf we see 327
Old time, the porter of our years 406
Old time was charg'd with manners rude 384
Old time, who eats, nor drinks, nor sleeps 449
Old time, who listens to no pray'r 559
Old time, who marks decay on all that pass 875
Old time, who moves with steady pace 486
Old time who still his course pursues 551
Old Time, (whom none can check in race) 553
Old Time with a visage, which most men of his age 931
Old time, with his scythe, in the midst of last night 596
Old time's industrious charioteer 465
Old time's rapid stream has put out, like a dream 539
Old winter, in his northern icy car 851
Old year now is past and gone 61, 941
Old year's past, time ushers in the new 487
Omnipotent is habit—from the child 896
On Christmas Day, I have heard say 787
On fiery chariot and in smoking gear 672
On fiery chariot, and in smoaking [sic] gear 855
On frosty wings with rapid flight 616
On New-Year's day, by custom old 587
On rapid wings last year has fled 691
On the first of the year, 'tis a natural case 479
On the pinions of time, lo! the seasons return 359
On this auspicious, festive day 432
On this auspicious—happy day— 218A
On this day when the world and his wife all appear 974A
On this gay morn, when ev'ry care's at rest 706
On time's swift wings, again, has flown 772
On western plains, where lofty turrets rise 129

Once every week our Spy comes out 515
Once in a year, O! 'tis a day of joy 399
Once in a year, to bend the suppliant knee 293
Once more 774
Once more awake the strain of grateful praise 259
Once more, dear friends, you see me here 873
Once more I have come with my compliments annual 338
Once more in these eventful times 621
Once more indulgent heav'n rolls round the year 940
Once more, kind friends, we greet with hearty cheer 711
Once more kind masters, if you can dispense 230
Once more my annual round has been perform'd 49
Once more my days their circling race 947
Once more my friends I do appear 86
Once more my kind patrons with joy we behold 245
Once more, my kind patrons, with pleasure I meet you 916
Once more, my masters all, and you 175
Once more old Time, with never-ceasing haste 602
Once more old time's untired career 651
Once more our little globe has run 693
Once more permit the news-boy to appear 364
Once more revolving Earth has run 405
Once more round the monarch of light has earth roll'd her 643
Once more the all-enliv'ning sun 195
Once more the annual glass of time 979
Once more the carrier brings addresses 507
Once more the earth has circled round the sun 745
Once more the good angel who always protects 276
Once more the humble carrier of your news 286
Once more the muse attempts th' accustomed lay 821
Once more the New Years morn returns 189
Once more the poor boy who distributes the news 106
Once more the steady wheel of time has wound 597
Once more the wing of hoary time 650
Once more, with frank, well-wishing tones 838
Once more with our humble address 662
Once more your humble votary must appear 279

Once more your old news-boy, appears with his
    rhymes 310
Once more your young news-man appears with
    his rhymes 285
Once the refulgent ruler of the day 138
One year has gone—fled like a ghost! 789
Onward rolling waves of time 435
Our boat, which always keeps a look 666
Our eagle shall soar till time is no more 626
Our good friend, Time, still on his way 505
Our news-boat now no longer trips 732
Our old and worn-out year 'tis said 831
Our old master time, a printer of fame 324

Patrons accept on this New Year 677
Patrons accept the salutation 763, 765
Patrons, again you see me here 431
Patrons and friends, O! may you hail 757
Patrons and friends! The tide of time 770
Patrons and friends whose glowing smile 430
Patrons, and friends, whose soften'd smile 386
Patrons and friends! With welcome meet 918
Patrons and friends, your printer's boys 584
Patrons, another year is past 800
Patrons good day a novice carrier sues 690
Patrons! expecting and sincere 901
Patrons—revolving time's career 847
Patrons, that carrier of all truth and lies 933
Patrons we hail you! Time's impetuous sway 640
Peace to the world! Columbia cries 314
Peaceful year with olive crown'd 667
Pendant toute la guerre 995
Pensive muse, who long has ceas'd to sing 883
Perhaps it might be expected that I should 301
Permit a bashful, inexperienc'd boy 992
Permit me, sirs, upon this day 997
Permit my friends, the printers boy 264
Pity the pockets of a poor young man 578
Plague on the practice (some pendant's invention
    509
Plus on vit, glose qui glose 950
Poets invoke their muse for inspiration 254
Poor Robert would invoke a muse 218
Poor Tom's a cold—God bless you, masters 158
Pour me conformer à l'usage 954
Pray gentlemen be kind and civil 263
Precious time, how important 'tis to man 826
Precisely twelve o'clock, last night 396
Prince of the months, in youthful prime 452
Printer's boy (he seeks no better name) 120

Progressive time, whose rapid wings— 713
Pythagoras, that learned wight 506

Que dans Paris on s'applique 963
Qu'on ne me parle plus de vers 942

Reader, when you and I met last 804
Readers, good morn 499
Rejoice, Columbia's sons rejoice 636
Replete with much event—important—vast! 773
Republican patrons, attend to my song 416
Respected public, lend and ear 226
Resume the song O! muse of fire 348
Revolving seasons, and returning time 156
Revolving seasons usher in the year 480
Revolving scenes attend revolving years 105
Revolving time, bless'd year-renewing time 117
Revolving time has roll'd another year 413
Revolving time, in his career 518
Revolving time, that ever steady friend 574
Rhyming season's come again 927
Rising year, with glory bright 199A
Rising glory of my nation 249
Round about the bursting sun 744
Round creation's red centre our planet has run
    704

Said Ned unto Sam, what's the news of the day?
    108
Says Charon to Mercury, how goes it above? 41
Scarce had this morn gleam'd faint along 424
Scarce has the new-fledg'd year its flight begun
    845
Schon wieder sinket uns ein Jahr 608
Scowl'd from the presence of the epic bard 349
Season of song, hail! once again 850
Season's circling round is past 632
See! another year is gone! 809
See honest Wiley still appear 64
See! Patron's see! your faithful boy appear 714
See winter, with forbidding brow 590
Serious and solemn be the song 946
Seventeen hundred ninety-six 333
Seventeen times the earth's revolv'd 664
She comes! She comes!—I hear the festive sound
    83
Shining orbs that cheer our sight 814
Should I vain boy? alas! the task's too great 239
Si je viens vous importuner 990
Si souvent on ne critique 984

S'il faut que dans les premiers jours 945
Silent, unseen, unweari'd, endless, slow 813
Simple acorn, dropping once, 'tis said 759
Since fortune first, to 'gild my humble name,' 368
Since I the news-boy's toilsome trade profest 363
Since its freedom the press triumphant maintains 954
Since last I pass'd the threshold of your door 500
Since last the carrier greeted you, the sun 833
Since last the sun his southern visit paid 556
Since mankind had rather, on ev'ry occasion 421
Since now we see the Constitution 242
Since now, with peace and plenty blest 73
Since one more stage, on life's long road, is run 688
Since the storm's overblown, and the skies almost clear 26
Since time, the old bald-pate, leads in a New-Year 949
Since 'tis a custom ev'ry year 20
Sing muse the tenth, whose annual voice 330, 345
Smiling muse, on rosy wings 513
So fühlten begeisterte Dichter 192
Sol revolving still runs on 252
Sol's fiery coursers to the south have sped 806
Some miles above the milky way 221
Some New-Year's rhymes your news-boy sends 282
Some people think Life like the ocean 982
Some poets mount upon Pegasus 908
Some travel East, some travel West 990
Stern winter now crowns the chill brow of the mountain 837
Stern winter now in pomp despotic reigns 340
Stern winter now with all her gloomy train 516
Still as emerges from the womb of time 60
Still as the circling seasons roll 475
Still pain'd suspense awaits the lazy joy 118
Still pressing on thy rude and powerful path 926
String of rhymes but once a year 326
Struggling with modesty and pride 1000
Subscrirer [*sic*] (By the fireside, with his waiter by him.) See who knocks at the door? 508
Such is the fashion of the time 610
Suffer my muse with soft address 89
Sun and moon and this fair world 736
Sun in roseate beauty drest 82
Suppose a man's ailment admit not of cure 46
Swift and perpetual is the lapse of years 504

Tempest tolls the knell of parting year 888
Thanks to my stars—the unweari'd sun 236
That rolling planet called the sun 439
There is a strain belov'd by all 891
There's not an ear that is not deaf 4
There's nothing new beneath the sun 895
This chilly morn I take my stand 450
This day the annual wishing muse 255
This day, when smiling friends, and (foes) 849
This festal morn once more your carrier brings 642
This morn I arose with thoughts on my mind 775
This morn, my patrons, with a heart sincere 794
This year's begun my humble muse 97
Tho' Borea's chill blasts curls the hair of my head 628
Tho' custom would lead us to pass in review 754
Tho' war's dark tempest frowning lowers 670
Tho' winter bends the floods in chains 387
Tho winter with his surly blast 861
Thou New-Year's muse, who condescends to sing 385
Though cheerless winter closes round 588
Though in my teens, unskill'd in learned lore 476
Though nations rage with hostile jars 313
Though past events are hourly read 238
Though time retains its antient sway 247
Through every age—o'er every clime 932
Through wet and dry, and frost and snows 227
Through wet and dry, and heat and cold 194
Throughout the long-year past, in good or in bad weather 104
Time, ever varying, ever changing 877
Time flaps his snowy pinions at the goal 925
Time has been, your printer's boy could bring 788
Time has revolv'd another year 715
Time hurries on with rapid bound 919
Time like a quick stage rushes on 550
Time, like a river, rolls its varied stream 842
Time, like the dove of rapid flight 701
Time, on his rapid wings, demands again 820
Time runs his ceaseless race,—another year 865
Time shakes his plumes, and from December's night 580
Time, urging on his swift career 225
Time was the muse could sing of peace 186
Time when advancing spreads his plumes 930

Time, who as every poet sings 603
Time, whose unwearied pinions bear 445
Time with a rapid flight and even 655
Time, with his pinions broad and strong 902
Time's annual circuit has again come round 892
Times are hard and money scarce 557
Times, in ever variable display 447
Time's measurer, the radiant sun 14
'Tis New Year's Day again! Your new's-boy
    comes! 469
'Tis New Year's day, and all expect to find 881
'Tis not for me to sweep the sounding strings
    166
'Tis past, the fatal year is past 107
'Tis past! 'Tis gone! th' important day has fled 79
'Tis roll'd away! another year 836
'Tis strange, but true, that in this isle 609
To all gentlefolks in town, and every, and any 55
To all his patrons, sage divines 582
To ask! or not to ask? That is the question.— 353
To bring New Years, revolving time makes haste
    3
To custom's voice, the news-man still attends 777
To day a new year opes to view 377
To fulfill the agreement I made in my last 244
To give his friends pleasure the new [sic] boy
    with pain 96
To our illustrious Gore 577
To patrons, num'rous and so kind 604
To rhyme without reason a fault would appear
    834
To scenes of blood, and dreadful deeds of arms
    200
To song return ye tuneful nine 367
To tune his gratulary strain 320
To wake the soul by transient gleams of reason
    793
To wish his patrons many happy years 742
To wish you happy thro' the coming year 30
To you my patrons, I present my strain 267
Too long has discord, bath'd the earth in gore
    440
Toujours de mes devoirs fidele observateur 962
Towne's Evening Post!—Good masters pray 165
True as the rising sun, thro' wet and dry 481
True to my trust, as is old Father Time 455
Tune the harp and fiddle-string 478
Twas a cold rainy night, when the carrier's
    mother 776
'Twas said, by one who saw with piercing eyes 716

Twelve fleeting months their course have run
    611
Twelve months my weekly course I've run 960
Twelve toilsome months have slowly pass'd 448
Two annual courses time has run 15
Two years have passed, since news-boy's lays 735

Un pais autrefois soumis au despotisme 956
Upon the stage your news-boy comes once more
    296

Various comforts of the changeful years 325
Voice l'aimable saison 966
Vous favez qu'a tout nouvel an 969

Warrior so bold, and an army so brave 681
We, heralds, sirs, of Father Time 576
We hunted up the man of rhyme 569
We, news-boys, so smart, have long time found it
    thus 798
We young Mercuries wish, that with all who sub-
    scribe 237
Web of life is a mingled yarn 784
Week after week, I, constant as the sun 124
Welcome day of joy and gladness 767
Well, Christmas and New-Year, these holiday
    times 477
Well, now my lad, what brings you here? 594
Wet from the types and scarcely born 343
Wet, shivering, cold, the sport of every blast 527
What bold, adventurous, tuneful sprite 573
'What does not fade?' the poet sung 689
What here again?—Why sure it is not Tuesday—
    491
What means this clamour? Why this strife? 131
What scripture pronounces, experience proves
    true 496
What shall the muse of western climes 427
What tempests gloom'd the by-past year— 207
What time bears on his rapid wing 78
What vast advantages we find 443
Wheel of time 627
When blissful numbers swell the song 696
When first by freedom fired our sires began 552
When last we pour'd the unassuming lay 822
When now the circling year is past 829
When on the printing duties I attend 90
When princes, arm'd with power 541
When rival nations, great in arms 749
When winter with his raging winds 601

Whence come the ills of life? 756
Whence this tumultuous noise, these dire
    alarms? 24
Where are the Caesars, Alexanders now 911
Where e'er the mouth of man is found 270
Whereas by use, time out of mind 532
Whereas, when New Year's day doth first come
    843
While all the wise heads of the nation 571
While at the genial board you pay 899
While busy mortals stretch their sanguine views
    155
While chilly winds of cold December blow 222
While folks of all sorts are their compliments
    paying 309
While gladsome notes of joy resound 525
While in a chilly winter night 422
While in this festive season all rejoice 339
While New Year's morn each breast with joy
    inspires 328
While northern lads thro' hills of snow 248
While o'er his drear and desolate domain 663
While o'er the earth's expanse, the golden ray
    312
While others sing, in harsher strains 418
While pompous players, in this happy age 141
While slumb'ring on bed, having scarce clos'd
    my eyes 256
While storms and tempests spend their furious
    force 268
While Washington, with conduct sage 336
While Whitehead signs his New-Year's ode 162
Whilst genial friendship on this festive day 379
Whilst happier brutes th' inspiring God obey 10
Whilst innovation, with destructive rage 408
Whilst old Time presents another year 619
Wide flood of time whose rapid career 722
Will you think of the news, I have carried for
    you 912
Wind it was cold, and the fast falling snow 467
Winter, again, like pilgrim old 630
Winter appears—the hoary monarch of the year
    355
Wir haben, Gott sey Dank! ein neues Jahr erleht
    280
Wir treten jetzt, walt's Gott! ins Neue wieder ein
    76
With congee, bending to right angle 607
With constant pace earth rolls her seasons round
    122

With dawning of the New Year's Day 917
With ever steady and unerring pace 528
With heavy heart and pocket light 48
With hope elate, with heart sincere 618
With humble hope—a heart with zeal 555
With joyful heart and gratitude sincere 868
With joyful heart I now appear 456
With merry heel, and heart full light 437
With my bundle and cane, at your doors I appear
    869
With pleading prospect we behold 179
With rapid speed, the swift wing'd flight of time
    586
With scarce a smile to greet the new-born year
    758
With silent step another year 639
With sithe [*sic*] and glass, and phiz profound 733
With withering touch, though winters hoary
    hands 341
With yesterday another year's withdrawn 854
Within a circle of a year 768
Wo ist der Weg zum Glück der Liebe? 906
Would you read of great battles and marvellous
    things 39
Wrapt in his robes of frost, another year 823

Yankee boy once more essays 922
Ye friends of good order, ye men of reflection
    369
Ye friends of truth and freedom's reign 489
Ye gen'rous patrons of our annual song 151
Ye Louisianan nymphs begin the song 337
Ye patrons kind, whatever name 401
Ye sons of Freedom's peaceful soil 583
Ye viewless sylphs and elves and fairy trains 410
Ye, who my monthly pages turn 725
Year after year we still have hop'd to find 707
Year eighteen hundred and fifteen is done 797
Year has pass'd from human sight 812
Year now dawns, what tribute shall I bring? 58
Year of our Lord, eighteen hundred and four 484
You, friend and patron of the Hive 473
Young misses have their valentine 635

Zum jez'gen lieben neuen Jahr 785
Zum kunft'gen lieben neuen jahr 858
Zum Neujahr wünsch' ich euch und mir 747
Zwar wünsch ich zu jeder Zeit 882

Name Index

Alsop, Richard 283, 443
Barlow, Joel 168, 208, 217, 222
Biglow, William 357
Bond, Tobias 173
Bowen, Abel 892, 921
Bowman, Godfrey 343
Caldwell, Charles 393
Caleb 211
Child, Nathan B. 104
Cobbett, William 363
Cogswell, Mason Fitch 263
Coles, Dennis 454
Cree, Joseph 154
Dearborn, Samuel 921
Dorman 792
Doughty, John 702, 736, 773
Duncan, Hugh 148
Dwight, Theodore 443
Elliot, Samuel 335
Ellsworth, John 411
Epenetus 615
Evans, Nathaniel 60
Everett, David 476
Freneau, Philip 191, 194, 198, 201, 204, 207,
    215, 220, 223, 238, 360, 361
Gerrish, William 394
Hall, Ebenezer 115
Heartt, D. 675
Honeycomb, Will 287
Hopkins, Lemuel 299, 317, 330, 345, 348, 367
Hutton, Joseph 643, 645, 674
Jones, Daniel 757, 800
Kellogg, John 547
L'Hommedieu, Stephen S. 818
Liddel, John 278
Lincoln, Daniel W. 504
Linn, John Blair 458
Little Jack 368
Livingston, Henry, Jr. 227, 436, 902
M'Bride, John 486
McCurdy, James 347
Marshall, Stephen 635

Martin 212
Modish, Ned 143
Monroe, William 737
Nurse, John 147
Paine, Robert Treat 322
Parks, Daniel 225
Parrish, William 752
Parsons, Frederick T. 817, 930
Patton, John M. 717
Peirce, T. 852
Peirce, Tom 876
Philanthropos 65
Pole, Thomas, Jr. 362
Ray, William 835
Robbin 341
Robert 235
Rolla 920
Rose, Aquila 1, 2, 3
Simmons, Wm. 827
Smead, Wesley 818
Swinney, Laurencius 55
Swinney, Lawrence 91
Symmes, Peyton S. 818, 932
Tracey, Joseph W. 536
Trimble, John 289
Trumbull, John 190, 199A
Vardill, John 73
Vernon, Nancy 48
Ward, Abram 656
Waterhouse, Samuel 81
Webster, Noah 249, 250
Weeden, Job 133
Welch, Benjamin 173
Weston, Tom 173
Wheeler, J. 315
White, Thornley L. 669
Whitehead 162
Woodworth, Samuel 734
Worth, Gorham A. 851
Wright, Mr. 875
Wrigley, Francis 198